The Guillotine
And
The Cross

Warren H. Carroll

Distributed by:
ANGELUS PRESS
2918 Tracy Ave
Kansas City, MO 64109 USA
1-800-966-7337 • 1-816-753-3150

Christendom Press
MANASSAS, VIRGINIA

ISBN 0-931888-45-X

DEDICATION

*To the community of Carmelite Sisters in Buffalo
whose prayers have been the shield and buckler
of Christendom College*

"What man of you, having a hundred sheep, if he has lost one of them, does not leave the ninety-nine in the wilderness, and go after the one which is lost, until he finds it? And when he has found it, he lays it on his shoulders, rejoicing. And when he comes home, he calls together his friends and his neighbors, saying to them, 'Rejoice with me, for I have found my sheep which was lost.' Just so, I tell you, there will be more joy in heaven over one sinner who repents than over ninety-nine righteous persons who need no repentance" Luke 15:4-7.

Table of Contents

Table of Contents

I.

"Ça ira!" "Here it Goes!"
(August 10, 1792)

It was three-quarters of an hour past midnight of August 10, 1792, hot and sultry, when the bells of Paris began to ring. They were church bells, whose primary purpose was to call the faithful to worship; but now the churches were empty and dark, and only the bells sounded. At first some of them tolled slowly, but others quickened the beat—ringing and rising, ringing and rising, until it was an almost continuous, ear-splitting *ding-ding-ding-ding*; and this was the tocsin, the city alarm, the call to arms, which it was a capital offense to sound without orders from the government. Yet in Paris that night there were three governments—that of the King, that of the Assembly and the Mayor, and that of the insurrectionary Commune; the third of these was invisible because it had been created, secretly, that very evening. It was the Insurrectionary Commune that had sounded the tocsin. All through the night before it began to ring, rumbling rumor had swept the streets: the time had come; the time was now; the time was tonight. "Here it goes!" men said, not really knowing why they said it, but saying it over and over again. "*Ça ira!* Here it goes! *Ça ira!* Here it goes!"[1]

In an unpretentious street-level apartment at 24 rue des Cordeliers (Street of the Franciscan Friars) three women were weeping, frightened by the sound of the tocsin. After some minutes of distress, they heard a familiar heavy tread and an extraordinary figure emerged from the room where he had been trying to catch a few winks of sleep. He was a brawny mountain of a man, with a booming voice and an overpowering presence. His huge, grotesquely flattened face looked as though it had been kicked and gored by a bull. (It had—by two different bulls—and had also been trampled by a herd of pigs.) He sought, with a kind of rough tenderness, to comfort them:

9

his wife Gabrielle, whom he loved genuinely and profoundly; Lucile Desmoulins, one of the most beautiful women in Paris; and Louise Robert. Nothing to worry about, he told them; all part of the plan for the night. They were in no danger, for they were under his protection; and he was Georges-Jacques Danton, leader of the French Revolution.

At one o'clock in the morning a gun boomed from the New Bridge over the Seine, and the ringing of the tocsin continued. Hundreds of armed men were gathering in the Place de Grève which sloped down to the bank of the Seine in front of City Hall. Conspicuous among them was the solid block of 516 men who had marched all the way from Marseilles, France's second city on its south coast, singing the fighting and marching song—the Marseillaise—which they had already made famous. But, though there were reports of up to 2,000 more armed men gathering in the St. Antoine Quarter where the Bastille had stood, long known as the focus of the revolution, the response was not as large or quick as the Insurrectionary Commune had expected. From City Hall they sent a delegation to Danton at his apartment. One of its members was a prosecuting attorney, cousin to Camille Desmoulins, Lucile's husband, who had been the first to arouse the mob for the storming of the Bastille three years before. The prosecuting attorney was tall and robust, but of strange appearance, with thin downward-turning lips under a sharply pointed nose, very high arching eyebrows, an almost permanent frown, and shifting, darting eyes. His name was Antoine Quentin Fouquier-Tinville. Danton promised that night to make him his aide. Fouquier-Tinville was later to prosecute almost all the victims of the guillotine during the Terror, and to be recalled by Lenin when in December 1917 he founded the first Soviet secret police, progenitors of the KGB: "Where are we going to find our Fouquier-Tinville?"[2]

Soon after Fouquier-Tinville and his companions departed, at about two o'clock in the morning, Danton decided the leader's presence was needed at City Hall. "It's no good," he told Gabrielle, who obviously did not want him to go, "I have to go down there."[3] Upon arriving, he proclaimed to the National Guard and others in and around City Hall the establishment of the authority of the Insurrectionary Commune of Paris. The Mayor of Paris, Jérôme Pétion, was nowhere to be seen; he had been told what was coming, and had decided not to resist it. But the commander of the National Guard, Antoine-Jean Galliot, Marquis de Mandat, a brave and loyal officer who was at the post of danger at the royal palace, was ready to fight the insurrectionists.

A mile and a half down the Seine from City Hall the royal family of France was confined in the palace and gardens of the Tuileries, as they had been confined since that fearful day in October 1789 when they had been brought there from Versailles by an armed mob like the one now gathering, led by men carrying severed human heads on their pikes. More than a year ago they had made a dramatic attempt to escape, slipping out of the Tuileries and out of Paris just after midnight, riding for their lives all the next day until they were recognized and stopped, just short of safety, in the little town of Varennes. But they had ridden for their lives not on horseback but in an enormous lumbering carriage, carrying their children's governess instead of an armed guard, with the Queen's hairdresser as an outrider and one of their scouts too nearsighted to see much; while the man who caught them, the 28-year-old postmaster Jean-Baptiste Drouet, rode to cut them off gripping his horse's mane on a wild gallop through woods on a stony ridge in deepening dusk at the risk of his life. Now they were back in the Tuileries; and when they heard the tocsin, they knew it sounded for them.

His Most Christian Majesty Louis XVI, King of France, was moderately tall, blond and blue-eyed, and running to fat. A kindly, pious man of no more than average intelligence, he would have been somewhat miscast as a ruler in any age, but probably would have coped well enough in a time of stability and peace. But France had been gripped for more than three years in such a convulsion as no nation in Christendom for centuries had seen or imagined, which this king—knowing that he personally had done almost nothing to arouse it—could neither understand nor bring under control. Despite being shut away in the Tuileries, he had sensed the menace of this night even before the tocsin began to ring. For the first time in his reign he had refused the ancient ritual of the *coucher*, the ceremonial putting of the king to bed. He had thrown himself on his bed fully clothed, sleeping only for brief intervals. At other times he paced about the palace in his rumpled purple suit, his usually carefully curled and powdered hair dishevelled, gripped as ever by the fatal indecision that was so fundamental a part of his character. Louis XVI was in no way a coward; but he had an unconquerable aversion to shedding the blood of his own people, and his personality was not one that could dominate any difficult situation.

His wife, Marie Antoinette, was made of different stuff. To the memory of no other woman, and of few of either sex, has the verdict of her time and of history alike been so unjustly and vindictively destructive. The worst of the pamphlets written against her, just before

and during the Revolution, still require special credentials even to
read at the National Library of France. Though the most savage and
obscene calumnies are no longer believed, the fetid odor of scandal yet
hangs about her name, laced with the acrid tang of contempt. Didn't
she say of starving people, "Let them eat cake!"?

No, she didn't. The one who said that was the wife of Louis
XIV, Marie Antoinette's husband's great-great-grandmother.[4]

Marie Antoinette, married to the heir to the throne of France at
only sixteen, had been rather frivolous in her first few years as
princess and then queen. But time and especially motherhood had matured her. She was devoted to her fourteen-year-old daughter, Marie-
Thérèse Charlotte (named for Marie Antoinette's splendid and heroic
mother, for forty years Holy Roman Empress of the Habsburg dynasty), and to her seven-year-old son Louis Charles, the Crown Prince
since his elder brother had died of a tragic, wasting disease during the
first days of the Revolution back in 1789. Marie Antoinette was a
deeply believing Catholic. She had oppressed no one. More intelligent,
more sensitive and more decisive than her husband, she had understood the Revolution almost from the beginning much better than he.
She sensed the black malignancy at its heart, seeming drawn from
wellsprings below the world, calling up the fountains of the great
deep. She and her husband and her children had been prisoners of the
Revolution for three long years. After their escape was so barely
foiled at Varennes, on the endless, frightful journey back, with mobs
threatening their lives almost every step of the way, her once lovely
auburn hair had turned dead gray. (Of those who rode in the royal
carriage back from Varennes, only two survived the Revolution.) All
her vivacity and most of her beauty had gone. Calvary lay ahead, her-
alded by the endless clanging of the tocsin.

Members of the National Guard posted to the Tuileries were arguing vociferously whether or not they should do their duty and defend the royal family. Their shouts, recriminations and threats penetrated the royal chambers. Only the Swiss Guard stood firm and silent,
nine hundred farm boys from the Alpine valleys of strongly Catholic
Luzern canton, the last wholly loyal body of fighting men left in Paris,
iron-disciplined, unyielding; but they had only thirty rounds of ammunition per man, because Mayor Pétion had refused to approve issuing
them any more. And the men from Marseilles had brought cannon.

It was nearly four o'clock in the morning. The tocsin was finally
stilled, but now the drums were beating in the streets, punctuated by
the periodic booming crash of signal guns. The sky was beginning to
redden in the east; it would be a beautiful sunrise. Princess Elizabeth,

the King's gentle and holy sister, took the trembling Queen by the arm and led her to a window overlooking the garden of the Tuileries. "Come, Sister," she said, "let us watch the dawn break."[5]

There were a few brief, precious moments almost of peace; then a wild-eyed National Guard officer rushed into the royal quarters. "This is your last day!" he cried. "The people have proved the strongest. What carnage there will be!" Marie Antoinette burst into tears. "Save the King! Save my children!" she cried to the heedless, excited officers in the King's Chamber. She ran into her little son's room. Alone of all the household he had slept through the night, but he was awake now, and asked: "Mama, why should they hurt Papa? He is so good."[6]

With a great effort Marie Antoinette gained command of herself. She seated herself by the fireplace in the room of the King's valet, with her back to the windows, and addressed herself to Pierre Louis Roederer, the Attorney-General and representative of France's second government, the Legislative Assembly, who earlier had informed the royal family that even as chief law enforcement officer of that government he could do nothing about what was happening, because an insurrection, unlike ordinary crime, was beyond his powers. He had urged the royal family to leave the Tuileries and place themselves under the protection of the Assembly, which had convened at two o'clock that morning under the presidency of the famous lawyer and orator Pierre Vergniaud of the Gironde region in the south of France, to debate—of all subjects at such a moment—Negro slavery. Now she asked Roederer again: "What is to be done?" He repeated his earlier recommendation.

"Monsieur, there are troops here," said Marie Antoinette; and in that moment there spoke through her the heritage of half a thousand years of Habsburg Holy Roman Emperors, from whom she was descended. "It is time to know who will triumph: the king and the constitution, or factionalism."[7]

Roederer retired in some confusion. Evidently he had not expected this kind of courage. The King, inspired by his wife, for the moment echoed it. He had no confidence in the Assembly. He would fight for his crown and his life. In a few minutes he would review his troops.

It was now five o'clock in the morning. The loyal commander of the National Guard, Marquis de Mandat, had been at the Tuileries most of the night. He received a second summons from City Hall, calling on him to report there. From whom did the summons come—the "legitimate" city government headed by Mayor Pétion, or the mysterious insurrectionists? It appeared to come from the regular city government, approved by the Legislative Assembly, and Roederer persuaded Mandat that it was his duty to obey it. Neither the King nor the Queen intervened. Mandat leaped on his horse and rode along the right bank of the Seine toward City Hall. On the way he saw large numbers of armed men forming up and preparing to march.

Arriving at City Hall, Mandat issued orders almost at the moment of dismounting "to disperse the procession marching on the Palace by attacking it in the rear." The battalion commander who received the order, perhaps still unsure of which government to obey, took it to Police Commissioner Rossignol, who brought it to Danton. Danton strode menacingly into Mandat's office with Rossignol and demanded that he come before the councillors of the insurrectionary Commune to explain himself. Mandat faced him—the smaller man, the aristocrat, looking up at the giant with the smashed face who had said some days earlier, when Pétion proposed removing Mandat as National Guard commander once the insurrection had begun: "What do you mean, remove him? Kill him, man! The dead can't come back."[8]

"This so-called Commune of yours is nothing but a bunch of seditious rebels," Mandat declared, his eyes kindling, "and I have no intention of appearing before them."[9] Danton reached out a vast hand and seized Mandat by the scruff of the neck. He was thrown into prison and declared to be deprived of his command, being replaced by Santerre, a brewer from the Saint-Antoine Quarter. About three hours later Mandat was brought out of his cell under guard and led to the steps of City Hall, where Police Commissioner Rossignol coolly drew his pistol and shot him dead.

"Mandat had given orders to fire on the people," Danton later explained. "I therefore transferred the death sentence to him."[10]

Just a few minutes after Mandat's arrest, the King finished buckling on his ceremonial sword, and still in his rumpled purple suit, with his cocked hat under his arm, went down into the Tuileries gardens to review and if possible inspire his defenders. On the way he passed members of the Swiss Guard, who were stationed inside the palace; they called to him: "Down with the factions! Down with the Jacobins!"[11] (Mercenaries these farm boys may have been, but they knew what they were fighting.) But out in the courtyard where the National Guard units were drawn up, the first cries of "Long live the King!" were soon drowned out by "Long live the nation!" and "Down with the tyrant!"[12] Some of the guardsmen actually broke ranks and crowded around the King, shaking their fists in his face and calling him a fat pig. Nevertheless he continued, saying to each company he reached, "I love the National Guard!"[13] When he did not meet an obviously hostile response, he would say, pathetically: "We must defend ourselves, don't you think?" With reference to the attackers, he said: "They are certainly coming. What do they want? I will not separate myself from good citizens; my cause is theirs."[14] At length he desisted, and returned to his family deathly pale.

It seems to have been almost exactly at this moment that Roederer, who had left the Tuileries to find out more about what was going on outside, encountered Danton. He had been drinking heavily; Roederer could smell the alcohol on his breath.

"The whole thing's planned; we're sure to win," the giant said, confidently. "But the thing is, people are set on killing the King today, and I don't regard this as necessary in the circumstances. . . . His death would complicate things enormously, and I am therefore against the whole idea of the King's execution. What I want *you* to do is put the fear of God into him—persuade him to leave the palace and seek asylum with the Assembly. There we shall have him surrounded, and can proceed to arrange his deposition at our leisure."

Roederer hesitated. Suddenly Danton seized him by the throat.

"Take care," he thundered, in the voice that had sometimes been heard all the way across the Seine. "In this tragedy everyone has his allotted part to play. Anyone who thinks he can be a mere onlooker will find it costs him his head. Don't falter now, or you'll regret it later. I will be watching you." Suddenly there was a roar of cannon fire. "Do you hear that?" bellowed Danton. "The ball has begun! This time we are calling the music, and people must dance to our tune!"[15]

At the Tuileries the King sat at a table next to the entrance to his reception room, his hands on his knees. Everyone could see that he had no idea whatever what to do. The shouting grew louder as more and more revolutionaries poured into Carrousel Square in front of the palace. Roederer reappeared.

"Your Majesty has not five minutes to lose. You will be safe only in the National Assembly. The opinion of the Department is that you go there without delay. You do not have enough men to defend the chateau. They are no longer well disposed toward you. The artillerymen have unloaded their guns. . . . There are twelve piece of artillery and a huge crowd is arriving."

Louis XVI rose and went to a window which had a partial view of the front of the palace.

"I don't see a very large crowd," murmured the bewildered King.

Gerdret, a colleague of Roederer, shouted in exasperation; the Queen reproved him, and turning again to Roederer, said that the palace still held many men who would defend the royal family.

"Madame, all Paris is marching," responded Roederer.

"Are we totally deserted?" Marie Antoinette asked, fighting despair. "Will no one act in our favor?"

"Resistance is impossible," said Roederer flatly. "Do you wish to make yourself responsible for the massacre of the King, of your children, of yourself, of the faithful servitors who surround you?"

"God forbid!" said the Queen. "Would that I could be the only victim."

"Time presses, Sire," said Roederer coldly, turning his eyes to the King, who had remained completely silent as his life and his family's were being debated. Nor did he speak, even now.

"Monsieur Roederer," said Princess Elizabeth, in his stead, "Will you answer for the life of the King?"

"Madame, we will answer for dying at your side; that is all we can promise."

The King rose and moved over to the noblemen and officers who had assembled in his reception room, swaying a little as he walked.

"Gentlemen, I beg you to withdraw and abandon a useless defense. There is nothing to be done here for you and for me. *Marchons!* (Let's go!)"[16]

Escorted by a double column of Swiss and National Guardsmen, with Roederer in front and the King following him, the royal party set out for the Assembly across the gardens of the Tuileries. Birds were singing, the sun was shining, the grass was a brilliant green. Marie Antoinette followed her husband, holding her son's hand; right behind her was Princess Elizabeth, holding the hands of her niece Marie-Thérèse Charlotte and the Queen's dearest friend, the Princess de Lamballe. Tears streamed from the Queen's eyes. At one point, for a moment, she felt she could not continue walking, and leaned for support on the arm of La Rochefoucauld of the Guard; he could feel her whole body trembling. Yet still she struggled against despair, calling out to her ladies-in-waiting: "We shall see you again." But Princess de Lamballe whispered, "We shall never return."

As they approached the Assembly, they had to push their way through the angry crowd, but no serious attempt was made to stop them. Vergniaud the orator was presiding—large-featured, strongly built, with heavy, wavy hair carefully dressed over a high forehead, and dark eyes that looked indolent in repose but filled with fire when

he began to speak. He may not have been surprised at the arrival of
the royal family, but most of the deputies were. The proceedings came
to an instant halt. The King walked up to Vergniaud and said: "I have
come to prevent a great crime and I believe that I cannot be safer
anywhere than in the midst of the representatives of the nation."
Vergniaud replied: "You can count on the firmness of the National
Assembly. It knows its duties and its members are sworn to uphold the
rights of the people and of the constitutional authorities."[17]

Those kind words from the uncompromising republican Vergniaud were later used as evidence of "royalism" by Fouquier-Tinville in
the prosecution which sent Vergniaud to the guillotine.

Somewhere in the distance, shrewdly placed at a vantage point
never revealed, a 23-year-old lieutenant of artillery from the island of
Corsica, a short man with lank brown hair and large, masterful gray
eyes, had been watching everything that had happened, and was to
happen later that morning, at the Tuileries. He shook his head grimly
as he watched the King and his party depart.

"Ah, if I had been in command!" said Napoleone Buonaparte.[18]

All revolutions have moments of madness even by their own
standards, of searing irony and low comedy, as the world crumbles
while odd bits of flotsam spin and drift on the surface of the tide. One
of them came at this point. The royal family was in the Assembly; but
François Chabot, the unfrocked priest who was a master of bitter in-
vective, particularly against the Church he hated, rose to protest: the
Constitution of France forbade the Assembly of the nation to debate
in the presence of the sovereign. (It is not recorded that anybody then
pointed out that the Constitution of France also guaranteed the personal inviolability of the sovereign, and that the Assembly was only in
his presence because his personal inviolability had just been violated.)
Vergniaud, stiff and pompous, led the Assembly in a solemn debate on
this difficult question of constitutional law. They could not proceed in
the presence of the King; Heaven forbid that they not proceed! But
they could not send the King out of their presence, for that would
probably mean his death, from which they could protect him nowhere
else. What to do? The Alice-in-Wonderland solution: confine the royal
family in the stenographer's box, a stifling little closet six feet high
and twelve feet wide, separated from the Assembly by an iron grill.
While he was in this cell, the Assembly was technically not in the
King's presence. The royal family went into the box. The children
fussed. The Queen was still fighting for control of herself, clasping
and unclasping her hands in her lap. The King, in the words of a
German observer, seemed "stunned and helpless."[19]

The royal family remained in this hot, almost airless prison for the next fourteen hours.

At the Tuileries, within a few minutes of the departure of the King, the attackers burst through the gates, meeting no resistance; the French National Guardsmen remaining there either fled or joined the revolutionaries. Then they saw before them, on the grand staircase of the palace, the Swiss Guard drawn up in battle array.

Shouts of hostility and demands for surrender rose from the attackers. François-Joseph Westermann, one of their commanders, a German-speaking Alsatian, called out: "Surrender to the nation!" "We should think ourselves dishonored!" came the reply. Then some of the attackers who spoke German tried to persuade the non-commissioned officers and men to turn against their officers. "We are Swiss, and the Swiss only lay down their arms with their lives," one of them, Sergeant Blazer, replied.[20]

Frustrated and increasingly angry, the attackers began trying to pull the Swiss off the stairs with hooks on the end of their halberds. They succeeded with five of them, disarming and then butchering them. Higher up on the stairs, Captains Zusler and Castleborg gave the order to fire. The disciplined volleys swept the mob and drove the gunners from their cannon. The attackers fell back from the palace into Carrousel Square where they had gathered earlier. Captains Durler and de Pfyffer led a sortie. Sixty Swiss formed a hollow square and advanced, sweeping Carrousel Square with fire. The Swiss brought up the cannon they had recaptured and fired on the attackers fleeing into the narrow streets opening off the square. Among those fleeing in disorder were the men of Marseille.

"The Swiss handle their artillery with vigor," Lieutenant Buonaparte noted approvingly from his vantage point.[21]

But the men of Marseille rallied when out of cannon shot and began to return the fire of the Swiss, who with only thirty rounds per man were now low on ammunition. Westermann rallied the Parisians, and a fierce musketry duel began, with hand-to-hand fighting as well. As the roar of battle rose, it began to drown out the sonorous deliberations of the Assembly, just five hundred yards away from the Tuileries; a few stray bullets even came through the windows of the Riding School building where it met. Near panic, with its speakers shouting to be heard over the din, the Assembly passed an incredible decree placing "the security of all persons and all property under the safeguard of the people of Paris."[22] Several members urged the King, in his box, to order the Swiss to cease firing. He agreed at once, sending an elderly retainer, retired General d'Hervilly, himself a Swiss, to carry the message. D'Hervilly made his way at great peril through the storm of fire to the palace, found Captain Durler, and gave him the order.

Captain Durler refused to accept it. He had seen his five men who had been captured and disarmed by the revolutionaries at the foot of the grand staircase killed before his eyes. He knew these foes would give no quarter. Surrender meant death. He ran to the Assembly, pushed his way into the suffocating cabinet where the King was confined, and pleaded with him to allow his faithful Swiss to continue defending themselves.

Louis XVI made his last decision as King of France. It was like so many of his other decisions, or the lack of them, that had brought ruin to himself, to his family, and to his people—while meaning only the best.

"Lay down your arms. Place them in the hands of the National Guard. I do not wish brave men to perish," he said to Captain Durler.

Captain Durler could not accept a verbal order alone, even from his supreme commander, that would condemn most of his men to death. He asked for the order in writing. Louis XVI gave it to him.

"The King orders the Swiss to lay down their arms immediately and to withdraw to their barracks. Louis."[23]

And so the drums of the Swiss Guard beat the retreat before the Revolution. Back through the gardens of the Tuileries they marched; the treacherous National Guardsmen assembled there opened fire on their unresisting ranks as they passed. One column went to their barracks, the other to the Assembly; in both places, they stacked arms. Then, disarmed and defenseless, they were set upon. Wherever they went, wherever they fled, wherever they hid, they were seized, dragged out in triumph, and slaughtered. Many of them were horribly mutilated. Before it was over, an observer said he did not believe there was a single street in Paris that had not seen at least one Swiss head on the end of a pike. At the end of the day, children were rolling some of the heads along the streets. Women like vultures were tearing strips of flesh off the naked corpses of the King's defenders.

More than six hundred of the Swiss Guard died in that massacre, one of the most repulsive history has recorded. (Far more were killed at Auschwitz and places of its kind—but even that killing was not done in the streets of the capital city of a nation with women and children cheering on the killers and mutilators of men who had only done their duty in defense of the legitimate sovereign, and were no longer even attempting to resist.) The remainder were thrown into prison, almost every one of them to die in the same fashion less than a month later. Still there have been historians who have found their fate palatable, and even in some ways admirable. It has been remembered in a different way in Luzern. There stands today in that beautiful city a stone lion erected in memory of her sons who gave their lives in a foreign land, in defense of a foreign king. The lion is dying, struck down by a lance. Faithful unto death, it holds in its paws a shield emblazoned with the fleur-de-lis, ancient symbol of the kings of France. Below it are engraved the names of the fallen.

Nor were the Swiss Guard the only victims in the Tuileries that day. The storming mob killed and mutilated every man they could find who had served the King, from noblemen to cooks, totally without regard to age or station, to the number of more than two hundred; they were only just persuaded to spare some of the women, by no means all. Says Christopher Hibbert:

> They threw the bodies out of the windows, impaled heads on pikes, looted the rooms, smashed furniture and windows, pocketed jewelry and ornaments and scattered papers over the floors. Fugitives who tried to escape were struck down as they ran across the garden and hacked down under the trees and beside the fountains. Some clambered up the monuments but were prodded down with pikes and bayonets by the assailants who, forbearing to fire for fear lest they injure the marble, stabbed them as they fell at their feet.[24]

Wooden buildings adjoining the palace caught fire; the killers drove away the fire brigade with gunfire, and let them burn until the fire spread to parts of the palace.

Not all the French noblemen and soldiers at the Tuileries that cataclysmic morning were cowards, traitors, or fools. Because none could know whether the man to his right or his left fell into one of those categories, no firm united defense, such as the Swiss had made until the order came to lay down their arms, had been possible; yet there were men present who would have been willing to lay down their lives for the royal family. Among them were two young noblemen soon to make their mark upon the history of the Revolution and the resistance to the Revolution: François-Athanase Charette from the coastal region at the mouth of the Loire River, thirty years old, keen-featured with a high forehead, athletic, gallant and dashing with a theatrical flair; and Henri de la Rochejaquelein, 20, ardent, courageous and eloquent, tall and fair-haired, with lively eyes in an oval face. He was the eldest son of the Marquis de la Rochejaquelein, from an old through by no means rich noble family of the Bocage, the country of small fertile fields and almost impenetrable hedgerows in the west of France south of the Loire's mouth. Henri's father and brother had fled to England in the emigration of the nobles, but Henri had stayed with his king; his family had an ancient tradition of special loyalty to the monarch. Henri's cousin, Louis-Marie Joseph, Marquis de Lescure, 27, thoughtful, reserved, and utterly loyal, whose bride Marie-Louise Victoire de Donnissan was god-daughter to one of Louis XV's daughters (an aunt of Louis XVI), had tried all during the early hours of the morning to reach the Tuileries to aid the King, but was unable to gain admission.

Abandoned by their king, swept up in the tornado of looting and massacre that followed the royal order to the Swiss to lay down their arms, Charette and La Rochejaquelein managed to escape unharmed. Charette was in the greatest danger; caught in a crowd ransacking the royal apartments, he saved himself by putting on one of the revolutionary jackets known as the *carmagnole*, taken from the body of one of the attackers shot down by the Swiss, and by slinging over his shoulder the severed leg of one of the Swiss victims of the mob. (That such an object should serve as an effective disguise is an especially memorable example of the character of the massacre of the Swiss Guard.) Neither man ever forgot the scenes he had witnessed that day in the Tuileries. Both were to fight for Catholic France after Louis XVI had been executed, as he had allowed no man to fight for her while he lived.

But that was in the future. For now there was no recourse, nowhere to turn but the Assembly; and the Assembly itself was gripped by terror. Some of the looters and killers of the palace invaded the Assembly chamber, shouting and screaming, literally with blood on their hands. Guadet, who had replaced Vergniaud in the chair at ten o'clock, greeted them obsequiously: "The Assembly applauds your zeal." One of the men of the Insurrectionary Commune sprang to the rostrum and cried: "Learn that the Tuileries are on fire, and that we shall not hold our hand until the people's vengeance is satisfied!"[25] Men and women, howling threats, stood on chairs and even climbed columns to catch a glimpse of the royal family in their tiny prison. Marie Antoinette sat white-faced and shaking; incredibly, the King seemed calm. The standards of the Swiss Guard were brought in and deposited on the president's desk. Loot from the palace followed, as an "offering to the nation," piling up on a table set in front of the desk. Some of the Queen's jewels appeared on it. Then, perhaps borne by a bloody hand, came the golden ciborium from the tabernacle in the royal chapel, still containing the Body of Christ.

With Guadet in the chair, Vergniaud joined the special Committee of Twenty-One that was deliberating the fate of the monarchy.

The committee members were soon agreed, and Vergniaud reported their agreement to the Assembly. There was no longer any way to pretend that the much-hailed Constitution of 1791 was still in effect. It and the King were suspended, and the election of a new national legislative body, the Convention, was ordered. Meanwhile the royal family was declared to be "under the charge of the legislative body until tranquillity is restored to Paris."[26]

It was to be a very long time before tranquillity was restored to Paris: more than seven years.

The revolutionaries had gained their essential objectives; those who stridently demanded the immediate deposition and execution of the King did not (as we have seen) have the support of Danton, the architect of the insurrection. The call for a National Convention meant the end, at one stroke, of the monarchy, the constitution, and the existing Assembly. The other two governments which had existed in Paris when the tocsin began to ring on August 10 had now been set aside. Only the Insurrectionary Commune remained.

Danton was asleep while this was going on, absolutely confident of the outcome. In the middle of the afternoon he was awakened by an excited Camille Desmoulins to tell him that the Assembly, by 222 votes out of 284, had just elected him Minister of Justice in the new provisional government.

Evening fell. In the Hotel de Diesbach, the Marquis de Lescure and his 19-year-old wife of less than a year, Marie-Louise Victoire, knew that it was only a matter of time before the killers found them, for they were known as supporters of the King who lived in that hotel. Marie-Louise was seven months pregnant. They left the hotel in disguise. At first the streets through which they made their way were ominously quiet. They saw flames around the Tuileries. Groups of armed men passed them, roaring drunk, bellowing revolutionary slogans. On the Champs-Elysées they met a woman pursued by a man with a gun, threatening to kill her. She seized Lescure's arm, begging him to save her; Marie-Louise seized his other arm; in any case, he carried no weapons. The pursuer said: "I have killed several aristocrats today, and this will be some more." Why was he angry with the woman? "I asked her the way to the Tuileries, to go and kill the Swiss," but she had not answered him. Lescure answered: "You are right; I am going there also."[27] Then he persuaded the man that he had to find a safe place to leave the women, before they could go to the Tuileries to kill more Swiss; and so they parted. At last Lescure and his wife found refuge in the dwelling of his former housekeeper, with Marie-Louise Victoire in the last stages of exhaustion and weeping uncontrollably.

Meanwhile, in the Jacobin Club, hotbed of revolution, a little man was speaking. He was not prepossessing: his voice was weak and scratchy; his pale face had a greenish tint, and was occasionally afflicted by a tic. His jawbone was long, his chin prominent, his eyebrows bulging. His near-sighted gray-green eyes had a curious, glittering intensity, magnified by his habit of covering them with glasses and then frequently raising them to his brow so that the eyes could be more clearly seen. He dressed lavishly and meticulously; otherwise he was abstemious and puritanical. He disliked women. He loved power, but did not yet have much. He despised wealth, and was known as "the Incorruptible." He came from Picardy, the province which had given John Calvin to the world. His name was Maximilien Robespierre, and he was to become the lord of the Terror in the French Revolution.

He spoke of the great importance of the forthcoming National Convention, and of the election of its members. He urged the Jacobins to send representatives to the provinces to explain the events of this day, and to see to the immediate release of all imprisoned revolutionaries. But in the events of the day he himself had played, so far as history has been able to determine, no part.

Shortly before midnight the royal family was at last released from their box and taken to the Convent of the Feuillants, just behind the Riding School building where the Assembly met. Revolutionaries surrounded them. Their way was lighted by candles affixed to muskets. They were put in four musty cells, unused for years, unfurnished. One of their few surviving retainers brought mattresses. Outside, the revolutionaries could be heard still shouting threats, particularly against the Queen. Some men, climbing up a grating overlooking the corridor upon which the cells opened, were calling: "Throw down her head!"

Louis de Bourbon, no longer King of France, wrapped his head in an old cloth and lay down on his mattress. His last words before falling asleep were: "People regret that I did not have the rebels attacked. But what would have been the result?"[28]

The long day was done; the hour bells tolled midnight. Now, anyone who wished to secure justice in France would have to see Georges-Jacques Danton.

NOTES

[1]This pungent phrase, probably the most historically famous idiom in the French language, is impossible to translate accurately. Its literal meaning is "here it shall go," quite close to the sense of the English idiom "here it goes!" or "here goes!", which also conveys some (though not all) of the sense of confidence, purpose and determination of the French idiom.

[2]Harrison E. Salisbury, *Black Night, White Snow: Russia's Revolutions, 1905-1917* (New York, 1978), p. 545.

[3]Robert Christophe, *Danton* (London, n.d.), p. 226.

[4]Vincent Cronin, *Louis and Antoinette* (New York, 1975), p. 13.

[5]Stanley Loomis, *The Fatal Friendship; Marie Antoinette, Count Fersen and the Flight to Varennes* (Garden City NY, 1972), pp. 249-250.

[6]Rupert Furneaux, *The Bourbon Tragedy* (London, 1968), pp. 11. 22.

[7]David P. Jordan, *The King's Trial; the French Revolution versus Louis XVI* (Berkeley Ca, 1979), p. 6.

[8]Christophe, *Danton*, pp. 226-227.

[9]*Ibid.,* p. 227.

[10]*Ibid.*

[11]Jordan, *King's Trial*, p. 7.

[12]Furneaux, *Bourbon Tragedy*, pp. 24-25.

[13]Louis Madelin, *The French Revolution* (New York, 1925), p. 268.

[14]Furneaux, *Bourbon Tragedy*, p. 25.

[15]Christophe, *Danton*, p. 228.

[16]Furneaux, *Bourbon Tragedy*, pp. 27-28; Jordan, *King's Trial*, p. 8.

[17]Furneaux, *Bourbon Tragedy*, pp. 29-30.

[18]*Ibid.,* p. 16; Madelin, *French Revolution*, p. 269.

[19]Madelin, *French Revolution*, p. 269.

[20]*Ibid.,* p. 270; Furneaux, *Bourbon Tragedy*, p. 32.

[21]Furneaux, *Bourbon Tragedy*, p. 33.

[22]Madelin, *French Revolution*, p. 270.

[23]Furneaux, *Bourbon Tragedy*, p. 34; Cronin, *Louis and Antoinette*, p. 354.

[24]Christopher Hibbert, *The Days of the French Revolution* (New York, 1980), p. 160.

[25]Madelin, *French Revolution*, p. 272.

[26]Claude G. Bowers, *Pierre Vergniaud, Voice of the French Revolution* (New York, 1950), p. 230.

[27]Marchioness de La Rochejaquelein, *Memoirs* (Edinburgh, 1816), p. 24.

[28]Furneaux, *Bourbon Tragedy*, p. 41.

II.
For Christ or the Revolution
(May 5, 1789-September 9, 1792)

Of all the great human upheavals in history, none came as so great a surprise as the French Revolution.

This fundamental historic truth has been obscured by the clouds of legend and groundless assumption that have gathered about the shattering event that, more than any other political occurrence, has shaped the history of the West for the past two centuries. But the facts are—and honest, thorough historians grant them—that none of the horsemen of the Apocalypse, none of the traditional harbingers of disaster, rode in France during the reign of Louis XVI before the Estates-General convened in Paris in May 1789. There was no war, to sap the country's strength and strike down its young men. When the Revolution began, France had enjoyed complete peace for six years. There was no famine, though much is often made of the narrow margin by which the poor of France were able to afford the bread which was their staple of life. But the margin was there. For the most part, there was enough for the people to eat. Certainly there was no change in the availability of food from the pattern of most people's lifetimes. There was no pestilence. There was no great change of religion; for all the growing, fashionable unbelief in some upper-class circles, for all the popularity of the vehemently anti-Christian Voltaire and Diderot and Rousseau among a number of articulate intellectuals, these ideas and tendencies had barely touched the ordinary people of France in 1789. There was no organized political opposition, no group which had dedicated itself to revolution or anything like it. This was at least partly due to the fact that there was no serious and widespread political oppression. Here is where the legends and groundless assumptions cluster most thickly. But the government of France in 1789 suffered primarily from neglect, not oppression. Most members of the royal family and most upper-level aristocrats simply did not take their governmental responsibilities seriously. A number of evils, and some actual instances of oppression, arose because of their neglect. But they were not part of, nor the result of any policy or plan; they were not very severe; and, despite all his shortcomings as an efficient ruler, Louis XVI was a principled monarch who wanted to do his duty and had undertaken a number of important initiatives, especially in the area of taxation, to try to counter the effects of the neglect.

Fairly serious economic problems did exist, due to the inadequacy and unfairness of the taxation system and the substantial burden of debt from the war ending in 1783 in which aid from France had enabled the American colonies to become independent of Great Britain, but without gaining much in tangible immediate benefit for France. These problems had induced the King and his counsellors to call the Estates-General, a national representative body of three houses—clergy, nobility, and commons—into session for the first time in no less than 175 years. But they were not problems of the catastrophic kind that the whole nation would be aware of. In all probability most Frenchmen barely recognized, if at all, their existence.

Nevertheless there were real, long-standing grievances. There was need for reform. The very fact that the Estates-General had not met for 175 years showed how far the government had withdrawn from the people. This withdrawal took the form of a political structure of royal absolutism; but with the important exception of Louis XIV (famous for his saying, "L'état, c'est moi!"—"The State, that's me!") none of the kings of those years had in fact ruled strongly, nor made much use of their power. It was diffused among their ministers and courtiers, who were inclined to be much more interested in their social prestige and personal pleasures than in any aspect of the business of governing. Probably the most serious grievance was the impenetrability of the body of aristocrats who dominated society and government. Unlike England, where titles of nobility could directly or indirectly be bought, in France the only way to be an aristocrat was to be the biological descendant of an aristocrat. Those who were not (nor devious and skillful enough to deceive or defraud others by a false pedigree into accepting them as aristocrats) were shut out. With the rarest of exceptions (such as Jean Bart, the son of a Dunkerque fisherman who became an admiral for Louis XIV), the commoner had no hope of advancement beyond the middle levels of French society. All high offices in government, the military services, and the Church were closed to him and to his descendants forever. Along with many other

evils, over the generations and the centuries this rigid biological strati-
fication had created the feeling in many (though by no means all)
French aristocrats and commoners that they really were made of different stuff.

But when all is said and done, when the evils and shortcomings
of the French political and social system in 1789 are stated frankly but
without exaggeration; when the economic problems of the nation at
that time are given their full just weight; when the impact of the destructive criticism and widespread intellectual vogue of the *philoso-
phies*—Voltaire, Rousseau, Diderot and their followers and admirers—is duly evaluated; the sum total does not come close to account-
ing even for the events of the day of the tocsin, August 10, 1792, to say
nothing of the grisly horrors that were to follow it. Other Western nations had endured, and were to endure far worse afflictions than those
of France in 1789 without bursting forth in an explosion that released
the fountains of the great deep. France herself had known, and was to
know far greater evils and dangers than any which faced her then,
without repeating the Revolution. In fact, the French Revolution has
never been repeated. It is unique. Only one other event bears close
comparison with it: the Communist Revolution in Russia in 1917. But
then all the precipitating factors of war, famine, pestilence, and previously organized political opposition were present, that had not existed
in 1789 in France—and, above all, the well-remembered example of
the French Revolution itself, to which Lenin, the maker of the Bol-
shevik Revolution, often referred.

Why then did the French Revolution come?

Honest history is silent. The answers ideologues are so ready to
give are all verdicts of hindsight, cheating time and reality, which only
go forward, while it goes backward. This world's time and reality give
us no answer; for no man predicted the French Revolution.

Yet there were foreshadowings. They were all on the side of the
revolutionaries and their precursors; no one else felt them. Let us consider two. One came to an old man, and one to a man very young.

The old man was François-Marie Arouet, who wrote under the
name of Voltaire. He was seventy-nine years old when in 1773 the Je-
suit order was suppressed by Pope Clement XIV, under immense pressure from Prime Minister Pombal of Portugal, King Charles III of
Spain, and powerful figures at the French court. Voltaire disliked the
regime of the kings, but he disliked the Roman Catholic Church much
more; he called it *l'infame*, the infamous thing. He knew that the Jesuits constituted the strongest and most effective body within the
Church in his time. "Once we have destroyed the Jesuits," he said, "we

shall have it all our own way with the infamous thing."[1] When their
suppression came he welcomed it with the greatest satisfaction, saying:
"In twenty years there will be nothing left of the Church."[2] Twenty
years from 1773 was 1793—the year of the Terror, the year when the
French Revolution abolished first the Christian era and then the worship of God.

The young man was Louis Antoine Saint-Just, twenty-two years
old when the Estates-General met in 1789, from Nivernais in the heart
of France, handsome as an angel, dark-haired and pale. In that year
1789 he published a satirical poem entitled *Organt au Vatican*. Much of
it was a bitter, scatological attack against the Church and her bishops,
priests, monks, and nuns. It included a barely veiled excoriation of
Louis XVI and Marie Antoinette. Of man in general Saint-Just wrote
thus: "Man is an animal, like the bear or lion, his characteristics error
and foolishness, malice, pride, and ambition . . . His heart, com-
pounded of pride and self-interest, fears what it hates and scorns what
it loves."[3] In this condition, he said, men can get help from Satan. In
the most revealing passage of the poem, Saint-Just describes an invasion of Heaven itself by the devils, who entrench themselves there.

It is Hell's most cherished though impossible dream, from the
time when Christ's sacrifice on Calvary opened Heaven. Louis Antoine Saint-Just became, under Robespierre, the architect of the Terror in the French Revolution, his pale icy countenance untouched by
any of the blood he shed. Men called him then "the Angel of Death."

Within days of its convening in May 1789, the Estates-General,
without precedents in living memory and stirred by tumultuous demands for fundamental change from the lawyers and journalists who
dominated its largest house, the Third Estate, was careening from crisis to crisis. Bewildered Louis XVI did not know how to put it back on
course. Expelled by royal order from the Hall of Diversions in the
royal palace at Versailles where it had been meeting, the Third Estate
and its allies in the First and Second Estates met on a tennis court and
proclaimed itself a National Assembly which would not disband until
France had a constitution.

The King's more vigorous younger brother, the Count of Artois,
thought he knew just what to do about that. The next day he reserved
the tennis court for a game.

These things happened late in June 1789. On July 14 the ancient
fortress-prison in Paris called the Bastille was stormed by a mob stirred
up by the oratory of Camille Desmoulins and led by the sinister
Stanislas "Strike-Hard" Maillard, tall, dark, saturnine, and tubercular.
Only seven prisoners were found inside—four forgers, a count

charged with incest, and two madmen, one of them an Irishman with a three-foot beard who thought that he was God. But when the day was done, the mob had torn Governor de Launay of the Bastille and Mayor Flesselles of Paris to pieces and paraded their heads on pikes. Less than three months later a similar mob, again led by Maillard, almost killed the Queen at Versailles and brought the royal family by force to the Tuileries (where they lived in captivity until August 10, 1792), once again with pikes bearing human heads leading their march.

During the captivity of the King the revolutionaries dismantled virtually the entire political and social structure of France. The constitution, which they claimed to have been their original and primary objective, was adopted in 1791 and a new national representative body, the Legislative Assembly, took the place of the National Assembly; but that constitution went down in flames on the day of the tocsin. The really important work of the Revolution was the work of dismantling—actions such as wiping out by a stroke of the pen all the historic provinces of France, deep-rooted in the past and rich in tradition, which gave each Frenchman the name for the region of his home, and replacing them with twice their number of "departments" whose boundaries were drawn totally without regard to where the provinces had been.

Most important of all was the dismantling of the Church in France. As early as November 1789, less than a month after the royal family was taken by force from Versailles, all Church property was taken over by the national government. In August 1790 the Civil Constitution of the Clergy became law, reluctantly accepted by Louis XVI on bad advice. This totally reorganized the church in France, making each of the new departments a diocese and prescribing the manner of choosing both bishops and pastors of parishes, without reference to the Pope or to the existing structure of church government. When Pope Pius VI rejected the Civil Constitution of the Clergy (though not yet in a formal public statement), the Assembly demanded that all clergymen in France be required to take an oath to uphold it. In a moment of terrible weakness for which he never afterward ceased to condemn himself, Louis XVI signed the law requiring this oath on December 26, 1790, believing that most of the clergy of France would take it anyway.

They did not. A substantial majority heroically rejected it, though it cost them their positions, and many of them ultimately their lives. In the Assembly itself, which had passed both the Civil Constitution of the Clergy and the requirement for the oath to uphold it, only two bishops out of the 49 who were members, and only one-third of the priests who were members, would take the oath. In the country as a whole, only 45 per cent of the priests took it, and many of these retracted publicly as soon as Pope Pius VI solemnly condemned the French Civil Constitution of the Clergy as schismatic in March 1791. Only six out of the total of 134 bishops would take the oath. (The contrast to the bishops of England under Henry VIII could hardly be more striking.) At the head of the six was Talleyrand, who became a legend for always choosing the winning side in time. With him were Loménie de Brienne, whom Louis XVI had refused to recommend for Archbishop of Paris because "the Archbishop of Paris must at least believe in God";[4] Jarente of Orléans, "a ruffian"; Savine, "a madman"; Gobel, who was to be named "constitutional" archbishop of Paris and then to repudiate his priesthood before the National Convention in the terrible November of 1793, when Christianity was abolished in France; and Miroudot who was, quite appropriately, titular Bishop of Babylon. All the other 128 said no. The aged Bishop of Poitiers spoke for them all, in January 1791 in the Assembly: "I have been a bishop for thirty-five years. Though bowed down with age and study, I will not dishonor my gray hairs. I refuse the oath."[5]

Before August 10, the only penalty enforced against clerics refusing to take the oath (known as "non-jurors") was removal from their parishes and dioceses. This was severe enough, at least for the parish priests, since in most cases it separated them from their only source of income. Religious orders had already been outlawed and their property legally declared forfeit to the government, though before August 10 this had not been generally enforced. But in the new climate all non-jurors were seen as traitors. Many of them in Paris were among the first victims of a law passed by the Assembly August 11, the very day after the deposition of the King, which recognized the effective rule of the insurrectionary Commune in the capital by authorizing it to investigate "crimes against the security of the state"[6] and to arrest and indict suspects. Non-juring clergy were high on the Commune's list, and by August 15—the feast of the Assumption, which had been the national feast of Catholic France—they began to be arrested.

On that day Nicolas LeClercq of Boulogne, a professed member of the Christian Brothers for twenty-four years, whose name in that order was Solomon and whose mission was to provide education for children without charge, wrote a letter from one of his order's schools in Paris to his sister in Boulogne, Marie-Barbe. He suggested to her that if it were no longer possible to attend Mass said by a priest in communion with Rome, she and her family should still recite the prayers of the Mass daily. Then he said:

If God permits, I shall come and join you and mingle my tears with yours. But no! What do I say? Why should we weep since the Gospel tells us to rejoice when we have something to endure for the name of Christ? Let us then suffer joyfully and with thanksgiving the crosses and afflictions which He may send us.[7]

That evening, soon after arranging for the dispatch of the letter, Brother Solomon found his school building surrounded by fifty members of the National Guard (which five days earlier had refused to defend their King). They searched the building, and took him with them to the nearby seminary of Saint-Sulpice, which the Commune had seized. There he was interrogated. The interrogation was brief.

"What is your name?"

"Nicolas LeClercq."

"Are you a priest?"

"No."

"Do you belong to a religious order?"

"Yes, the Brothers of the Christian Schools."

"What was your position?"

"Secretary to the Superior-General."

"Have you taken the oath?"

The interrogator meant, of course, the oath to accept and uphold the Civil Constitution of the Clergy, and thereby reject the authority of the Pope and the Catholic Church.

"No."

"Lodge him in the hotel of the Carmelites."[8]

The "hotel of the Carmelites" had been a great Carmelite monastery, whose cornerstone had been laid 180 years before, just thirty years after the death of St. Teresa of Avila. Now it had been taken over by the Commune for use as a prison. The Revolution had moved first of all against the contemplative orders, since the revolutionaries saw them as utterly useless and parasitical upon the "real world." A prison was much more practical than a contemplative monastery! Within a few days at least a hundred others were confined there, mostly non-juring priests. Included among them was John de Lau, Archbishop of Arles, an ancient see in the south of France which went back to Roman times.

On August 13 the Commune had demanded from the Assembly the creation of an extraordinary tribunal to "judge the crimes of August 10th."[9] (By this they meant resisting the assaults of that day, or planning or hoping to defend the King, or notably lacking sympathy with what had happened.) The Assembly had already turned the de-

posed King and his family over to the Commune, which lodged them
in the Temple tower, one of the grimmest keeps in Paris, and on August 11 had authorized the Commune to make arrests. Now they were
asked to authorize the Commune to act as judge, jury, and executioner
as well, and to deny all appeal from their decisions. The Assembly hesitated; but their position had been fatally weakened by the fact that
they had already voted their own dissolution on August 10 as part of
accepting the downfall of the constitution and the monarchy. On August 15—the very day Brother Solomon was arrested—Robespierre
appeared before the Assembly with blunt words to hurry them along:

> Since the 10th the people's just desire for vengeance
> has not been satisfied. I cannot conceive of what insur-
> mountable obstacles apparently stand in the way. . . . Refer-
> ence is still made only to crimes committed during the rising
> of August 10, and this is to restrict the people's vengeance
> too much, because these crimes go back well before then. . . .
> We demand that the guilty be tried by commissioners taken
> from each section [of the city of Paris], sitting as a court of
> final appeal. (Applause.)[10]

Chabot, the ex-priest deputy who had forced the royal family
into the stenographer's box August 10, at once moved that Robespierre's wish be made law; but Girondin leader Brissot still disap-
proved. Therefore on August 17 "a provisional representative of the
Commune" came before the Assembly to remind them who had the
pikes and the guns.

> I come to tell you, as a citizen, as a magistrate of the
> people, that at midnight tonight the tocsin will be rung and
> the alarm drum beaten. The people are weary of waiting to
> be avenged. Beware lest they carry out justice themselves. I
> demand that you decree on the spot that one citizen per sec-
> tion be nominated to form a criminal tribunal. I demand that
> this tribunal be established at the Tuileries and that Louis
> XVI and Marie Antoinette should slake their great thirst for
> the blood of the people by seeing that of their villainous
> satellites flow.[11]

The Assembly surrendered at once, passing the bill exactly in the
form demanded. Once again it was made clear who really governed
France.

The new tribunal soon went to work. In the morning of August
21 it heard the case of Louis Conolot d'Angremont, charged with attempting to raise a body of armed men to defend the King. Before the
hour bells struck noon he had been tried and condemned to death for
his fidelity to his sovereign and to the clause of the constitution which

guaranteed the King's personal inviolability. Since it was expected that Conolot d'Angremont would be only the first of many condemned, the Commune had prepared for the coming stream of executions by erecting in Carrousel Square in front of the Tuileries palace, where the mob had assembled for the attack of August 10, the very latest in killing machines, the dread invention of a piano maker named Schmidt, but popularly associated with the name of Dr. Guillotin, who recommended its use as a more humane way of killing than hanging. The thing was tall and black, with two high poles between which a great knife fell with immense force. Below it, where the knife struck, was stretched a neck. The victim's head, cut off, fell into a leather bag. It had come into use just that year, to execute a few ordinary criminals. That day, in a warm and pleasant afternoon, it claimed in Louis Conolot d'Angremont its first political victim. It was called the guillotine.

On August 24 the guillotine took its second victim, Arnaud Laporte, secretary to the Civil List; and on the 25th its third, Durozoy, a writer for the *Paris Gazette*. It is not often remembered by the zealous admirers and defenders of the French Revolution and its alleged commitment to democratic liberties that the third of the guillotine's thousands of political victims during that revolution was a newspaper reporter.

But Minister of Justice Danton was not happy with the pace of the extraordinary tribunal's work. He did not think they were killing fast enough. He knew just the man to speed them up. Before the end of August he added his useful aide Antoine Quentin Fouquier-Tinville to the tribunal. During the next two years, Fouquier-Tinville was to come to know the guillotine very well.

On August 26, the day after reporter Durozoy went to the guillotine, news came to Paris that a Prussian and Austrian army accompanied by exiled French aristocrats had invaded the country and taken the border fortress of Longwy.

In April that year the revolutionary government, with the very reluctant assent of the imprisoned King, had declared war on Prussia and Austria. Their governments had been sharply critical of the Revolution, and French interests clashed with Austrian in Belgium (which Austria ruled, but mostly spoke French) and in Alsace (which France ruled, but mostly spoke German). But there was no good reason—certainly no necessity—for the war. The Girondins, leaders of the Assembly at that time, supported it in a desperate attempt to knit a dissolving nation together by appealing to patriotism against a foreign enemy; many royalists favored it in the forlorn hope that a foreign war would reawaken support for the monarchy. For both groups it was a fatal miscalculation which was to cost most of their leaders their lives. The war which had not been there to explain the French Revolution's origins was later begun by its own leaders who were beginning to draw back from their handiwork, hoping in vain to change its course.

The French army, like every other institution in France, had been largely dismantled by the Revolution, and was close to chaos. Its one reasonably competent general still in service August 10—Lafayette—turned himself over to the Austrians on the 19th rather than fight for a regime that had overthrown his King. The remaining officers from the old regime were men with little conscience or ability, who had stayed either out of inertia or because of the vastly expanded opportunities for promotion created by the departure of the many officers who remained loyal to the King or were dismissed for opposition to the Revolution. There were also much younger officers jumped far up in rank by the revolutionary government, in whom no amount of ability could make up for lack of experience, and very young officers just enlisted, whose time would come but was not yet. (The fact that the volunteers of 1791 included seven future marshals of Napoleon has often been remarked, but did not much help the army in 1792; they were all still much too young.) The combined Austrian and Prussian forces under the Duke of Brunswick on the eastern border of France were approximately equal to the French in numbers, but far superior in discipline and leadership. Fire, if not cohesion, was added to Brunswick's army by some five thousand bitterly angry French aristocrats driven from their country by the Revolution, determined and personally brave, but not used to fighting as a unit. Despite this problem and continuing difficulties of cooperation between the Prussians and Austrians, it was generally believed in Europe that this invading force was sure to prevail. Longwy had fallen almost without resistance, and by August 30 the Duke of Brunswick invested the greater fortress of Verdun.

There was substantial, though by no means universal public alarm over the invasion, and the Paris Commune moved at once to take advantage of it to consolidate its power and make itself even more feared. On the evening of the 28th Danton went before the Assembly to declare the Commune's intention to search every house in Paris for arms and suspected traitors. "When a ship is wrecked," he thundered in his booming voice, "the crew throw overboard anything which might place their lives in peril. Similarly, all potential dangers to the nation must be rejected from its bosom."[12] In view of both the past authorizations by the Assembly for the Commune to proceed against suspects and the fact that the Commune already held effective power in Paris, he did not really need Assembly approval for this action; but he felt it would strengthen his hand to have it, and he obtained it easily. He left the Assembly at midnight, climbed into his carriage (the Minister of Justice rode in state), and ordered the coachman to bring its horses to a gallop. He clattered through the streets to City Hall (did he spare a glance for its steps where the Marquis de Mandat had been shot down in cold blood by his order, just nineteen days before?) and passed on the search decree to the designated commissioners of the Commune.

> Domiciliary visits shall be announced by the beating of drums. The visits shall be made by the commissaries of the sections, assisted by a sufficient number of armed troops. In the name of the nation they shall demand of each individual an exact declaration of the number of arms in his possession. After the declaration, if the individual is suspect, his home shall be carefully searched. In case the declaration is false, the declarer shall be immediately arrested. Every individual having a domicile in Paris, who shall be found in the home of another during the domiciliary visit, shall be considered suspect, and as such shall be put under arrest. The commissaries of the sections shall have a register upon which they shall exactly inscribe the names of those individuals visited and the number of arms found. They shall inscribe with the same exactitude the names of persons who are absent from their homes, and affix seals to the doors of their apartments. Houses in which no one can be found, and which the commissaries are unable to enter, shall be padlocked.[13]

The search was carried out that evening, the 29th, during a period of two hours. The brewer Santerre, Mandat's successor as commander of the National Guard, was in charge. Only two thousand muskets were found (Danton had said he expected to find eighty thousand). The real purpose of the search was not to look for arms, but for people known or suspected to be hostile to the revolutionary regime. About four thousand were arrested and imprisoned. Available evidence suggests that, while Danton agreed to the plan and took the public lead in carrying it out, the idea came from the fevered and probably diseased brain of Jean-Paul Marat, and included from the beginning the intention to massacre many of those to be seized.

Marat belongs to that fortunately small band of history-makers of whom the Christian can truly say, in charity, that he hopes they were only insane. Even the most fervent admirers of the French Revolution shrink from Marat now, as many did in his own time, with a shudder. A quack doctor and scientist, he had purchased a medical degree from the University of St. Andrews in Scotland and claimed to have developed an electrical theory that explained the workings of the physical universe better than Newton's; he raged when the French Academy of Science, unimpressed by his theory, refused to elect him to membership. His name was originally spelled Mara; his father was an apostate Catholic from Cagliari in Sardinia and his mother a Calvinist of Geneva. Left an orphan in his teens, he roamed Europe as a vagabond, ending up in London, where he seems to have led a life of crime. J. M. Thompson says:

> There are almost sufficient grounds for identifying Jean-Paul Marat, during some otherwise unaccountable gaps in his English career, with 'John Peter Le Maître, alias Mara,' who taught French first at Warrington Academy, and then at Oxford, where he lived with a wife in a house at the corner of the Broad and the Turl, and had a child christened at St. Michael's in the Corn; who robbed the Ashmolean collection of a number of valuable medals; fled, pursued by Sir John Fielding's runners, to London, Norwich, and Lichfield; was arrested at Dublin, imprisoned in Oxford Castle, and condemned by the Vice-Chancellor's court to the hulks at Woolwich.[14]

Escaping or released from the English prison hulks, Marat reappeared in Paris in 1777 and managed to get himself hired as doctor to the household troops of the King's brother, the Count of Artois (he whose answer to the Tennis Court Oath was to reserve the tennis court for a game). Marat also conducted a considerable private practice revolving around the administration of "artificial anti-congestive fluid" (*l'eau factice anti-pulmonique*), a concoction consisting mostly of chalk and water. When the Revolution came he embraced it with the greatest enthusiasm. The vehemence of his language was almost beyond belief, and well in advance of its time. During the first few weeks of the Revolution he wrote: "When a man is in want of everything, he has a right to take from another the superfluity in which he is wallowing: nay, more, he has a right to cut his throat and devour his palpitating flesh."[15] In September of that year he launched his own newspaper, *The Friend of the People*, which soon gained wide readership largely from pure shock effect; here is a typical passage: "Rise up, you unfortunates of the city, workmen without work, street stragglers sleeping under bridges, prowlers along the highways, beggars without food or shelter, vagabonds, cripples, and tramps. . . . Cut the thumbs off the aristocrats who conspire against you; split the tongues of the priests who have preached servitude."[16]

In person Marat was unforgettable. By 1792 men were calling him "the monster." He was very short, barely five feet tall, with black hair, protruding greenish-yellow eyes, and an olive complexion, thin but strong and muscular, afflicted with a virulent skin disease and agonizing headaches for which he wore a red bandanna soaked in vinegar over his head. He wore open-necked shirts to the most solemn occasions and usually carried pistols in his belt. But the aspect of his extraordinary physical appearance most remarked by his contemporaries was its constant agitation. He was never still. His face and his whole body jerked as he walked; one contemporary said, "he did not walk; he hopped."[17] His wide mouth twitched and grimaced; his eyes rolled; his hands and arms gesticulated. Day after day he wallowed in his hatreds.

On August 19, 1792 Marat had written in *The Friend of the People*: "The wisest and best course to pursue is to go armed to the Abbaye [the Abbey of St. Germain des Prés, another church building taken over by the Commune for use as a prison], drag out the traitors, especially the Swiss officers and their accomplices, and put them to the sword. What folly it is to give them a trial!"[18] He had appointed himself head of what he called the "Committee of Surveillance" under the Commune, which designated him the official reporter of its acts. This committee drew up a long list of suspects whose names were turned over to the house searchers of August 29 for automatic arrest wherever found.

Marat's Committee of Surveillance included two later members of the Committee of Public Safety of the Terror, Jean-Nicolas Billaud-Varenne and Jean-Marie Collot d'Herbois. Billaud-Varenne was a native of the long-time Calvinist stronghold of La Rochelle, "badly brought up by a feeble father, a mother who combined immorality with religion, and a libertine abbé."[19] A failed lawyer and a failed writer, before the Revolution he was an "ineffectual drifter."[20] In 1789 he published *The Last Blow Against Prejudice and Superstition*, a violent attack on the Catholic Church. He called for the government to take over its property and control its clergy. Most Catholic doctrinal teachings should be abandoned, religious vows and clerical celibacy forbidden, bishops abolished, and the liturgy of the Mass simplified. Any Catholics who might oppose such changes were dismissed in one scathing sentence: "It is possible, no doubt, that a vile interest, seconded by a stupid ignorance, may still dare to rise up against so advantageous a reform; but its motives will be too contemptible for anyone to give ear to its clamor."[21] As for Collot d'Herbois, he was a native Parisian, an actor and a failed theater manager, bitter at the low social

esteem in which his theatrical profession was generally held, angry
and excitable, with a touch of paranoia.

It is quite clear that the inner circle of leadership in the Commune had decided by the time the night arrests were made, and very
likely several days before, to kill large numbers of the prisoners.
Prudhomme, an eyewitness, reports a discussion among members of
the Surveillance Committee on their disposal:

> Marat proposed to set the prisons on fire, but it was
> pointed out to him that the neighboring houses would be en-
> dangered; someone else advised flooding them. Billaud-
> Varennes proposed butchering the prisoners. "You propose
> butchering them," someone said, "but you won't find enough
> killers." Billaud-Varennes answered warmly, "They can be
> found." Tallien showed disgust at the discussion, but did not
> have the courage to oppose it.[22]

As for Danton, he was later to say regarding this decision: "I
looked my crime steadfastly in the face, and I did it."[23]

On August 30 the Assembly, following the lead of Jacques Brissot, the Girondin, who had learned on a six months' visit to the United
States in 1788 the difference between a law-abiding and a revolutionary republic, made a last spasmodic effort to check the power of the
Paris Commune. Angered and deeply alarmed by the arrest that day
of Girey-Dupré, editor of the principal Girondin newspaper in Paris,
The French Patriot, Brissot led the Assembly in acting not only to free
Girey-Dupré immediately but to order the dissolution of the Commune. "At last," Brissot said with an optimism which the history of
the next two years was to prove utterly unjustified, "good citizens
[have] opened their eyes, and perceived that they had not twice conquered liberty in order to hand it over to intriguers, and that they
ought not to raise upon the ruins of royal and patrician despotism a
despotism more oppressive and more hateful."[24]

This sudden burst of courage caught the Commune by surprise,
but was foredoomed by the events of the day of the tocsin. The Legislative Assembly was, in modern political parlance, a lame duck. The
voters were already meeting to choose the electors who in turn would
choose the delegates to the National Convention that would take its
place. It had destroyed the basis of its own authority by suspending
King and constitution August 10. All it had left was a rapidly dwin-
dling prestige—higher in the country, which by and large had not
kept up with the incredibly rapid march of events in Paris; lower and
steadily declining in the capital. The Commune acted promptly. Pli-
able Mayor Pétion, almost in eclipse since August 10, was trotted out

to head a deputation to the Assembly urging reversal of its action, and Robespierre drafted a long memorandum on how necessary it was to keep the Commune in being. Both deputation and memorandum reached the Assembly before the end of the day of Brissot's action, August 30. For one more day the Assembly waited; then on September 1 delegate Thuriot, after receiving what was doubtless a very blunt message from Danton, rose to urge it to rescind its action and "restore" the Commune (which actually had never ceased functioning). This was immediately done.

On that same day, September 1, a pamphlet was distributed all over Paris with the sensational title *The Great Treason of Louis Capet. Discovery of a Plot for Assassinating All Good Citizens during the Night between the 2nd and 3rd of This Month.* No historian has identified the author of this screed, but its publication must have been known to the leaders of the Commune, and was probably sponsored by them. Cynical falsehood could go no farther; there was indeed a plot for assassinating many good citizens during the night between the 2nd and the 3rd, but it was not by "Louis Capet,"[25] but by the Commune itself which oversaw the distribution of the pamphlet.

On September 2 the fortress of Verdun surrendered to the Prussians, and its commander Beaurepaire blew his brains out.

The news did not arrive in Paris until two days later, but the revolutionaries had anticipated it. September 2 was a Sunday, with few people at work; there was every opportunity for inflammatory oratory, not only in the Assembly and at announced meetings in halls used by the Commune in the Paris sections, but on street corners and in parks throughout the city. At dawn the Commune issued a proclamation, posted up all over Paris: "TO ARMS, CITIZENS, TO ARMS, THE ENEMY IS AT OUR GATES!"[26] (So far was the enemy from being at the gates that it required two days of hard riding to reach Paris from the lost fortress, and the Duke of Brunswick managed to use up the next twelve days in advancing just twenty miles.) The orators whipped all who would listen to them into a frenzy of mingled anger and fear. Danton donned a scarlet coat and went to the Assembly, insisting that his wife Gabrielle (who hated crowds and public debates) come with him to the galleries, where she sat watching him in a taffeta dress and a lace cap. He explained measures being taken for the city's defense and the need for all citizens to be ready to fight. The tocsin was about to be rung again, he declared:

> Whoever refuses to serve in person, or to return his arms, will suffer the death penalty. When the tocsin sounds, it is not an alarm signal; it sounds the charge against our

country's enemies. And to defeat them, gentlemen, we need audacity, yet more audacity, always audacity, and France will be saved!"[27]

"A gigantic ovation rose from the benches and poured down from the galleries," says a recent biographer of Danton. "Even his fiercest enemies applauded him. As one of them afterward wrote: 'When he uttered those final words, this hideous man was beautiful.'"[28] Danton's *toujours de l'audace* is as famous in French history and popular lore as Patrick Henry's "Give me liberty or give me death!" is in America. Rarely if ever has so thrilling and eloquent a commitment been followed through in so strange and ugly a manner.

And so the endless, hammering *ding-ding-ding-ding* of the tocsin was heard again in Paris at two o'clock in the afternoon of Sunday, September 2, 1792. Signal guns boomed, drums beat, militia assembled, a red flag rose over City Hall. About thirty minutes later, four carriages were lurching through the echoing streets on their way from City Hall to the Abbey of St. Germain des Prés which was being used as a prison. The carriages were filled with priests and religious who had refused to take the oath to accept the Civil Constitution of the Clergy and with it, the schismatic church the Revolution had set up in France in defiance of the Pope. When they had nearly reached the Abbey, a man leaped upon one of the carriages and plunged a sword through the window. He withdrew it with blood dripping from the blade and waved it in the air, screaming to the bystanders: "So this frightens you, does it, you cowards? You must get used to the sight of death!"[29] Then he began slashing wildly at those inside the carriage, and was joined by several others including some of the men who were supposed to be guarding the prisoners. The terrified horses tried to escape. They dragged the carriages, now full of dying and dismembered men and their killers, to the gates of the Abbey. The surviving prisoners jumped out. Two of them were killed instantly upon dismounting; the others were pursued into the Abbey courtyard and hunted down like rabbits. Only one of the 24 occupants of the carriages, Father Sicard, lived to tell the tale in his memoirs.

Two men strode into the corpse-strewn courtyard of the Abbey just as the last of these victims was expiring: Billaud-Varenne of Marat's Committee of Surveillance, wearing a red jacket and sash and an enormous wig; and beside him, a long sword bumping against his knee, the cadaverous figure of Stanislas "Strike-Hard" Maillard, the herald of death, the man who had led the assault on the Bastille, the assault on the King and Queen at Versailles, and the assault on the King and Queen at the Tuileries, each one characterized by the dismemberment of helpless victims. Billaud-Varenne made a short speech, ending with: "Citizens, in sacrificing your enemies you accomplish your duty!" Then Maillard growled: "There's no more to do here for the moment; let's go to the Carmelites." "To the Carmelites!" his hired assassins (some of them convicted felons just released from the prisons for this "duty") responded, and hurried off while the bodies were being dragged feet first out of the courtyard.[30]

The faithful priests and religious imprisoned at the former Carmelite monastery were taking their daily exercise in the garden when the killers entered shortly after three o'clock, armed now with pistols as well as swords and pikes, shouting for the Archbishop of Arles who was confined there. Abbot Hébert, Superior-General of the Eudist Congregation, was standing with the Archbishop; Hébert stepped forward to ask for a trial before they were executed, and was promptly shot through the shoulder. The Archbishop fell to his knees for a moment of prayer; then he arose and said, echoing his Lord at Gethsemane: "I am the man you are looking for."[31] Instantly a sword slashed across his face; then a pike plunged into his chest. At almost the same moment, the same happened to the other episcopal prisoner in the Carmelite monastery, the bishop of Beauvais. The priests in the garden who were able to reach the church that opened upon it, came in to kneel before the tabernacle and give each other the absolution of the dying.

Then Maillard arrived, carrying a list of all the prisoners. "Don't kill them so quickly," he said. "We are meant to try them."[32] He set up a table in the corridor as the judge, and assembled a group of the killers as a jury. The corridor was poorly lit; a single candle stood upon the table, surrounded by pipes and bottles, casting gigantic and hideous shadows on the wall. The surviving prisoners were brought in two by two, each one escorted by three men with swords crossed over his breast. Two men in blood-spattered shirts guarded the door. Maillard peered at his list in the flickering light through silver-rimmed spectacles (later carefully preserved by his descendants) and timed the proceedings with a gold watch. To each prisoner Maillard said: "Your name and your profession. Take care; a lie will be your ruin."[33] Each man was then asked whether he had taken the oath to accept the Civil Constitution of the Clergy; when each responded in the negative, he was then asked whether he was now prepared to do so.

It is not recorded that a single one took the oath. It is because of Maillard's clear implication that they could have saved their lives by swearing to obey a schismatic church, that the Catholic Church has beatified 191 of these men as martyrs.

As each pair was condemned, they were pushed along the corridor to the steps going down into the garden, and at the foot of the steps they were stabbed or beaten to death with shouts of "Long live the nation!" Each conviction and execution, timed by Maillard, took no more than two or three minutes. Some of the 119 bodies were taken away, but most were dumped in the monastery well under a covering of bottles, brooms, cases, and dishes, where their battered bones were found by excavators seventy years later.

When all the prisoners at the Carmelite monastery were dead, except for the handful who had managed to escape in the confusion, Maillard and his killing team went back to the Abbey. After all, they had only killed there the prisoners who had arrived in the carriages; the building held more than 300 who were still alive. Maillard set up his court again. It was night now; two great bonfires were lit in the Abbey courtyard where the massacre had begun. Not all the prisoners in the Abbey were priests and religious, and Maillard amused himself by letting some of the laymen go free. The condemned were hacked to death in the courtyard. The slaughter continued all night. A passer-by, Philip Morice, actually saw the gutters of the Street of the Seine outside the Abbey running with blood.

At some point during that hellish night one desperate victim tried to escape up a chimney. Maillard was informed by a guard. He ordered him to fire shots up the chimney, and warned him that if the prisoner escaped the guard himself would be killed. When the shots did not dislodge the prisoner, straw was set afire under him. When he fell, almost unconscious from the smoke, he was promptly killed on the hearth.

At about one o'clock in the morning an English doctor, John Moore, was writing in his journal in his hotel room in Paris on the almost inconceivable events of the past day, which were still in progress:

> Is this the work of a furious and deluded mob? How is it that the citizens of this populous metropolis remain passive spectators of so dreadful an outrage? Is it possible that this is the accomplishment of a plan concerted two or three weeks ago, that those arbitrary arrests were ordered with this in view, that rumors of treason and intended insurrections and massacres were spread about to exasperate the people and that, taking advantage of the rumors of bad news from the frontiers, orders have been issued for firing the cannon and sounding the tocsin to increase the alarm and terrify the populace into acquiescence; while a band of selected ruffians was hired to massacre those whom hatred, revenge or fear had destined to destruction, but whom law and justice could not destroy?

It is now past twelve at midnight and the bloody work still goes on! Almighty God![34]

Nor had the dissolving Assembly been forgotten. The Count of Montmorin, once the Foreign Minister of Louis XVI, had been given special treatment by Maillard when he was found at the Abbey. Impaled on a pike, he was carried into the Assembly chamber, still writhing. When someone ventured a mild protest to the Minister of Justice, Danton responded: "To hell with the prisoners! They must look after themselves."[35]

Incredible as it must seem, the horror was not yet over when sunrise at last ended the night of the long knives of September 2-3. The massacre continued for *four more days*. There is unquestionably authentic documentary evidence that the killers were paid for their work from the public funds of Paris, administered by the Commune.[36] On the 3rd the former royal family—themselves also among the imprisoned—were barely saved by the quick tongue of Jean-Pierre André Daujon, himself an active member of the Commune who had been charged with their safety. He convinced the killers who came to the Temple that the Queen and her children were hostages of special value to the state and that the King would undoubtedly be executed by judicial process soon. Marie Antoinette's dearest friend, the Princess of Lamballe, was not so fortunate.

There are depths beneath depths, and we have now reached the pit. Legend to the contrary notwithstanding, very few of the victims of the September massacres were aristocrats—only about thirty out of more than 1,400.[37] The Princess of Lamballe was much the highest-ranking and best-known victim. She had been incarcerated in La Force prison. The main killing team, having spent the afternoon at the Carmelite monastery and the night at the Abbey, came to La Force in the morning of the 3rd. Close to exhaustion, utterly debauched by sixteen hours of constant murder, many crazed by drink, the killers when they reached La Force had almost ceased to be recognizable as human beings. "Strike-Hard" Maillard was still their leader. Torture, rape, and cannibalism were now added to the other horrors that had become routine. Brought into a corpse-filled room before Maillard, the Princess of Lamballe was ordered to swear hatred to the King and Queen. She refused, and was killed at once with swords and pikes, and decapitated. Then, as Stanley Loomis tells us, "her still beating heart was ripped from her body and devoured, her legs and arms were severed from her body and shot through cannon. The horrors that were then perpetrated on her disemboweled torso are indescribable; traditionally they have remained cloaked in the obscurity of medical Latin."[38]

Two hundred and eleven years before in Guatemala City in Central America an aged man had died: Bernal Diaz del Castillo, last of the conquistadors of Mexico, their historian. He would have understood, better than any man who lived after him, what had happened to the Princess of Lamballe; for he had seen those things done every day upon the altars of the Satanic empire of Aztec Mexico which he and his companions and his captain, the great Hernan Cortes, had expunged from the face of the earth.[39]

The head of the Princess of Lamballe was carried through the streets of Paris on a pike. In Bastille Square it was taken to a hairdresser's to be cleaned and made more recognizable; then it was brought to the Temple. Singing the Marseillaise and the song *Ça Ira*, the crowd intended to show it to Marie Antoinette.

Warned by a frightful scream from one of her attendants, the former Queen refused to come to the window. A National Guard officer entered the room and told her that the people had brought something to show her "how they avenge themselves on tyrants." What had they brought? "The head of the Lamballe woman."[40]

Marie Antoinette collapsed and lay unconscious, unresponsive even to the caresses of her children. A commissioner of the Commune, who still retained some remnant of human feeling, mercifully drew the blinds. She never saw the head. When he heard that later, Collot d'Herbois of Marat's Committee of Surveillance expressed his regrets, saying that "if he had been consulted he would have had the head of Madame de Lamballe served in a covered dish for the queen's supper."[41]

There was yet no man to draw again the sword of Hernan Cortes.

There were more than 1,400 victims of the September massacres; but Marat was dissatisfied. For him, it was not nearly enough. On September 10 another member of the Committee of Surveillance wrote: "Marat states openly that 40,000 heads must be knocked off to ensure the success of the Revolution."[42] On September 3 the Commune sent an announcement to all the departments of France, over Marat's signature, "that many ferocious conspirators detained in its prisons have been put to death by the people—acts of justice which seemed to be indispensable in order to terrorize the traitors concealed within its walls at a time when it was about to march on the enemy. The whole nation will without doubt hasten to adopt this measure so necessary to public safety."[43]

This document was despatched from the Ministry of Justice.

But the Paris Commune had other business than killing during these ghastly days. They also had an election to supervise. Deputies from Paris to the new National Convention were being chosen. On this very same September 3 that the body of the Princess of Lamballe was being mutilated with indescribable horror and her head paraded through the streets of Paris, the electors met in the impartial precincts of the Jacobin Club, after having been duly purged of anyone not clearly in sympathy with the actions of August 10. They had met the previous day in the former palace of the Archbishop of Paris, and had convened there first on September 3 as well; they were then conducted from the palace to the Jacobin Club. On their way, crossing the Seine on the Pont-au-Change (Bridge of the Money-Changers), they passed between a double stack of ravaged bodies, victims of the massacre in nearby Châtelet prison. When voting for the deputies began September 5, there was no secret ballot.

It is impossible to appreciate fully the character of the National Convention, which played a central role in all that happened in France throughout the Reign of Terror, without keeping constantly in mind these circumstances in which its members from Paris were elected.

Robespierre was elected first, with 338 votes to 136 for Mayor Pétion. Next it was Danton's turn, by 638 votes out of about 700 on the 6th. Elected with him was Collot d'Herbois, who had wanted to serve Marie Antoinette the Princess of Lamballe's head on a platter. The next day it was Billaud-Varenne ("Citizens! In sacrificing your enemies you accomplish your duty!") and Louis-Pierre Manuel, public prosecutor of the Commune, who declared: "The moment has come *to un-nail Jesus Christ!*"[44] Also elected were Camille Desmoulins; the butcher Legendre, active in the massacres; two candidates with a touch of culture, David the painter and Fabre d'Eglantine the poet; and the erstwhile Duke of Orléans, heir to the throne should Louis XVI and his brothers and his son not survive, who sought to insure his own survival by taking the name of Philip Equality. Last of all, on September 9, came the election of Marat, chosen over the distinguished scientist Joseph Priestley by a vote of 420 to 101 after Robespierre's bodyguard had threatened Louvet, trying to speak against Marat's election, and prevented him from speaking.

On that same day, 43 important state prisoners who had been sent to Orléans by the Assembly to try to save their lives, were brought back on demand of the Commune by Fournier "the American," an agent of Marat's Committee of Surveillance, and slaughtered to the last man at Versailles.

Georges-Jacques Danton had the final word. A few days later he was speaking with Louis-Philippe, son of "Philip Equality" and long afterwards to be King of France himself. The young man, then an officer in the army, remembered the conversation vividly, and frequently recounted it in later life. When Louis-Philippe expressed horror at the massacres, Danton said:

> Do you know who gave the orders for those September massacres you inveighed against so violently and irresponsibly? ... It was I. ... I did not want all these Parisian youths to arrive in Champagne until they were covered with blood, which for us would be a guarantee of their loyalty; I wanted to place a river of blood between them and the *émigrés* ... We are not asking for your approval; all we are asking from you is silence, instead of making yourself the echo of our enemies and yours.[45]

Danton's devoutly Catholic wife Gabrielle, who in her taffeta dress and her lace cap had listened so proudly to him in his scarlet coat crying out to the Assembly of France, "audacity, yet more audacity, always audacity, and France shall be saved!" knew now that the husband she had adored had the blood of 1,400 of history's most horrible murders on his hands, that he and his colleagues had been directly responsible for the martyrdom of more than two hundred priests and religious of Jesus Christ because they would not abandon His vicar on earth. Danton could feel her withdrawing from him, feel a shadow of repulsion where there had been so much love; but he could not yet feel her prayers. The Duke of Brunswick was on the march again at last, and he had to deal with him now.

NOTES

[1]Martin P. Harney, *The Jesuits in History* (New York, 1941), p. 298.

[2]Vincent Cronin, *Louis and Antoinette* (New York, 1975), p. 225.
[3]*Ibid.*, p. 234.
[4]*Ibid.*, p. 263.
[5]J.M. Thompson, *The French Revolution* (New York, 1945), p. 165.

[6]*The Cambridge Modern History* (first edition), Volume VIII, "The French Revolution" (New York, 1908), p. 240.

[7]W.J. Battersby, *Brother Solomon, Martyr of the French Revolution* (London, 1960), p. 7.

[8]*Ibid.*, p. 10.

[9]Claude G. Bowers, *Pierre Vergniaud, Voice of the French Revolution* (New York, 1950), p. 237.

[10]Louis-Philippe, *Memoirs, 1773-1793*, ed. John Hardman (New York, 1977), p. 256.

[11]*Ibid.*, p. 257.

[12]Robert Christophe, *Danton* (London, n.d.), p. 251.

[13]E.L. Higgins, ed., *The French Revolution as Told by Contemporaries* (Boston, 1938), pp. 245-246.

[14]Thompson, *French Revolution*, p. 328.

[15]Bowers, *Vergniaud*, p. 241.

[16]Stanley Loomis, *Paris in the Terror* (Philadelphia, 1964), p. 90.

[17]*Ibid.*, p. 92.

[18]Hippolyte Taine, *The French Revolution*, tr. John Durand (New York, 1881, 1962), II, 211.

[19]*Encyclopedia Britannica*, 11th edition.

[20]R.R. Palmer, *Twelve Who Ruled; the Year of Terror in the French Revolution* (Princeton, 1941, 1969), p. 12.

[21]*Ibid.*, p. 13.

[22]Loomis, *Paris in the Terror*, p. 77.

[23]Bowers, *Vergniaud*, p. 244.

[24]Eloise Ellery, *Brissot de Warville, a Study in the History of the French Revolution* (Boston, 1915), p. 299.

[25]Louis XVI's family name was Bourbon, not Capet. Capet had never been a family name, but simply the personal surname or nickname of Hugh, the first French king of the new dynasty that followed the Carolingians beginning in 987, from which all later French kings were (however distantly) descended. The name meant "head" or "big-head."

[26]Louis-Philippe, *Memoirs*, p. 259.

[27]Christophe, *Danton*, p. 254, except that the translation of Danton's famous cry of *de l'audace, encore de l'audace, toujours de l'audace* has been slightly altered from that of Christophe's translator, who says "boldness, and yet more boldness, boldness at all times." "Audacity" is the cognate word in English and seems to give more of the flavor of Danton's own language, while there is no "and" before *encore*, and "always" is the normal translation of *toujours*.

[28]Christophe, *Danton*, p. 255.

[29]Christopher Hibbert, *The Days of the French Revolution* (New York, 1980), p. 170.

[30]Battersby, *Brother Solomon*, p. 22.

[31]Hibbert, *Days of the French Revolution*, p. 170.

[32]*Ibid.*, p. 171.

[33]Higgins, ed., *French Revolution*, p. 249.

[34]Loomis, *Paris in the Terror*, pp. 81-82.

[35]Cronin, *Louis and Antoinette*, p. 358.

[36]Thompson, *French Revolution*, pp. 332, 336-337; Taine, *French Revolution*, II, 221-222.

[37]Loomis, *Paris in the Terror*, p. 82.

[38]*Ibid.*

[39]See my *Our Lady of Guadalupe and the Conquest of Darkness* (Front Royal VA, 1983).

[40]Cronin, *Louis and Antoinette*, p. 359.

[41]Taine, *French Revolution*, II, 216n.

[42]*Ibid.*, II, 218n.

[43]Loomis, *Paris in the Terror*, p. 96.

[44]Madelin, *French Revolution*, p. 301.

[45]Louis-Philippe, *Memoirs*, p. 308.

III.
Strange Victory
(September 10-November 30, 1792)

Karl Wilhelm Ferdinand, the Duke of Brunswick, prided himself on being an enlightened despot. His hereditary domain, situated in rolling country north of the Harz Mountains in central Germany between Magdeburg and Hanover, was of only moderate size and historical importance in the patchwork of petty German states that had once (but not for a long time) been drawn together under the Holy Roman Empire. But the Duke was a very wealthy man with a Europe-wide reputation as a general. Though not a citizen of the kingdom of Prussia, he had fought with distinction under Frederick the Great (his nephew) in the Seven Years War, and in consequence received the rank of field marshal in the Prussian army. He had married the daughter of the Prince of Wales, during the period when the kings of Great Britain were Germans of Hanover who could barely speak the language of their British subjects. After the Seven Years War ended in 1763, he had travelled widely in Europe, spending considerable time in France, and visiting Voltaire in Switzerland during the last years of his life. In 1780, at the age of forty-five, he succeeded his father as Duke, and in 1787 commanded a Prussian army which invaded the Netherlands, attaining its objectives rapidly, easily, and completely. When the French Revolution broke out, the reputation of the Duke of Brunswick both as a liberal and as a gracious aristocrat was so high that in 1792 he found himself in the unique position of playing host to the refugee brother of Louis XVI, the future King Louis XVIII, while also being offered command of the French revolutionary army—an offer he turned down.

In private life, the Duke's great wealth gave him ample opportunity to gratify his personal tastes to the full. He surrounded himself with an odd combination of liberal intellectuals and spiritualist mediums. He adorned his ducal palace with ostentatious luxury; it had doors of malachite and ivory, and what were called "Babylonian staircases." But his greatest material passion was for his diamond collection. When he died under the sword of Napoleon's Field Marshal Davout at the Battle of Auerstadt in 1806, the inventory of his estate showed no less than 2,400 diamonds "of all sizes, variously cut, rosettes, brilliants, and briolettes."[1]

Because of his reputation, once he had turned down the French offer of command earlier in 1792, there was no opposition to the Duke of Brunswick being given the command of the allied army whose objective was to march on Paris and save the French monarchy. In the courts of King Frederick William II of Prussia and of Emperor Leopold II of Austria there was only a glimmer of understanding of the magnitude and character of the forces unleashed in France since 1789, and none at all of the events of August 10, of which those courts had barely heard by mid-September. The whole eighteenth century had been characterized by pervasive, purblind nationalism. The very idea of a truly international cause hardly existed. Every man in Europe had been familiar with that idea from 1517 to 1648, all through the long struggle between Catholics and Protestants for the future of Christendom; but that had ended, at least in its political phase, with the Treaties of Westphalia in 1648 and their principle "the religion of the country shall be the religion of the king" (that is, of the king ruling in 1648—later conversions were not allowed). The last truly international cause had been the struggle against the Turkish assault of 1683, hurled back from the gates of the Austrian capital of Vienna by the great John Sobieski of Poland; but no man living in 1792 could remember that, and now Poland was in the process of being carved up by the very powers which were marching against France. The French refugees from the revolution—the émigrés—had done their best to explain to the leaders of Prussia and Austria what was at stake. They had had some success, or there would have been no expedition into France for the Duke of Brunswick to command. But the Prussian and Austrian leaders did not yet really take it all quite seriously. They were at least as much interested in fishing in troubled French waters for whatever they could get out of them to their national, dynastic, and territorial advantage as in ending the horrors of revolution, saving the lives of the French royal family, and returning the émigrés to their homeland. There were only five thousand *émigrés* in arms; without foreign help they could do nothing.

But the Duke of Brunswick commanded 36,000 of the best soldiers in the world.

The quality of Prussian military training had become legendary; but the legend was founded on solid fact and historical achievement. With a relatively small force of Prussian soldiers, vastly outnumbered by a host of enemies, King Frederick the Great of Prussia had defeated the best armies of Europe in the Seven Years War. Many of the Prussian soldiers in the army of the Duke of Brunswick were the sons of Frederick's veterans, and all were heirs of the military tradition which he had raised to its summit. They and their kind had made the little kingdom of Prussia, no more than a principality around Berlin less than a hundred years before, one of the great powers of the world. Now they faced on the ancient battlegrounds of Lorraine a confused and disorganized French army which had lost all its best and experienced commanders; whose line regiments had been deprived of their colors and their identities (to take just one example, the Navarre Regiment of the French army was the direct descendant of the band of warriors formed before 1500 by Chevalier Bayard of song and story, the knight "without fear and without reproach"; it had been redesignated by the revolutionary Assembly as simply the Fifth of the Line); and many of whose recent recruits were as likely to kill their own officers by the inimitable revolutionary methods, as the enemy. Almost everyone assumed that the Duke of Brunswick and his Prussians would cut through this demoralized force with little difficulty and liberate Paris from the murderers of September.

Those who reckoned thus, reckoned without Georges-Jacques Danton. The giant from Arcis-sur-Aube, the River of Dawn, with his pig-trampled face and his voice of thunder and his will of iron, was more than a match for the Duke of Brunswick with his ivory doors, his spiritualist mediums, and his diamond collection.

Toujours l'audace! he had cried, audacity always! It was no mere oratorical slogan. Danton meant exactly what he said—and he was not talking only about reckless bravery on the battlefield.

Danton was nothing if not a realist. He knew exactly the condition of the French army. As he said coldly to young Louis-Philippe of Orléans before that world-shaking September was over: "Don't think that I am deceived by these spurts of patriotic enthusiasm . . . No, I know what reliance to place on this inconstancy, on these rapid transitions that so often expose us to panics, flight, shouts of 'everyone for himself' [*sauve qui peut*], and even treason."[2] Danton could have had little doubt that the Duke of Brunswick and his Prussians were fully capable, with sufficient determination, of thrusting aside any resistance the French troops before them were then capable of offering, and crossing in a few days the roughly one hundred miles that separated them from Paris. And *toujours l'audace* meant more than simply throwing oneself into the path of the advancing military machine to be ground under its wheels.

What then did Danton do?

History has never been sure. Academic historians have tried to avoid what they felt would be unscholarly speculation; historians with axes to grind for any of the combatants in September 1792 have all had much to lose by admitting even the possibility that the most persistent legend about the events following the Duke of Brunswick's capture of Verdun might be true. But that legend persists. Unflattering though it is to the national pride of both the French and the Prussians, it fits the facts. More important, it fits the character of the principal actors, the men of destiny at this turning point of history, that strangely ill-matched pair: the mountainous, bellowing orator, shrewd unscrupulous planner, and reckless killer Danton; and the fussy, courtly, "benevolent" diamond collector sympathizing hypocritically with both sides, the Duke of Brunswick.

Let us review the course of various relevant events whose occurrence is firmly established historically.

Verdun fell September 2. During the next twelve days the Duke's army advanced, very slowly indeed, into the Argonne Forest separating the Meuse River on which Verdun stands, from the Aisne to the west. So slow was the advance that the American Ambassador to France, Gouverneur Morris, confided to his diary on the 13th: "The inactivity of the enemy is so extraordinary that it must have an unknown cause."[3] On September 14 the Duke turned the French position in the forest at a place called Cross in the Wood (Croix-aux-Bois). The French army, commanded by General Dumouriez, at once retreated in disorder, forcing Dumouriez to withdraw the following day to the little town of Sainte-Ménéhould on the Aisne.[4]

Meanwhile some very curious things were happening in Paris. When King Louis XVI and his family had been taken by force from Versailles by the revolutionary mob in October 1789 and brought to the Tuileries, they had almost nothing with them but the clothes on their backs. The contents of the immense, luxurious palace of Versailles fell into the hands of the revolutionaries. Those contents included all the crown jewels of France. They were kept in Versailles under lock and key and guard until 1791. Then they were moved to the National Archives building on Louis XV Square in Paris, still under the pretense that they remained the property of the King, who theoretically continued to reign under the constitution of that year. Their custodian was royal archivist Lemoine-Crécy, who had the crown jewel collection inventoried. The list of jewels filled fifty pages, and included some of the largest diamonds in the world, so large and famous that they had names: among them the Regent, 137 carats; the Sancy, "only" 53 carats; the Tavernier; the Dragon; and the Blue Diamond of the Golden Fleece, which had been a particular favorite of King Louis XIV and weighed 115 carats. Upon the overthrow of the monarchy August 10, the revolutionary provisional government, with Danton as Minister of Justice, took custody of the jewels and assigned a new custodian, Citizen Restoul, to take the place of Lemoine-Crécy. Since the National Archives building was located in Paris and the only real government in Paris during this period was that of the Commune, it was the responsibility of the National Guard under Santerre, the brewer who had replaced the murdered Mandat, to supply its guards.[5]

Guards were not much in evidence around this fabulous collection during the second week of Brunswick's snail-like advance through the Argonne Forest. The few who were present seem to have spent most of their nights on duty sound asleep. On the night of September 16—the day after the panicky retreat of the French army before the Duke of Brunswick—a patrol happened by Louis XV Square, now renamed Revolution Square (Place de la Révolution), where the guillotine was to stand during the Reign of Terror. In the flickering light from the lantern at the corner of Saint Florentin street and the square, the patrol spied a startling sight. One man was throwing small objects down from the second story window of the National Archives building; a second was carefully picking them up from the street and stuffing them into his pockets; a third was climbing up to the second story window with a basket in his hand, presumably to hold larger or more precious objects of the same kind. (One would hardly want to throw a 137-carat diamond into the street, even in an ornate setting. What if it fell in a hole?) In the ensuing confusion all the thieves escaped; but it was soon learned, when some were arrested on an informer's tip, that this was the last of four burglaries, the first three having been carried out on the 10th, 11th, and 14th of September; and that before the final burglary of the 16th, the thieves had amused themselves by eating a candlelit picnic supper with vintage wine in the drawing room of the Archives building. They had certainly felt remarkably secure.[6]

The jewels were almost all gone. Out of more than 24 million pounds' worth, all but 600,000 pounds' worth had been taken, including the Regent, the Sancy, the Tavernier, the Dragon, and the Blue Diamond of the Golden Fleece. An investigation followed, during which the odd details mentioned above were revealed, and a number of the jewels—including the Regent and Sancy diamonds, but not the Blue Diamond of the Golden Fleece—were recovered, though stories differed as to where they were found. At one time or another no less than 51 persons were fingered as principals or accomplices in this series of burglaries; yet only 17 were arrested, and of these, five were acquitted, and seven others received only short prison terms; some were even allowed to keep some of the jewels they had stolen. Only five of the 51 went to the guillotine. The merciless Revolution was uncommonly merciful to its jewel thieves. All this was done under the authority of Minister of Justice Danton.[7]

One of the most active members of the Jacobin Club of Paris, chief nursery of the Revolution, was a man named Carra. He had lived for some years in Germany, and had come to know the Duke of Brunswick personally—perhaps due to the fact that both men were Freemasons. Carra was also a close friend and associate of Danton. On July 25 Carra published a column of opinion in a periodical called *Patriotic Annals (Les Annales Politiques)* in which he delivered himself of the following sentiments about his friend the Duke, quite extraordinary for a revolutionary:

> The Duke of Brunswick is the greatest soldier and statesman in Europe. Perhaps all he lacks now is a crown to make him, I do not say the greatest king in Europe, but certainly the true redeemer of European freedom. If he does reach Paris, I would wager that his first act will be to visit the Jacobin Club and don the red cap of liberty.[8]

On September 17, the day after the theft of the crown jewels from the National Archives building was finally discovered, the Paris Commune chose Carra as one of two delegates to go to the headquarters of General Dumouriez at Sainte-Ménéhould, where he was now facing the Duke of Brunswick's advancing army. The Duke and Dumouriez knew each other well, and had already exchanged messages under flags of truce. Carra unquestionably met and talked with Dumouriez; it is not known if he met and talked with the Duke of Brunswick.

Three days later, on September 20, was fought—in a manner of speaking—the Battle of Valmy. This critical encounter occurred near a windmill along the direct route to Paris from the Argonne Forest, a route which Dumouriez, shunted aside in Sainte-Ménéhould, was no longer in position to block. Valmy is often included among the decisive battles of world history. The cannon of both armies fired at each other through most of a misty morning; it had been a very rainy September, and the resulting mud and disease have often been held responsible for the slowness of the Prussian advance. Several hundred casualties—perhaps as many as two thousand—were inflicted on both sides by the cannonading. Those casualties represented less than five per cent of the troops engaged. At two o'clock in the afternoon the Duke of Brunswick finally marshalled his forces in column for attack. Many of the French soldiers shouted defiantly in response, "Long live the nation!" Dumouriez's second, General Kellermann, put his cocked hat on the end of his sword and twirled it about. But no charge came from the Duke of Brunswick. The attack columns stood easy. Then he formed them up a second time. Again, no charge came. Then he formed them up a third time. Again, no charge came. Questioned by the bewildered and not overly bright King of Prussia, who was with him, as to what he was doing, the Duke of Brunswick called out to the King: "We will not give battle here, under any circumstances."[9]

The day closed with the decisive battle that should have ended the French Revolution still essentially unfought, and with a sudden, almost universal conviction on both sides that it was not going to be fought after all. The famous German literary figure and intellectual Wolfgang Goethe, author of *Faust*, who was with the Prussian army at Valmy, said: "From this place and from this day forth begins a new era in the world's history, and all who were here today can say they were present at its birth."[10] On September 22 the Duke concluded an armistice with Dumouriez. Dysentery spread rapidly in the Prussian camp, and on the night of the 29th the Prussians began to retreat, moving steadily out of France. On October 4 Danton appeared before the newly elected National Convention to announce that Paris was out of danger; on October 22 Brunswick recrossed the French frontier, while a French army under General Custine was already operating with considerable success in German territory and had taken the large city of Mainz on the Rhine. The allied invasion, thought certain to succeed, had come and gone without even one real battle.

When in 1806 the Duke of Brunswick died of his wounds at the Battle of Aüerstadt and the inventory of his estate showed the more than 2,400 diamonds mentioned earlier, among that hoard of precious stones was the Blue Diamond of the Golden Fleece—missing a 40-carat fragment. Earlier, in 1795—just three years after Valmy—the Duke's daughter Caroline had married George, Prince of Wales, son of King George III of England. The marriage was not a happy one, but endured after a fashion until the Prince was crowned King George IV in 1820 after years of ruling as Prince Regent during his father's terminal insanity. In the crown placed on the head of George IV at his coronation was the missing 40-carat fragment of the Blue Diamond of the Golden Fleece. As king, George IV demanded that he be freed from the wife he so thoroughly disliked, and the House of Lords obliged. However, since Caroline was widely thought by the English people to have been wronged, she was allowed to take her "personal jewelry" back to Germany with her. The Lords permitted her to include the 40-carat fragment of the Blue Diamond of the Golden Fleece in her personal jewelry. When she died, she bequeathed it to an Italian, who sold it to an American millionaire named Hope. That 40-carat fragment of the Blue Diamond of the Golden Fleece, which first appears as the property of the Duke of Brunswick's daughter, is the famous and allegedly accursed Hope Diamond, now in the Smithsonian Institution in Washington. The 75-carat larger portion of the Blue Diamond of the Golden Fleece passed to the Duke of Brunswick's elder son. Overthrown by revolution, he travelled through Europe with a suitcase full of diamonds, finally finding refuge in Geneva, where he died in 1871 and willed his fortune to that city. Some years later the city authorities sold the Blue Diamond to a banker named Victor Lyon, who died in 1963 at the age of 85, still in possession of it.[11]

Did Danton save the Revolution by buying victory at Valmy from the Duke of Brunswick with the Blue Diamond of the Golden Fleece? For two hundred years the legend has persisted that he did. If any leader in history could have persuaded the enemy commander to "throw" one of the decisive battles of the world, it would have been Georges-Jacques Danton. *Toujours l'audace!*

On the day after the "Battle" of Valmy, the newly elected National Convention held its first regular session in Paris.

We should pause to take a careful look at these men and the place where they were meeting, where so much history was to be made.

There were 749 members authorized to sit in the Convention. Not one had called himself a royalist during the elections. About one-third had served in either the original National Assembly (83) or the immediately preceding Legislative Assembly (194). About half of them were lawyers, far more than any other professional or occupational category. Younger men predominated; few statistics point more clearly to the destructive passion of the Revolution for rejecting all that was older and traditional than the age distribution of the delegates to the National Convention: no less than 85 per cent were under fifty. The wisdom of years was not wanted in that gathering.[12]

They met, as had their predecessor assemblies ever since the Third Estate was locked out of the Hall of Diversions in Versailles and went marching to the tennis court, in a peculiar building which had been a royal riding academy. It was in shape a long rectangle, designed to include a racing oval and tiers of benches for spectators at horse shows, with overhanging galleries on each of the four sides. Never intended for regular daily use by hundreds of people, it was poorly lit and poorly ventilated; the windows were few and small, high up near the ceiling. The only source of heat for winter sessions was a single porcelain stove which was (one of the many weird ironies of the Revolution) a model of the destroyed Bastille. The floor was the old racing oval, somewhat constricted to allow placement of the maximum possible number of benches. The president sat in a chair elevated above the oval, with the tables for the recording secretaries immediately below him. Directly across the oval from the president's chair was the podium or "tribune" from which delegates addressed the Convention. All around the oval were the deputies' benches; the public was admitted only into the galleries above, which had no connection with the floor. In the middle of the building, next to the long sides of the oval, the benches were lower but laterally more extended; on either end, next to the short sides of the rectangle and back from the short ends of the oval, the benches rose up to a considerable height. In the Legislative Assembly, the more violent revolutionaries had congregated, at first simply by chance, on the higher benches to the left of the president's chair, from which they became known as "the Left" or "the Mountain." (The persistence to this day of the former term, along with its opposite "the Right," is a forceful reminder of how much the legacy of the French Revolution is still with us.) Perhaps in a feeble attempt to defuse political labels and hatreds, when the National Convention met the president's chair had been set up on the opposite side of the Riding School, so the high benches where the radicals had sat were now on his right. But they held resolutely to their benches, and so marked had the political connotation of the term "the Left" already become that it did not matter to anyone that the Left in the National Convention was now physically on the right. The deputies opposite them were the Girondins, who at first had been the radicals, and were quite uncomfortable with their new role as conservatives. Those in between, because their seats were lower down, were known as "the Plain." As they skulked lower and lower with the passing months in an increasingly desperate effort to keep out of sight and trouble, some wits began calling them "the Marsh."

The most thorough recent study of political alignments in the early National Convention shows 178 Girondins (led by an "inner sixty"), 215 Jacobins and others of the Mountain, and 250 of the Plain (many of whom rarely attended the sessions).[13]

Though only 371 deputies had arrived, the first regular session of the Convention met September 21, and proceeded at once to vote on the abolition of the monarchy. Since no royalists had been elected, the outcome of the vote was a foregone conclusion; but the vehemence of the language of the motion is well worth noting. The abolition of the monarchy was moved by a priest, Henri Grégoire, who had become a bishop in the schismatic "constitutional" church. Active in the national assemblies from the beginning, Grégoire had presided in the original one on the day the Bastille was taken. He has often been held up as proof that there were genuine Christians and clergymen supporting the Revolution, and it is true that Grégoire never disavowed Christianity itself; but he disavowed the Pope and the Catholic Church, and his language was full of hate and ended in blasphemy as he introduced his motion for the abolition of the monarchy September 21, 1792:

> Kings are in the social order what monsters are in the natural order. Courts are the factories of crimes and the dens of tyrants. The history of kings is the martyrology of nations. Certainly none of us will ever propose to retain in France the fatal race of kings.
> We know only too well that all the dynasties have never been anything but a devouring breed living off human flesh. But we must measure the friends of liberty! We must destroy this magic talisman whose power may still bewitch many men. I demand, therefore, that you consecrate the abolition of the monarchy by a solemn law.[14]

Christians do not "consecrate" abolitions and destruction.

There was no debate at all on Grégoire's motion. It passed unanimously. Insofar as the Convention—the only national governing body then existing in France—could manage it, France's thousand-year-old monarchy had been destroyed.

Eight days later, on September 29, the second and third floors of the Great Tower of the Temple were deemed ready for occupancy by the royal family, although still being painted and papered. This forbidding structure, Paris' equivalent of the Tower of London, had been built by the Knights Templar in the thirteenth century and left essentially unchanged for five hundred years. It was a dark square keep with turreted ramparts all around it, 150 feet high with walls nine feet thick. The eight-inch-thick outer door was secured by iron bands and four enormous bolts. The windows—little more than peepholes through the nine feet of masonry—were blocked by iron bars and shutters; very little light came through them, and no air. No less than 250 men were on guard at all times, on the first and second floors and around the building. The prisoners had to pass through seven checkpoints to reach the enclosed garden for their daily exercise. Throughout the entire period of their imprisonment this devoutly Catholic family was never allowed to attend Mass or to see a priest, except for Louis on the day before his execution.

The ex-King was lodged on the second floor and Marie Antoinette and the children on the third floor. On their first day in the Great Tower they were not even permitted to see each other. The commissioner of the Commune on duty that day was Antoine Simon, a shoemaker. Sobbing, Marie Antoinette begged Simon at least to let her and the children have dinner with the ex-King. He grudgingly agreed. Almost moved for a moment, Simon turned to a companion saying, "I believe those bloody women will make me cry." But then, throwing off the temptation to sympathy, he said to Marie Antoinette: "When you murdered the people on August 10th *you* did not cry."[15]

On October 4 Marat made his first appearance before the Convention. (He had not been a member of either the National Assembly or the Legislative Assembly, the national legislative bodies which had preceded the Convention.) In late September the Girondins had launched a major oratorical assault on the Paris Commune, keyed to the massacres of September. They were aware that some of them could have been included in those massacres, and that Marat and Robespierre had wished to do so, but had been prevented by Danton. Investigating committees had been appointed, but no concrete action had been taken. A furious demonstration greeted Marat when he stepped to the "tribune" to speak; deputies from the left and center of the rectangular hall shouted that he was a monster and a disgrace to the Convention and should not be heard. "Give him a glass of blood!" one member shouted, and others joined in, "Blood! Give him blood!"[16]

Eventually, however, the Convention decided that since Marat was a duly elected member, he must be heard. He called bluntly for a dictatorship (without naming his prospective dictator) and denounced the Girondin leaders (calling them "Brissotins" for one of their leaders, Brissot). In a melodramatic gesture, Marat put a pistol to his head at the tribune and vowed to shoot himself if the Convention passed a decree against him. The pistol was not loaded. Finally he sat down, to

cries of "monster" and "scoundrel" and "to the Abbaye" (the prison
where the massacre he had instigated had begun).[17]

The day after Marat's address to the Convention, Dumouriez
temporarily left his army, being now quite certain that the Duke of
Brunswick was withdrawing completely from France, to come to Paris
to urge the Convention to authorize an invasion of Belgium. He had
Danton's strong support. The circumstances were uniquely favorable.
Half of Belgium was French-speaking, but the country was ruled by
the Austrians, who were much disliked there, especially after the attempt several years before by Joseph II—the only Habsburg emperor
in the whole history of their dynasty to be disloyal to the Catholic
Church—to take over the Church in Belgium. There was a Catholic,
local-rights party in Belgium and a revolutionary party; both, for different reasons, opposed the Austrians and favored French rule. The
Duke of Brunswick was headed home and was most unlikely to come
to the rescue of the Austrians, whose troops stationed in Belgium
could be heavily outnumbered by the French. On October 12 Dumouriez got his way. Four French striking columns set out for Belgium; on the 26th Dumouriez took personal command of them near
the frontier at Valenciennes and two days later marched into Belgium
with 78,000 men.

The following day, Maximilien Robespierre was called to account for the September massacres on the floor of the Convention.

Actually there is no solid evidence that Robespierre had been a
leader in planning—to say nothing of carrying out—the massacres.
But he was certainly undisturbed by them, and eager to profit from
them politically and personally. The Girondins knew him to be their
implacable foe, while they still hoped for a working alliance with
Danton, with whom they had often cooperated in the past. On October 29 Minister of the Interior Roland, one of the leading Girondins,
condemned the Paris Commune for usurpation of power and terror-
ism, and read a letter from the former vice-president of the Criminal
Tribunal in Paris which declared that Robespierre wanted to bring
about more prison massacres like those of September, and charged
him with seeking a dictatorship. Bedlam broke out on the floor of the
Riding School, with the loudest shouts coming from Robespierre's foes.
He rushed to the tribune, but his weak voice could not be heard in the
tumult. Then Danton rose, dominating the long hall from end to end
with his voice like the hammer of Thor.

"Let the orator speak," he roared. "And I demand to speak after
him—it is time that all was cleared up."[18]

Robespierre was not exactly a coward, but he hated rough-and-tumble. His eyes shifting wildly, he clutched the wooden railing in front of the tribune. But he managed to retain his customary supercilious air.

> "A system of calumny is established," said he with a lofty voice, "and against whom is it directed? Against a zealous patriot. Yet who is there among you who dares rise and accuse me to my face?"
> "I," exclaimed a voice from one end of the hall.
> There was a profound silence, in the midst of which a thin, lank, pale-faced man stalked along the hall like a specter, and being come directly opposite to the tribune, he fixed Robespierre and said, "Yes, Robespierre, it is I who accuse you."
> It was Jean-Baptiste Louvet.
> Robespierre was confounded: he stood motionless, and turned pale; he could not have seemed more alarmed had a bleeding head spoken to him from a charger....
> Danton, perceiving how very much his friend was disconcerted, called out: "Continue, Robespierre. there are many good citizens here to hear you."[19]

But Robespierre was overpowered by the dramatic intervention, and yielded the floor. Louvet was one of the Girondin "inner sixty," a close associate of Roland. He had been preparing this attack for a long time, and launched into it at once:

> Why were the massacres [of September] not prevented? Because Roland spoke in vain, because the Minister of Justice, Danton, did not speak. Because Santerre, in command of the Sections, was waiting; because municipal officers were presiding over these executions. Because the Legislative Assembly was dominated, and an insolent demagogue [Robespierre] came to the bar of the house to dictate the Commune's decrees, and threatened it with sounding the tocsin if it did not obey....
> Robespierre, I accuse you of having ceaselessly slandered the purest patriots. I accuse you of having spread these slanders in the first week of September, which is to say during days when these slanders were dagger blows. I accuse you of having degraded and proscribed the representatives of the nation. I accuse you of having constantly produced yourself as an object of idolatry; of having allowed people in your presence to designate you as the only man in France who could save the nation, and of having said it yourself. I accuse you of having obviously aimed at being the supreme power.[20]

It was not all quite true—yet. But it was coming true.

At this point, however, Danton was still in charge. The next day he spoke in his own defense, and carried all before him. He regretted the September massacres, but saw them as inevitable. "No throne was ever shattered," he proclaimed, "without some worthy citizens being wounded by the fragments."[21] Robespierre's own defense, delivered November 5 to galleries packed with his adherents, sounded the same theme. Violence is inseparable from revolution. "Citizens," he cried, "do you want a Revolution without a revolution?"[22] Louvet was denied permission to support his case further; the Mountain had won again.

The next day, November 6, Dumouriez's invading army of 78,000, despite its confusion and lack of discipline, by sheer numbers overwhelmed an Austrian force of only 13,000 at Jemappes ten miles inside the border on the way to Brussels, the Belgian capital. The Austrian authorities, sliding immediately from overconfidence, which had caused them to put their army into winter quarters even as Dumouriez was marching on them into a state of shock which seemed to paralyze their will, at once abandoned Brussels. Panic ensued. The city was full of French *émigrés*, many of them already sentenced to death by the Revolution, for whom capture meant the guillotine. "Without funds, without influence in high places, they had to flee the city on foot and carry their few valuable possessions with them in bundles attached to the end of a pole, which they put over their shoulders."[23] Dumouriez entered Brussels on the 14th; looting, rape, and bloodshed followed. Churches were ravaged; adorned crucifixes, reliquaries and candelabra were confiscated or destroyed. Even some van Eyck paintings were ripped up. Paris-style elections were held, and it was announced that the new French Revolutionary regime "would regard as its enemies" all Belgians "who rejected freedom and equality."[24] On November 19 the Convention passed a decree making this official French policy for the whole of Europe. The Revolutionary regime would aid anyone fighting against monarchy.

The news of Jemappes came to Danton as he was spending a few days in the country with Gabrielle, who was pregnant. Perhaps he was seeking to restore their relationship to what it had been before the September massacres. (He had resigned as Minister of Justice October 9, in order to concentrate on building up his power and influence in the Convention which was now the major center of power.) When he heard the news he returned at once to Paris. There he found the question of a trial for the ex-King the primary subject of discussion; but he did not speak on it. In his country retreat, Danton had been visited by Théodore de Lameth, who had left the Jacobin Club back in the summer of 1791 because of his disagreement with their increasingly violent and destructive course, and was now on the death list. He begged Danton to save Louis—by avoiding a trial or arranging his escape. Danton replied:

> Now, listen to me. I'll be as honest with you as I can. Though I don't believe the King is entirely blameless, both justice and expediency demand that he should be extracted from his present situation. I'll do everything I can to save him within the bounds of ordinary prudence. If I think there's a chance of my succeeding, I'm prepared to risk my own neck. But if I lose all hope, don't rely on me. In such a case, I freely admit that I shall vote with those who condemn the King. When his head rolls, I have no wish for mine to follow it.[25]

On November 30, the Convention appointed Danton as head of a special committee to go to Belgium to monitor the military occupation and administration there. By curious coincidence, one of his two colleagues on the committee was Gaston Camus, the man who had led the patrol that discovered the crown jewel thieves in the National Archives building on the night of September 16.

Ever since November 13, the great debate on whether, and how, to try the ex-King had been underway in the Convention. Even in that body, elected under the shadow of the swords and clubs and bloody corpses of September, there was at first hesitancy and doubt about going this far. It was a very serious matter to kill a king in order to destroy a monarchy. In all the history of Europe since the fall of the Roman empire, only one man had done that: Oliver Cromwell, whose memory was despised by royalists and revolutionaries alike as a fanatical dictator.

It was time for Louis Antoine Saint-Just, the "Angel of Death," the author of *Organt* in which Hell occupies Heaven, to make his first appearance at the tribune of the Convention. He did so on the first day of debate on the fate of Louis XVI, November 13. He wore black, with a huge white tie and a single gold earring. He did not smile. His dark eyebrows met when he frowned. His voice was laid on the delegates like a whiplash encased in ice.

> I undertake, citizens, to prove that the king may be tried; that the opinion of Morisson, which defends inviolability, and that of the committee, which would have him tried as a citizen, are alike false, and that the king must be tried under principles which derive neither from the one nor the other.... I tell you that the king should be tried as an enemy, that we have less to try him than to fight him, and that, since

we are no longer under the contract uniting Frenchmen, the forms of procedure are not in the civil law, but in the law of nations. . . . Some day people will be astonished that in the eighteenth century we are less advanced than at the time of Caesar; then the tyrant was immolated in the midst of the Senate with no other formalities than twenty-three dagger blows . . . I see no middle ground: this man must reign or die. . . . *No one can reign innocently [On ne peut pas régner innocement]*: the folly is too evident. Every king is a rebel and a usurper.[26]

"No one can reign innocently"! The French Revolution adopted those words of Saint-Just as a battle cry, which at one stroke condemned and dishonored a thousand years of the history of Christendom, many of its most revered leaders, and several canonized saints.

NOTES

[1]Robert Christophe, *Danton* (London, n.d.), p. 280.

[2]Louis-Philippe, *Memoirs, 1773-1793*, ed. John Hardman (New York, 1977), p. 308.

[3]Gouverneur Morris, *A Diary of the French Revolution*, ed. Beatrix Davenport (Boston, 1939), II, 541.

[4]Louis-Philippe, *Memoirs*, pp. 276-279; *The Cambridge Modern History*, Volume VIII (London, 1908), pp. 409-410.

[5]Christophe, *Danton*, pp. 266-267; Stanley Loomis, *The Fatal Friendship; Marie Antoinette, Count Fersen, and the Flight to Varennes* (Garden City NY, 1972), p. 262.

[6]Christophe, *Danton*, pp. 268-269, 272-273.

[7]*Ibid.*, pp. 265, 274-275, 283-285.

[8]*Ibid.*, p. 276.

[9]*Ibid.*, p. 279; Louis-Philippe, *Memoirs*, pp. 284-285.

[10]Loomis, *Fatal Friendship*, p. 260.

[11]*Ibid.*, p. 263; Christophe, *Danton*, pp. 283, 285.

[12]David P. Jordan, *The King's Trial; the French Revolution versus Louis XVI* (Berkeley CA, 1979), pp.46-47.

[13]Alison Patrick, *The Men of the First French Republic* (Baltimore, 1972), p. 30.

[14]Louis-Philippe, *Memoirs*, p. 310.

[15]Rupert Furneaux, *The Bourbon Tragedy* (London, 1968), p. 93.

[16]Louis-Philippe, *Memoirs*, p. 312.

[17]Claude Bowers, *Vergniaud, Voice of the French Revolution* (New York, 1950), p. 271.

[18]Jean Matrat, *Robespierre* (New York, 1971), p. 177.

[19]E.L. Higgins, *The French Revolution as Told by Contemporaries* (Boston, 1938), pp. 262-263 (from the journal of Dr. John Moore).

[20]Matrat, *Robespierre*, p. 178.

[21]Louis Madelin, *The French Revolution* (New York, 1925), p. 309.

[22]Jordan, *The King's Trial*, p. 54.

[23]Loomis, *Fatal Friendship*, p. 266.

[24]*Ibid.*, p. 267.

[25]Christophe, *Danton*, p. 310.

[26]Eugene Curtis, *Saint-Just, Colleague of Robespierre* (New York, 1935, 1973), pp. 37-39.

IV.
Execution of the Catholic King
(December 1, 1792-January 21, 1793)

Saint-Just's speech against the ex-King November 13 set the tone for all that was to follow in the great drama of his trial and execution. The Mountain never wavered from the position that Saint-Just and Robespierre marked out, and in the course of the ensuing two months won a total political victory on the issue of the ex-King's fate which put them in full control of France and its revolution.

Speaking at a Paris section meeting December 1, Jacques Roux, a leader in the Commune and a priest who had been forbidden by his bishop to exercise his priesthood after taking part in the sacking of several homes of noblemen in 1790, called explicitly for Louis' death, for "the head of the assassin of the French." "The liberty of the people," he said, should "be consolidated by the legal shedding of the impure blood of kings."[1] Roux was later to stand beside Louis at the guillotine and watch the great blade fall upon his neck.

The next day the Paris Commune sent a deputation to the convention, declaring that failure to act on Louis' punishment (his guilt was assumed) would be "a political blasphemy" and threatening a repetition of August 10 if action were not promptly taken.

The Convention reacted immediately to this undisguised threat. On the very next day, December 3, it voted by a large majority to put Louis on trial. Robespierre thought even this a concession. "Louis is not an accused," he said, "you are not judges. You are, you can only be, men of state, the representatives of a nation." If Louis was a defendant in anything resembling a court of law, he would have to be presumed innocent until proven guilty. But he could not be presumed innocent. Saint-Just had already declared that no man could reign innocently. "If Louis can be presumed innocent," said Robespierre, ruthlessly frank, "what becomes of the Revolution?"[2]

Here was the naked essence of all the proceedings against the former King of France. For even though the majority of the Convention in this instance rejected Robespierre's advice by voting to go through the form of a trial, this was in fact the view of most of its members: that Louis was guilty, not because of anything specific that he had done, but out of political necessity; the only real question was whether the penalty would be death. The man Louis de Bourbon disappeared into the symbol of the King of France—despite the fact that he was no longer King, the monarchy having been eliminated by the unanimous Convention vote September 21, and that he had numerous relatives, starting with his two brothers, ready to assume the claims of legitimate kingship for all who would accept them, as soon as he was dead.

The injustice was so flagrant that it is hard to believe that any later historian not blinded by the passion of revolutionary political partisanship could possibly defend it. Yet many have, although in truth the injustice grows even greater the more closely it is examined. There seems to be a widespread presumption that Louis must have been guilty of something serious, since not a single member of the Convention voted to acquit him.

Let us therefore look at the charges against him, as set forth by the official indictment drawn up by the Convention's special Committee of Twenty-One and reported to the full Convention December 10 by Robert Lindet, later a member of the Committee of Public Safety during the Reign of Terror, putting them in the context of the ex-King's actual situation during the preceding three years.

The first and most important factor to keep constantly in mind, though it is almost never mentioned in context of the charges against Louis even by writers and historians sympathetic to him, is that during the entire period from October 6, 1789 to the moment he went on trial for his life, Louis *and all his family—his wife, daughter, and little son*—were prisoners in the Tuileries, inadequately protected and in constant peril of their lives. They had been imprisoned without even the pretense of legality, with no charges, no trial, and no conviction. How anyone then or since, judging Louis' actions, could have ignored or forgotten this overwhelming fact staggers the imagination. When a man and his family are routed out of their residence in the middle of the night by a murderous mob and marched into the stronghold of their enemies behind the severed heads of their guards carried on pikes (as happened to Louis and his family October 6, 1789); then held in confinement under constant guard for two years and brought back from their only attempt at escape in a manner similar to their original abduction; then held in even closer confinement for another whole year until attacked in their place of confinement by thousands of armed men; and finally thrown into a 500-year-old dungeon behind walls nine feet thick, it would seem that no sane man could arrive at any conclusion other than that such a man is under duress. Being under duress, the first duty of King Louis XVI to his country, his family, and himself was clearly, unquestionably, to escape. He owed no duty whatsoever to his captors.

It may be argued that his captors, if they truly represented the people of France as they claimed to do, had a right to overthrow the monarchy and set up a republic. In the abstract sense, they may have had that right—if they truly represented the people of France. The fact that most of the King's captors did not openly avow support for a republic until well into the third year of his captivity strongly suggests that they did not think they had popular support for that action at least until then; and the lack of enthusiastic response outside Paris to the proclamation of the French Republic September 21 suggests that probably they did not have it even then. But even supposing that they did have popular support for the abolition of the monarchy, that could not possibly justify imprisoning their king and his family, keeping them all in prison until he was dethroned, and then killing them. At most, it could justify banishing the royal family from the country—a course of action followed many times in more recent years by European nations which have changed from monarchies to republics. This was suggested by many members of the Convention; in the final vote on Louis' fate (after finding him guilty without a dissenting vote, thereby fatally compromising their moral position) over three hundred of them voted to punish him only by banishment after the war with Austria and Prussia (which the revolutionary Assembly itself had forced Louis to declare in the spring of 1792) had come to an end. But the Revolutionary leadership in Paris never seriously considered any such action.

Another possible solution, abdication—either by the King's own volition or under pressure from the revolutionaries—was not urged by anyone because under French laws of dynastic succession it would make King either Louis' little son, also a prisoner, or if his father included him in the act of abdication, then Louis' brother who had escaped from France and was a far more vehement foe of the Revolution than Louis XVI.

The 33 counts of the indictment against Louis XVI were a grab-bag of mostly political complaints by the revolutionaries. The majority of them referred back to the period between October 1789 and September 1791 when, under the law as it then stood (France's first constitution, that of 1791, was not approved and put into effect until September of that year) Louis was still an absolute monarch, though illegally held prisoner. The actions for which he was indicted during that period mostly relate to his attempts to free himself and his family, to find and pay men at liberty in France who would defend his interests, and to provide financial assistance for some of his subjects, including some who had served him personally, who had been forced by the revolutionaries to flee the country. One of the documents introduced in evidence against him was a letter he had written in April 1791 to the Bishop of Clermont promising to restore the freedom of the Catholic Church in France from the governance of the state if he should regain the power to do so.

Other counts in the indictment referred to the period of less than a year, from September 1791 to August 1792, when the constitution was in effect. Louis was actually accused of criminal acts for having exercised the power of vetoing legislation which the constitution explicitly gave to him. He was also accused of not liking the constitution, calling it "absurd and detestable" (since he was still held prisoner under its regime, he could hardly have been expected to like it!). It thus became a criminal offense under the Revolution both to have abided by that constitution and to have criticized it. The fact that this constitution explicitly guaranteed the personal inviolability of the King, in no less than four different places, created a problem which the Convention evaded by saying that this guarantee need not be respected because what the sovereign people, through their elected representatives, could grant they could also take away. Again, in abstract theory, that was true. But could the sovereign people, or any just power on earth, guarantee a ruler inviolability, take the guarantee away from him, and then condemn him to death for actions taken or words spoken while he still had the guarantee? No one in the Convention wanted to ask that question. In all these kangaroo proceedings only one man had the courage to raise it: Louis' defense attorney, the fearless Raymond Desèze, the only real hero of these shattering two months when the moral stature of France descended to a level the world was not to see again until the days of Adolf Hitler.

As if all this were not enough, the indictment of Louis also included the killings of August 10, which, with a brazen effrontery that touched the edge of madness, it held that Louis had instigated—Louis who had not killed anyone, who had only tried to defend himself and his family, who had finally despaired of that defense and ordered his men to lay down their arms, thereby allowing their attackers to kill them! It is not as though these facts were unknown at the time and only established through later historical research. Anyone who had been anywhere near the Tuileries on August 10 or involved in any of the meetings of the Paris Commune and the sections at that time, knew them. As Desèze declared scathingly in his magnificent statement for the defense before the Convention December 26: "In this very hall where I speak members have disputed the honor of having planned the insurrection of the tenth of August."[3] Yet all agreed to painting the victim of the attack as the aggressor.

Louis' true guilt, if guilt he bore, was not that he had done the things the indictment charged, but that he had not done more of them, and more effectively—which might have enabled him to save his country, his family, and himself from the horrors now upon them all. When Robespierre said that if there was any possibility of Louis' innocence, the Revolution must be guilty, he was entirely correct. The Revolution was guilty. But in Paris at the end of the year 1792, it meant death for any man to say that.

There are only two moral responses to such a situation. If there is a reasonable chance to prevail, one may gather a group of brave men and fight. If there is no such chance, one may remain silent, as the martyred St. Thomas More in England remained silent, facing Henry VIII. But one may not vote to condemn a man—king or pauper—out of fear to speak known truth about his innocence.

When the time came for the Convention to vote on Louis' guilt, fourteen delegates abstained. We may hope that, for some of them at least, it was for St. Thomas More's reasons. All the rest present—no less than 707—voted him guilty.[4]

Raymond Desèze had said, to all these men, in his statement for the defense: "There is not today a power equal to yours; but there is a power you do not have: it is that of not being just. . . . Citizens, I will speak to you here with the frankness of a free man. I search among you for judges, and I see only accusers. You want to pronounce on Louis' fate, and it is you yourselves who accuse him!" He concluded: "I stop myself before History. Think how it will judge your judgment, and that the judgment of him [the king] will be judged by the centuries."[5]

History has not been worthy of Raymond Desèze.

So much attention has been focused on the close and dramatic vote on Louis' execution that many historical writers have lost sight of the even greater significance of his almost unanimous conviction for the legally fantastic "crimes" with which he was charged. Many Convention delegates, knowing in their hearts that Louis was innocent but lacking the courage to vote accordingly, seemed to have salved their consciences by assuming that at least they could spare his life. The vote on his guilt was taken first, in the afternoon of January 15, 1793—a month of cold winds, gray skies, and glare ice in Paris to open that fell year of the Terror. There had already been a long oratorical exchange between the Girondins and the Mountain, running from December 27 to January 4, on whether the decision on Louis' punishment should be made by the Convention or by special appeal to "the people" (meaning the 44,000 "primary assemblies" which chose the electors which chose the delegates to the National Convention). It was widely, and probably correctly assumed by both sides that this prolonged, difficult, and unprecedented appeal process would save Louis from a death sentence. Pierre Vergniaud, greatest of the Girondin orators, lavished all his eloquence on a philippic in support of this appeal, delivered December 31. Like most of Vergniaud's speeches, it drew a resounding chorus of admiration but changed few votes.

Much more important politically was the speech of Bertrand Barère of "the Plain" delivered January 4. Barère was the only outstanding orator of the Plain. He was a man whose best friend and worst enemy would not consider him principled. He always sought out the winning side, while keeping just enough distance from it to be able to switch again when the time came to do so. During the Terror, he was a "reluctant terrorist," a member of the Committee of Public Safety; he lived to be its last survivor, and was also a secret agent for Napoleon. Barère declared sanctimoniously to the Convention that it was under "the terrible necessity of destroying the tyrant in order to remove all hope of tyranny."[6] The king must die, and the Convention must order his death. "The tree of liberty could not grow were it not watered with the blood of kings."[7] Barère's speech was a signal to the Plain that the balance of power and influence in the Convention was swinging to the Mountain, which had dominated Paris ever since August 10. When the vote on the appeal to the people was taken in the evening of January 15, it was voted down by 424 to 284, a much wider margin than most of the members had expected.

On January 16 the Convention reconvened at 10:30 a.m. for the session that would vote on the execution of the King. It lasted 36 consecutive hours. Danton was there. The Convention had recalled him from Belgium a few days before to counter General Dumouriez, who had come back to Paris January 6 with many complaints about the

revolutionary regime in Belgium, which was rapidly alienating the
Belgian people. In the pile of mail awaiting Danton was a letter from
Bertrand de Molleville, a former French government minister now in
exile in London, trying to blackmail him into taking action to save
Louis' life by threatening to reveal evidence in his possession that in
the past Danton accepted money from the King. (Danton had; he
would accept money from anyone foolish enough to give it to him,
and then continue to do as he pleased.) He managed to convince the
recipient of de Molleville's letter that it was a forgery and to destroy
it. But in case some word of this should get out, it was now even more
essential for Danton's political future that he show himself as an uncompromising advocate of Louis' execution. So, early in the debate of
January 16, he trained the guns of his oratory on a proposal by the
deputy Lanjuinais, one of those most eager to save Louis' life, that a
two-thirds vote should be required for execution, and brought about
its defeat.

At eight o'clock in the evening in the Riding School, the Convention began voting on life or death for Louis de Bourbon. The day
had been heavily overcast and the night was exceptionally dark. The
galleries were packed, for the spectacle combined the highest political
drama with the ancient, savage appeal of the Roman arena: the life of
the former King of France was at stake, it would take all night to vote
on it, and the vote was likely to be extremely close. In the public galleries, scantily clad women sipped liqueurs and orange drinks while
hefty *sans-culottes* (the "trouserless ones" in whom the Mountain took
such pride) passed wine bottles back and forth. The single stove which
was a model of the Bastille smoked. The lighting was bad. Due to lack
of ventilation and extreme crowding, the smell was terrible.

Pierre Vergniaud, the Girondin orator, was in the chair. (Did he
think of that other time when he was in the chair of the Legislative
Assembly August 10, and Louis and his family had come in from the
killing ground to ask his protection, and he had answered: "You may
rely, Sire, on the firmness of the National Assembly; its members have
sworn to die in supporting the rights of the people and the constituted
authority"[8]?) Vergniaud had developed a unique method of keeping
order in the often tumultuous Convention (where one day a president
had broken no less than three bells ringing fruitlessly for order). When
the deputies were totally out of control, he would put on his hat and
rise from the chair. Since no one wanted this session abruptly adjourned, the hat signal always sufficed to restore enough decorum to
allow proceedings to continue.

It had been agreed that every one of the deputies present—721 eventually cast votes—would be individually polled, alphabetically by the department they represented, and within each department by the date of their election (the best known and most popular deputies had usually been elected first). Any deputy wishing to do so would also be allowed to explain his vote; and a majority took advantage of this special privilege. The voting and explanatory speeches took up fourteen hours of the marathon session, running entirely through the night into a new bleak winter's day. By what appears to have been a special arrangement by the Girondins, the vote began with Jean-Baptiste Mailhe of Haute-Garonne department, who had chaired the original committee that recommended the trial of the ex-King before the Convention. Mailhe explained his vote as follows:

> By a consequence that appears natural to me, as a result of the opinion I have already given on the first question [the guilt of the ex-King], I vote for death. I will make a simple observation: if death has the majority, I believe it would be worthy of the National Convention to examine if it might be useful to delay the time of execution. I return to the question, and I vote for death.[9]

When the weasel verbiage is stripped from this statement, it is clearly—as Mailhe, in fact, said twice—a vote for death, with no more than an expression of vague hope that the Convention "might . . . delay the time of execution." It could not even properly be called an amendment, not being concrete enough for that, though it has gone down in history as the "Mailhe amendment." At most, one might call it a vote for death with the possibility of reprieve.

The roll call continued, by department. In the French alphabetization of the departments, Haute-Garonne was listed under "G", followed by Gers, and then by Gironde. Throughout the trial, Louis' attorneys (there were three of them—François-Denis Tronchet and Lamoignon de Malesherbes, two very distinguished but elderly lawyers, and the younger and more dynamic Desèze) had necessarily pinned their hopes of saving their client's life on the Girondins, whose stronghold was this department. They had been the radicals of the early Legislative Assembly, universally republican and unquestionably revolutionary; but they had recoiled from the massacres of September, and it seemed that their recoil was not entirely due to fear that they themselves might have been among the victims, but included some genuine moral outrage. Most of the Girondins did not really want Louis executed. But they had been learning over the past several months that mere fastidiousness, occasional scruples, and brilliant oratory are not enough to brake or divert a revolution roaring ahead at full throttle. For that, two things are indispensable: truly exceptional courage, both physical and moral; and powder and shot (in the phrase Captain Bonaparte was later to make famous, "a whiff of grapeshot"). The Girondins had neither, as their most eloquent leader was about to demonstrate.

"The Department of the Gironde," intoned the secretary who was calling the roll.

Pierre Vergniaud laid aside his hat and beckoned Bertrand Barère temporarily to the chair, for Vergniaud was the first elected of the Gironde delegation and would cast its first vote. Louis' lawyers were standing in a narrow stairway which led up to the public gallery, from which they had a view of the tribune where each delegate announced his vote. They had just arrived, and asked where in the alphabet the roll call was. They were told "G." "Good," said Desèze, "that is the Gironde. Vergniaud's vote is favorable to us, and his influence will lead the others."[10] Desèze may well have known that just the night before Vergniaud had told Jean-Baptiste Harmand, a deputy of the Plain, that he would never vote for the death of the King.

A profound silence fell over what had been a noisy hall. Edmond Charles Genêt, later minister of the French Revolutionary government to the United States, described Vergniaud's appearance at this moment: "calm, lips compressed, eyes lowered toward the ground" as he ascended "slowly and solemnly" to the tribune.[11] His sonorous voice rang out:

> The law speaks. It says death. But in pronouncing this terrible word, worried about the fate of my country, about the dangers that menace liberty itself, about all the blood that might be shed, I express the same wish as Mailhe, and ask that it [the death penalty] might be submitted to discussion by the assembly.[12]

Heedless of the rules, Harmand rushed to the tribune, looking up in bewilderment at the great man. "What happened?" he cried, with mingled amazement and distress. "How can it be that you have changed your mind in so short a time?"

Often and eloquently Pierre Vergniaud had spoken against the evils of tyranny and how he intended to help free France forever from them. Now he gave to Harmand's question the answer of tyrants all down the ages: "I did not believe myself able to put the public good in the balance with the life of a single man."

On the stairway, something broke in the last heroic defender of Louis de Bourbon.

"All is lost," said Raymond Desèze.[13]

About three o'clock in the morning the vote reached Paris, thirtieth in the list of 83 departments. The Paris delegation, whose electors had passed by the corpses of the victims of September before they voted for the city's representatives in the Convention, voted 21 to 3 for death. Two votes from Paris were particularly remembered. The first was Danton's; he said:

> I am not numbered among that common herd of statesmen who have yet to learn that there is no compounding with tyrants, who have yet to learn that the only place to strike a king is between head and shoulders, who have yet to learn that they will get nothing from Europe except by force of arms. I vote for the tyrant's death.[14]

The other vote particularly remembered was that of Louis' own cousin, the former Duke of Orléans, now known as "Philip Equality." Having been last elected in the Paris delegation, he was its last member to vote. As he approached the tribune, a silence fell like that which had surrounded Vergniaud when he stepped up to it. "Philip Equality" spoke in a low voice.

> Solely concerned with my duty, convinced that all those who have attacked or will attack the sovereignty of the people deserve death, I vote for death.[15]

Jeers and boos resounded through the hall from the deputies who retained enough humanity to despise a man who would vote to kill his own relative. His son Louis-Philippe reports a meeting between his brother and his father the next day:

> My father, having returned from the Convention, sent for him. He found him dissolved in tears, sitting before his desk, both his hands over his eyes. "Montpensier," he said, sobbing, "I do not have the courage to look at you." My brother has told me that having himself lost the power of speech, he had wanted to embrace him but that my father had refused him, saying: "No! I am too wretched. I cannot now imagine what could have led me to do what I did!" and they remained for a long time in this attitude without uttering another word.[16]

Unfortunately the ex-Duke's repentance, or his courage, or both, were short-lived. Two days later he voted again for the death of his cousin, by voting against any reprieve in carrying out the death sentence.

When the roll call reached Hautes-Pyrénées, four departments after Paris, Barère, who represented it, handed the chair back to Vergniaud. The Convention took a short recess, its only one of this session. Deputies and spectators compared notes. The secretaries had announced no tally yet. Hundreds of people were keeping their own tallies, some pricked out with a pin on playing cards. Naturally, many of them did not agree. In fact 305 votes had been cast, and death held a narrow lead.

Eventually a cold gray dawn broke. Still the remorseless roll call went on, the deputies hanging on every vote despite their exhaustion. It seemed that every other member was voting "*la mort*." It was beginning to become evident that the votes for the Mailhe "amendment" could be decisive. If they were counted for death—as it seemed they must be—they gave death the lead it might need to prevail.

An absolute majority of the 721 votes cast was 361. It is not clear how many of the Convention members knew the exact number of votes that would be cast, but there must have been a general awareness that about 360 would prevail. As the wan winter's morning light filtered through the small, dirty windows high up near the roof of the Riding School and the roll call approached its end, those who had kept the most accurate tallies knew that the total for death, counting Mailhe votes as votes for death, stood at about 350. There were seven departments to go, out of the total of 83. The last two which had voted, Côtes-du-Nord (Breton peasants and fishermen, some of the most devout Catholics left in France) and Creuse (mountain peasants hidden away in their valleys, likewise) had cast only one vote each out of ten for death, with an additional vote from Creuse for the Mailhe "amendment."

Next was Dordogne department—fertile river valleys descending from the Central Massif, heavily Calvinist in the distant days of the Wars of Religion. The assemblies of Dordogne when the Convention was elected had been almost totally controlled by the Mountain. (Tragically for France, their power was not limited to Paris, despite the wishful thinking of the Girondins.) Dordogne's delegation voted nine to one for death.[17]

The verdict was decided. But two final acts of hypocrisy were still to come. Two of the principal Girondin leaders had yet to vote: François Buzot of Eure department, a handsome Norman dandy, the lover of Madame Roland; and Jerome Pétion, who had been mayor of Paris on August 10, but now represented Eure-et-Loir. Both voted for death à la Mailhe. Pétion had been in the carriage that bore the royal family back, prisoners again, from their flight which was intercepted at Varennes in June 1791. His companion on that ghastly journey, Antoine Barnave, had been brought by what he saw to understand the evil of the Revolution; he sought to the end to save Marie Antoinette and the children, and would die under the guillotine for it.

Buzot and Pétion perished in a different way. On June 18, 1794, long fugitives from the Terror which the vote on January 16-17, 1793 did so much to bring to France, they were found in a clearing in the wood of St. Emilion near Bordeaux, half-eaten by wolves. No man knows whether they died by their own hand, or by the teeth of the beasts.

About nine o'clock in the morning Vergniaud announced the vote. Three hundred and sixty-one deputies—an absolute majority of one—had voted unconditionally for death. Twenty-six had voted for death with the Mailhe reservation. If those votes were counted with the unconditional votes for death (as the Convention decided formally the next day that they should be) the margin was 387 to 334.

"I declare," said Vergniaud in his deep, solemn voice, "in the name of the National Convention, that the punishment it pronounces against Louis Capet is that of death."[18]

There was one last faint hope, that the Mailhe "amendment" had roused. The Convention might grant the condemned man a reprieve, and not execute him immediately. On the 19th another roll-call vote was taken on the reprieve. Tom Paine, the only member of the Convention not a Frenchman, spoke for it through an interpreter. He urged the Convention to allow Louis and his family to come to the United States of America, whose liberty Louis had helped to win. Vergniaud voted against reprieve, along with "Philip Equality." It failed by 380-310.

This last roll call ended at two o'clock in the morning of January 20. Louis was wakened early that morning and told that he would be taken to the guillotine the very next day. At two o'clock in the afternoon of the 20th he received the official notification of his sentence and the scheduling of his execution from Garat, Danton's successor as Minister of Justice. Louis responded by asking the Convention for three days to prepare himself "to appear in the presence of God"; to see a priest; and to see his family alone. (The Paris Commune had ordered Louis' complete separation from his family, for reasons never explained, from the time of his indictment and first formal interrogation by the Convention December 11.) He also asked the Convention to care for his family.

His request for a stay of execution was denied, but his requests to see a priest and his family were granted, both by the Convention

and the Paris Commune which was his actual jailer. The priest who
came to him was an Irishman, Father Henry Edgeworth de Firmont, a
convert and the son of an Anglican clergyman, who had been educated by the Jesuits in Toulouse, ordained in France, and had worked
for many years among the poor of Paris. He had escaped the September massacres by going into hiding, and had never taken the oath to
accept the Civil Constitution of the Clergy. Louis, as he faced the
Judgment, was haunted by the fact that, under enormous pressure, he
had signed the bill establishing the Civil Constitution of the Clergy
and the later bill requiring all priests and religious to swear to uphold
it. Louis was a faithful and devout Catholic and knew now, though he
had not understood clearly then, that the effect of these measures was
to establish a schismatic church in France, in defiance of the Pope. He
asked Father Edgeworth about Archbishop de Juigné of Paris, who
had refused to take the oath. "Tell him," Louis said, "that I die in his
communion, and that I have never acknowledged any bishop but
him."[19] Father Edgeworth remained with Louis from the afternoon of
the 20th until his execution the following morning. At dawn on the
21st he said Mass and gave Louis Holy Communion. It was the first
Mass he had been allowed to attend, and the first Holy Communion
he had been allowed to receive, since the day of the tocsin, August 10.

Louis saw his family for the last time on the evening of the 20th,
spending more than two hours with them. When she entered his room,
Marie Antoinette flung herself into his arms and could not speak or
move for more than ten minutes. She pleaded with him to let them all
spend the night with him; he refused, doubting that any of them could
endure it. His seven-year-old son asked that he might go out into the
streets and beg for his father's life. Louis calmed him, and made him
swear with uplifted hand that he would not seek to avenge his father's
death. His fourteen-year-old daughter wept incessantly and desperately
almost the whole time they were there, and collapsed completely when
her father said "adieu." Finally he had to promise that he would see
them again in the morning, though in the end he accepted Father
Edgeworth's advice not to do so.

When morning came, a cold rain was falling through a thick fog.
At seven o'clock Louis came out of his study where Father Edgeworth
had said Mass and given him *viaticum*, the last Communion for the dying. Louis gave to Jean-Baptiste Cléry, the only one of his former personal servants that the Paris Commune had allowed to remain with
him to the end, some special tokens of his love, saying to him:

> Will you give this seal to my son . . . this wedding ring
> to the queen. Tell her that I am leaving her with a great deal

of pain . . . This little package contains locks of hair of all my family. Give it to her too. Tell the queen, tell my dear children, tell my sister, that I had promised to see them this morning, but that I wanted to spare them the pain of such a cruel separation. How hard it is to leave without their final embraces![20]

When Cléry left the king, all these remembrances were confiscated by the guards and locked up in a drawer to which only they had the key.

At eight o'clock Santerre, the commander of the National Guard installed by the murder of Mandat August 10, arrived at the Temple with the Convention's official escorts to bring Louis to the guillotine: the two unfrocked priests Jacques Roux and Jacques-Claude Bernard, Roux having been one of the first to call for Louis' head. No less than a hundred thousand armed men lined the streets of Paris to prevent any last-minute rescue attempt. There actually was such an attempt, undertaken by an adventurer called Baron de Batz. He is said to have enlisted three hundred men for the effort, but when he and his equerry burst from the crowd crying "Join us, all you who want to save the King!"[21] only two men responded. They were instantly cut down; the baron and his companion escaped (how, we are not told—it could not have been easy under the circumstances).

About twenty thousand people filled every inch of Revolution Square, backed up against the National Archives building from which the crown jewels had been stolen. A carriage stood on the edge of the square with its blinds drawn; inside it sat "Philip Equality." The guillotine stood in the center of the square, on a platform six feet above the ground, its two tall upright timbers reaching up into the fog, its great blade glinting dully in the gray light. Louis de Bourbon removed his coat and his collar. After a protest he allowed his hands to be tied behind his back. He climbed the steps to the platform unflinching. The drums were beating. Louis signalled them to stop with a motion of his head. When he spoke, his voice was strong and clear.

"I die innocent. I pardon my enemies. I hope that my blood will be useful to the French, that it will appease God's anger. . . ." As though annoyed by the mention of God, Santerre ordered the drums to roll once more. Sanson the executioner strapped him to the plank, sliding him through the "widow's window." "Son of Saint Louis," Father Edgeworth cried over the beating of the drums, "mount to Heaven!"[22]

The guillotine fell with its horrible thudding crash. Sanson's son lifted Louis' severed head for all to see. Some of the crowd rushed up to dip their handkerchiefs in the blood of the man who had been King of France. Others danced around the guillotine, shouting "Long live the Republic!" and singing the Marseillaise. There was a salvo of cannon fire. Santerre had Louis' body taken immediately to the Madeleine Cemetery, where it was put in a plain open wood coffin and covered with a double layer of quicklime which ate it away like acid. When the grave was opened after the Bourbon Restoration twenty-two years later, nothing could be found of the body but a few unidentifiable fragments of bone.

In the Temple, Marie Antoinette and the children could hear the drums beating and the salvo of cannon fire, answered by a shout of "Long live the Republic!" from their guards. They knew what it meant.

> Madame Elisabeth [Louis' sister] raised her eyes as though in prayer and said, "Monsters! Now they are happy." The Dauphin [Louis' son] began to cry and his sister screamed. But according to Turgy the Queen was unable to utter a word. For a long moment she stood motionless and silent, beyond even grief. Then she turned to her son. Louis XVI may have been dead, but the King of France was not. The throne may have fallen, but its living symbol remained. So within the walls of their prison the three women, led by Marie Antoinette, made the ritual obeisance before the seven-year-old boy who had become Louis XVII.[23]

Among the guards assigned to the Temple in shifts during the whole period of the former royal family's imprisonment there, was one named François-Adrian Toulan. He had grown up in Toulouse in the south of France, had come to Paris in 1785, and had become an ardent revolutionary. He had commanded a battalion in the August 10 assault on the Tuileries. Rough in manner and wild in appearance, he had originally been to the prisoners one of the most frightening of their custodians.

But for all his appearance and manner, François-Adrian Toulan was a decent man, not a killer of the innocent or a manipulator of political symbols. Watching the prisoners even more closely than they watched him, he came to learn what no member of the National Convention had learned or at any rate dared to say: that they were human too, loving and suffering but without hope any longer in this world. As early as September he had given the prisoners some sign of his true feelings. But the commander of an assault unit on August 10 was no languishing poet of pity; François-Adrian Toulan was a man of action. Like Danton, he believed in *toujours l'audace*. Before the fatal month of January ended, he had chosen a moment when the guardroom was unattended except for himself, broke into the locked drawer where

Louis' last gifts to his wife and children—his wedding ring and the locks of their hair he had carried with him—had been put, retrieved them, and brought them to Marie Antoinette. For the next few days he was careful to denounce "the Austrian woman" with particular vehemence in the guardroom. The guard chiefs finally decided the disappearance of the ring and locket was due to an ordinary burglar.

Then Toulan began working out an escape plan.

NOTES

[1]David P. Jordan, *The King's Trial; the French Revolution versus Louis XVI* (Berkeley CA, 1979), pp. 70-71.

[2]*Ibid.,* p. 74.

[3]Vincent Cronin, *Louis and Antoinette* (New York, 1975), p. 362.

[4]Alison Patrick, *The Men of the First French Republic* (Baltimore, 1972), pp. 88-91.

[5]Jordan, *King's Trial,* pp. 131, 135.

[6]*Ibid.,* p. 150.

[7]*Encyclopedia Britannica,* 11th edition, "Barère, Bertrand."

[8]Claude G. Bowers, *Pierre Vergniaud, Voice of the French Revolution* (New York, 1950), p. 227.

[9]Jordan, *King's Trial,* p. 183.

[10]*Ibid.,* p. 186.

[11]Bowers, *Vergniaud,* p. 308.

[12]Jordan, *King's Trial,* p. 185.

[13]*Ibid.,* pp. 185-186.

[14]Robert Christophe, *Danton* (London, n.d.), p. 328.

[15]Jordan, *King's Trial,* p. 187.

[16]Louis-Philippe, *Memoirs 1773-1793,* ed. John Hardman (New York, 1977), p. 361.

[17]For the complete roll call of the Convention, including all delegates, on the votes involving the execution of Louis XVI, see Patrick, *Men of the First French Republic,* pp. 317-339.

[18]Jordan, *King's Trial,* p. 191.

[19]Cronin, *Louis and Antoinette,* p. 370.

[20]Jordan, *King's Trial,* pp. 215-216.

[21]*Ibid.,* p. 218.

[22]*Ibid.,* p. 220.

[23]Stanley Loomis, *The Fatal Friendship; Marie Antoinette, Count Fersen and the Flight to Varennes* (Garden City NY, 1972), pp. 274-275.

V.
Rising of the Catholic People
(January 22-May 27, 1793)

Whatever may be the case with later historians, contemporaries of the French Revolution living outside France had no doubt what the execution of Louis XVI meant. The news reached London at five o'clock in the morning of January 23. The French refugees, who formed a substantial community there, kept to their rooms in sorrow and in shame; the theaters did not give performances that evening, and Buckingham Palace was surrounded by crowds shouting for war with France. The next day the British Foreign Minister, Lord Grenville, sent a letter to French ambassador Chauvelin that might have come from the ice-cap of Greenland:

> I am charged to notify you, sir, that since the character and functions with which you were invested at this court are today entirely annulled by the death of His Most Christian Majesty, you have no longer any public character here, and His Majesty has judged it proper to order that you quit this kingdom within a week.[1]

Just a week later, Danton roared out from the tribune of the Convention a battle-cry that became almost as famous as *toujours l'audace*: "Kings and emperors threaten us; but now you have thrown down the gauntlet to them. That gauntlet is the head of a king!" He was speaking in favor of the immediate unconditional annexation of Belgium to France; once this had been decreed, he said, "you can apply the laws of France to Belgium—and then priests, nobles, and aristocrats will be swept away, leaving a land of freedom behind them."[2]

That very night Danton left Paris to return to Belgium. He had been in Paris for two and a half weeks. He had been present all

82

through the interminable sessions of voting on Louis' fate; he had spoken at the Jacobin and Cordelier Clubs, socialized with their members, joked with their women. His wife Gabrielle was far advanced in pregnancy and clearly not well. Lurid reports were circulating in Paris about orgies in French-occupied Belgium in which Danton had taken part. Gabrielle wept when she heard them. Her young friend Louise Gély did the best she could to comfort her. But Danton had little time for her, though he did come to say good-bye, that evening of January 31, before he set out again for the north.

He was never to see her again.

From London, at almost this same moment, came the measured words of William Pitt the younger, probably the greatest Prime Minister England has ever had, next to Winston Churchill—not directly in reply to Danton, whose speech he had probably not yet heard of, but to all that he and his revolution then stood for:

> They will not accept, under the name of liberty, any model of government but that which is conformable to their own opinions and ideas; and all men must learn from the mouth of their cannon the propagation of their system. . . . They have stated that they would organize every country by a disorganizing principle; and afterwards they tell you all this is done by the will of the people. And then comes this plain question: What is the will of the people? It is the power of the French. . . . This has given a more fatal blow to the liberties of mankind than any they have suffered, even from the boldest attempts of the most aspiring monarch. . . . Unless we wish to stand by, and to suffer state after state to be subverted under the power of France, we must now declare our firm resolution effectually to oppose those principles of ambition and aggrandizement which have for their object the destruction of England, of Europe and of the world.[3]

On February 1 the Convention declared war against Great Britain and the Netherlands, thereby committing Revolutionary France to hostilities against every major power in Europe west of Russia, except Spain (an omission rectified the next month). To fight such a war, many more soldiers would be needed. On February 7 a bill was introduced in the Convention to raise 300,000 of them. On the urging of Saint-Just, it was decided to abolish the distinction between the Line (the old regulars) and the volunteers, and to continue the practice of the soldiers in each unit electing their own officers, regardless of military competence. Each department was given a quota of men to raise. It soon became apparent that there would be nowhere near enough genuine "volunteers" to provide so many additional troops. To get them, there was no alternative to conscription—the draft. Never

in the history of France had it been used for national military service
in foreign lands.

Meanwhile Danton had returned to Belgium, reaching Brussels
on the evening of February 3, where he learned of General Dumouriez's plans to invade the Netherlands soon, since war had been
declared on that country, and plunged even more deeply into corruption and debauchery. By the later sworn testimony of General Mi-
aczynski, a Polish officer in the service of France, he actually set up a
press in Liège to print counterfeit promissory notes. His wild nights
there became the talk of Paris. But behind these age-old, all too common sins was one unique to Georges-Jacques Danton: he, more than
any other man, had created the death machine that now held France
firmly in its grip and was extending its arms to the whole of Europe,
that had struck down hundreds of priests and religious in the gardens
of the old monasteries of Paris for fidelity to Christ, His Church, and
the Pope.

February 10, 1793 was a Sunday, the day sanctified to the Lord
whom Danton had scorned. On that day, Gabrielle Danton died in
childbirth. She was only twenty-nine. Up to this pregnancy—her
fourth—she had always enjoyed excellent health. She died in agony,
her face brick-red from a raging fever, with Louise at her side.

The news came to Danton at a party in Belgium. He called for
his coach and set off at once for Paris. Over the steady clop-clop of the
horses' hooves and the creaking of the carriage wheels, the coachman
could hear him sobbing. When he reached Paris on the 16th, all that
remained on earth of Gabrielle was already in her grave.

Many messages of condolence awaited him. One was from Robespierre. It included this sentence: "Let us ensure that the effects of our
profound grief are felt by those tyrants from whom derive both our
public and our private misfortunes."[4]

Danton was a widower now, as Marie Antoinette was a widow.
They called her "the Widow Capet." The Polish painter Kocharski was
brought to her cell to do a pastel portrait of her in widow's veil and
mourning dress. Her hair was now completely white. She and her children and Louis' sister Elizabeth continued to be held in the 500-year-
old dungeon of the Knights Templar.

But François-Adrian Toulan, "the laughing cavalier of Gas-
cony,"[5] had just begun to fight. Within ten days of Louis' execution,
before the end of January, he had told Marie Antoinette that he
would help her escape from the Temple. She said she would never
leave without both her children and her sister-in-law. Toulan assured

her that he could get them all out. But he needed an outside contact. Could she suggest anyone?

She gave him the name of the Chevalier de Jarjayes, who had been her private secretary and the man who carried her correspondence to and from Antoine Barnave, the revolutionary who had been won over by her extraordinary courage in suffering during the terrible return from Varennes in 1791, and had also tried to save her and her family. Jarjayes was still in Paris, though preparing to leave, when Toulan went to him on February 2 with a letter from Marie Antoinette attesting her complete trust in him. On the 7th Toulan smuggled Jarjayes into the Temple disguised as a lamplighter. They worked out details of the escape plan, aided by the lessened sense of urgency among the Temple guards regarding security of the prisoners, following Louis' execution.

They had to bring another of the guards into the plot, a man named Lepitre—a former professor of Latin—who had also shown sympathy for the royal family before Louis' execution; he was head of the passport committee of the Commune, which meant that he could provide the documents necessary to get them out of Paris. They would drug the hostile Tison couple whom the Commune had permanently assigned to the Temple along with the guards, then go out and lock the doors, one of which was of solid iron. Marie Antoinette and Elizabeth would leave the Temple disguised as officers of the Commune, with large tricolor sashes and identity cards Lepitre would provide. Marie-Thérèse, daughter of Louis and Antoinette, would be disguised as the convenient lamplighter's son; young Louis, their son, would leave at the bottom of a large basket of laundry. Once out of the Temple they would take three light carriages and head for the English Channel, where a boat obtained by Jarjayes awaited them in a hidden cove near Le Havre.

It was an ingenious plan with good prospects for success. But the shadow of the guillotine hung over it. The prisoners had nothing to lose. Toulan and Jarjayes were brave as lions. But when the time came to act, ex-Professor Lepitre, no man of action, shrank back. He did not, after all, quite dare. And so he delayed and delayed until the opportunity had passed, until the increasing threat of the war arising from French defeats in the Netherlands and Belgium and the defection of French General Dumouriez to the Austrians at the end of March caused security to be tightened again. The plan had to be abandoned, and Jarjayes had to leave France. "We dreamed a beautiful dream," Marie Antoinette wrote to him, "and that is all."[6]

When Danton returned to Belgium March 5 he found its Catholic people rising against the Revolutionary occupation, the Austrians approaching the eastern border, and Dumouriez losing control of his army. (If Danton did obtain the French victory at Valmy by bribing the Duke of Brunswick, it is a fascinating question whether Dumouriez, the French commander there, knew it. The evidence suggests that he did not, and gained from that too easy triumph an inflated view of his own military abilities.) So threatening was the situation in Belgium that Danton had to turn around within twenty-four hours and rush back to Paris to get help in dealing with it. In a hard-hitting three-hour speech to the Convention March 8, he called for immediate heavy reinforcements for the army in Belgium (which would require all the more the conscription which the Convention had finally decreed explicitly on February 25), an emergency tax on the rich in the form of a capital levy, and the establishment of a special court, the Revolutionary Tribunal, to deal with treason. In arguing for the Tribunal, Danton harkened back to the crisis and massacres of September, recalling that he had told people at the time: "'What do I care for my reputation? Let my name be tarnished, if only France remain free!' I let myself be branded as a bloodthirsty monster, citizens. Should we balk at drinking the blood of humanity's foes, if need be, to win liberty for Europe?"[7] Under pressure from vociferous crowds called out by the Mountain and the Paris Commune and surrounding the Riding School, with the Girondins split on the question, the Revolutionary Tribunal—to become the chief legal instrument of the Terror—was established March 10. Fouquier-Tinville was appointed its prosecutor.

Meanwhile the conscription law was being proclaimed throughout the country. Its text was in the hands of every departmental government by the beginning of March. Only five days were allowed from receipt of the decree to try to obtain genuine volunteers, before beginning conscription by lottery. All government officials and all members of the National Guard were exempt—everyone, therefore, in the Revolutionary establishment. Almost all those subject to the draft were farmers or artisans. Earlier, in 1791 and even in 1792 in the aftermath of August 10, there had been much genuine patriotic eagerness to oppose foreign invaders. In many parts of France this patriotic fervor still existed. But the guillotining of the King had occurred since the last call for troops. And in one part of France, during the course of the year 1792, the laws exiling priests who would not take the oath to support the schismatic Civil Constitution of the Clergy had made a special impact.

This region was known to its inhabitants as the Bocage, the Hedge Country. From the name of one of the new departments including it, which the Revolution established, the whole of it came to be known as the Vendée. It ran some fifty miles south and southeast of the great port of Nantes near the mouth of the Loire River, which flows into the Bay of Biscay about midway down the west coast of France. Between Nantes and the mouth of the Loire the Bocage merged into a tract of former salt marshes, the Marais and the Pays de Retz, drained by Dutch engineers the previous century and transformed into farm and pasture land by a complex pattern of dikes and canals. The Bocage itself was fertile and not marshy, but had no substantial hills, and was cut up by a network of hedges and lines of trees into thousands of small estates and smaller peasant farms, a maze in which even a lifelong resident could become lost ten miles from home. With the exception of two reasonably good highways there were almost no real roads, only ancient tracks often sunken and lined with almost impenetrable bushes. The fertility of the soil ensured that most of the residents were not notably poor; the character of the country likewise prevented even the local aristocrats from becoming notably rich. Landowning aristocrats, smaller landowning farmers, and tenant farmers lived and worked together in substantial harmony, without nearly so much consciousness of class differences as characterized the rest of France. Life in the Bocage almost uniquely fostered freedom and equality—the real kind, not what the Revolution had sloganized.

But the most significant characteristic of the people of the Bocage was their profound and fervent Catholic faith.

Seventy-eight years before, now almost at the edge of living memory, St. Louis Marie de Montfort had preached his extraordinary missions and retreats in many of the isolated parishes of the Bocage. This saint, particularly distinguished for his devotion to the Blessed Virgin Mary and his emphasis on the Rosary, renewed and deepened their faith by his burning eloquence and all-encompassing charity. The devotion of the Sacred Heart of Jesus, launched in the preceding century by St. Margaret Mary Alacoque, had also taken deep root among the people of the Bocage. Nor was there a significant difference, as was common elsewhere in France, between the religious devotion of men and women. The people of the Bocage were almost untouched by all the sophisticated doubt about Christianity and the Catholic Church that had developed among those influenced by Voltaire and Rousseau and their colleagues. This was not because the Bocage was less literate than most of the rest of France; on the contrary, its literacy rate was unusually high for the time. But most of its people who were readers, read Catholic works. They did not read Voltaire and Rousseau.

The parish church was in many ways the center of the lives of these people. Their villages were small and poor, and they made the journey to them—often difficult due to the bad travelling conditions—only when necessity required. But they took their Sunday Mass obligation very seriously, which meant that most of them met together every week at their parish church. All important public as well as church announcements were made there, including announcements about hunts and dances as well as the rare matters involving the government. The great events in the lives of every farmer and his family—baptisms, first communion, weddings, funerals—all took place in the parish church.

As is almost always the case, the strength of faith of this Catholic people held their priests to a high standard of fidelity, as the priests in turn held their parishioners. When the great test of the oath to the Civil Constitution of the Clergy came, out of 474 priests in the region 367 refused it.[8] By the end of the year 1792, many of these priests had been exiled, and almost all had been forced to leave their parish churches. The effect of this, the quality of many of these priests and the loyalty of their parishioners, is unforgettably illustrated by what happened during 1792 in the tiny parish of Saint-Hilaire-de-Mortagne whose pastor, Father Paynaud, had refused the oath. When compelled by the Revolutionary law to leave his parish because of this, he told his people at his last meeting with them, at Sunday morning Mass at ten o'clock: "My brothers, I am going to leave you; but, wherever I go, my heart will be with you and I will pray for you. Each Sunday, so long as I am able, I will say Mass, at this same hour, for you. Join with it in your intentions and your prayer. Never assist at the Mass of an intruder!"[9]

Thenceforth, every Sunday, the faithful of Saint-Hilaire-de-Mortagne parish would meet at ten o'clock for the "invisible Mass." When the parish church was closed and locked against them, they went instead to the cemetery at this same hour. Asked by government men what they were doing, the peasant Lumineau answered for them: "We are at Mass. Our priest promised us when he left that he would say Mass for us, each Sunday, wherever he was." "Imbeciles!" they were mocked. "Your priest is a hundred leagues from here, and you think you are assisting at Mass?" "Prayer," Lumineau responded gently, "goes more than a hundred leagues; it ascends from earth to Heaven!"[10]

So it was that when the Convention's decree for conscription arrived at the Bocage, men knew that it meant not only exposure to all the normal hazards and horrors of war, but service to a government which had killed their King and was destroying their Church. It provided an occasion for resistance, and perhaps most important, a date to begin. For the drawing of the lots for conscription was set in many of the towns of the Bocage for March 12; and it was announced at the beginning of the month, allowing two intervening Sundays—March 3 and 10—for the news to spread and to be discussed when the people of the Bocage gathered at their parish churches which were still functioning, or for the many secret Masses offered by priests who had defied the laws requiring non-jurors to go into exile, and continued to live and serve their people at the daily risk of their lives.

Now at last the Revolution was to meet, not just individual heroes and bewildered victims, but a Catholic people in arms who knew how to draw the sword of Hernan Cortes.

The rising on March 12 was wholly spontaneous, as is shown by the fact that none of its later leaders were in position or ready to take command when it began. Two thousand peasants of the Bocage massed in the principal square of Saint-Florent-le-Vieil, a town of about 5,000 located on the south bank of the Loire about 25 miles upstream from Nantes, armed with shotguns, clubs, pitchforks, and swords made from scythe blades. They were led by a carpenter, a carter, a tailor, and a barrel-maker, and their sons. Nearly all of them wore the forbidden white cockade of the King, which the tricolor had replaced. When the drawing of lots for conscription was about to begin, a shot came from the crowd, which killed one of the Revolutionary speakers. The National Guardsmen present then fired in reply, killing four and wounding forty. Immediately the two thousand attacked, with echoing shouts of *"Vive le roi!"* and *"Vive les bons prêtres!"* (Long live the King! Long live the good priests!) The National Guard, greatly outnumbered, fled to an island in the river. The great Catholic rising in the west of France had begun.

Several of the principal leaders of the rising emerged within the next thirty-six hours. The first, because he lived in the parish of Saint-Florent-le-Vieil, was Artus, Marquis de Bonchamp. He was 33 years old, a regular army officer who had seen service in India, but had refused to swear loyalty to the Convention after the events of August 10. He had no illusions about the risk they were taking in challenging the might of the Revolution alone with almost entirely untrained fighting men, and repeatedly warned those who came to him to ask him to lead them, how small were their chances of success. But he said he would not refuse their appeal if they still made it knowing the odds against them; when they did, he took command.

Fifteen miles to the south, at the little village of Le Pin-en-Mauges, Jacques Cathelineau was baking bread at home on the morning of March 13 when he heard the news of the rising and how thousands of men of the Bocage were gathering in its support. Like Bonchamps, he was 33 years old. Tall and strong, with a young-looking, open face, he was a poor man, an itinerant peddler of woollen goods, modest and unassuming, deeply religious. His men were to call him "the saint of Anjou." He had a wife and five children. His wife begged him not to go. He told her that he must. He wiped the flour from his arms, put on his coat, and went out to take command of a contingent of twenty. It soon grew to four hundred, then to eight hundred. Many wore crosses and images of the Sacred Heart as marks of their allegiance; the spirit of the Crusades was upon them.

The two nearest towns were quickly occupied. At 11:30 in the morning they arrived before the town of Jallais. Seeing that here there would be opposition, Cathelineau halted, saying: "My friends, never forget that we are fighting for our holy religion."[11] He knelt, made the sign of the cross, and sang the "Vexilla Regis." He and his men carried the town at the first charge, capturing their first cannon, which they named "The Missionary." Between four and five o'clock in the afternoon, now well over a thousand strong, they reached the important town of Chemillé, taking it totally by surprise, pouring into the square shouting "Long live the King! Long live the Faith! Surrender your arms!" "Long live the King and our good priests! We want our King, our priests, and the old regime!"[12] After a brief exchange of fire Chemillé was taken, along with another cannon which Cathelineau's men named Marie-Jeanne. The "tree of liberty," one of which had been designated in most towns in France as a symbol of the Revolution, was cut down and used as fuel for a bonfire in which all decrees of the Convention which could be found in Chemillé, and everything tricolor, were burned.

In his very first day of battle, from the morning when he put down the bread he was baking to take command of his contingent of what was soon to be called the Catholic and Royal army, to the evening when he presided over the burning of the decrees of the Revolutionary government, Jacques Cathelineau had taken four towns, defeated two enemy detachments, captured two cannon, and secured the heart of the half of Maine-et-Loire Department which lay south of the Loire River. It was already becoming clear why one day Napoleon Bonaparte would say of this humble peddler, who had never before lifted a sword or fired a gun in anger, that he possessed "the first essential quality of a man of war, that of never resting either as victor or as vanquished."[13]

Meanwhile, on this same extraordinary day, fifty miles west of the region where Cathelineau was conducting his brilliant march, the peasants of the district of Machecoul in the reclaimed salt marshes of the Pays de Retz southwest of Nantes, known as the "black sheep" because they rode on black sheepskins instead of the saddles they could not afford, who had risen the previous day, were pleading with François-Athanase Charette to lead them. Charette was the dashing young nobleman who had barely escaped from the Tuileries August 10 after the King left his defenders behind to shift for themselves. Only 29 years old, trained as a naval officer, he was a native of this country, descended from an old but not especially wealthy noble family, generous and gregarious, famous among the common people for his splendid hunts in which many of them took part, in which he had often demonstrated his skill and endurance. Like Bonchamps, he was very reluctant to take the command offered him by the peasants who had risen against the triumphant Revolution, for he well knew the odds against success. They had to press him hard.

"What a disgrace," they said to him, "that a former officer of the King refuses to fight these sacrilegious men who despoil our churches, imprison our priests, and wish to carry off all our young men to fight in their wars."[14]

When he heard these words, François-Athanase Charette knew his duty and offered his life. No less than his life he gave. Three years later, after adventures that would fill a dozen books like this, he was caught at last by the Revolutionaries in the forest near Saint-Sulpice-le-Verdon and shot. He refused the traditional blindfold before the firing squad and, in a last gesture of magnificent bravado, himself gave it the order to fire.

Speaking to his officers in the course of the great rising in the west, Charette was on one memorable occasion to say:

> Our country is ourselves. It is our villages, our altars, our graves, all that our fathers loved before us. Our country is our Faith, our land, our King.... But their country—what is it? Do you understand? Do you?... They have it in their brains; we have it under our feet ... It is as old as the Devil, the world that they call new and that they wish to found in the absence of God ... They say we are the slaves of ancient superstitions; it makes us laugh! But in the face of these demons who rise up again century after century, we are youth, gentlemen! We are the youth of God, the youth of fi-

delity! And this youth will preserve, for its own and for its children, true humanity and liberty of the soul.[15]

The next day, March 14, a fourth leader joined the rising, bringing his men to join Cathelineau as he marched on Cholet, the principal town in Maine-et-Loire Department south of the banks of the Loire River. This was Jean-Nicolas Stofflet, the grandson of a German peasant from Swabia who had settled in Lorraine. For eight years he had served as an enlisted man in the Lorraine Infantry Regiment; then he became the gamekeeper of the estates of the Count of Maulévrier. Forty-one years old, strapping and vigorous, something of a martinet with a German accent, he was just the sort of commander these eager but wholly untrained and undisciplined fighting men needed. Cathelineau, with his profound humility, deferred to Stofflet, who wrote out the summons to the Revolutionary garrison of Cholet, consisting of less than 400 men facing a peasant host that had now grown to over 12,000: "The inhabitants of Cholet are ordered to surrender their arms to the commanders of the Christian army."[16] The garrison's brief attempt at resistance was blown away by the first cannonade from the Missionary and Marie-Jeanne, and Cholet surrendered.

Meanwhile the towns of Montaigu and Saint-Fulgent and the surrounding countryside, lying between Machecoul and Cholet, had been taken by yet another spontaneous independent uprising of the peasants of the region known as the Marches of Poitou and Anjou. Here the leadership fell to another minor nobleman named de Guerry, who accepted it March 14 after at first urging caution. His first act as commander was to order Mass said for all his men. About six thousand of them attended. As de Guerry describes it in his private journal:

> They presented a strange sight; some were armed with guns, others with scythe blades, bayonets, sabers, cudgels and pitchforks ... I held in my hand a pitchfork, whose shaft was at least six feet long; just before the *ite Missa est*, I handed it to its owner, proclaiming in a loud voice: *Tenez vrais défenseurs de la foi, allez et poursuivez les démons jusqu'à l'enfer!* [Keep yourselves true defenders of the Faith; go and chase the demons right back into Hell!][17]

The greater part of the Bocage and the Marais had been liberated in thirty-six hours by the Christian army, whose principal commanders were three minor noblemen, a gamekeeper, and a peddler.

South of the Bocage and the broad agricultural plain that adjoined it on the south in the departments of Vendée and Deux-Sèvres, the 12th Division of the Revolutionary army was stationed at the old Calvinist stronghold of La Rochelle. When the first reports of trouble in the north had reached La Rochelle, on March 10, 11, and 12 before the mighty upsurge of the 13th, the division commander had sent Lieutenant-General Marcé, an old soldier with 48 years' service, with 1,200 men and four cannon to join with a force from Nantes to put it down. This superannuated veteran was no match for the "youth of God." In a comic-opera promenade up the road from Chantonnay, he encountered at Gravereau Bridge a force which he could not identify, but decided must be friendly because it was singing the Marseillaise. What General Marcé did not know was that the Catholic and Royal Army had already supplied their own words to the famous tune; instead of "Come, children of the fatherland, the day of glory has arrived" they were singing:

> Come, armies Catholic,
> The day of glory has arrived!
> Against us from the Republic,
> The bloody standard has been raised.[18]

Marcé sent forward a herald and a trumpeter in the old style, to greet his supposed comrades. The peasants—totally unfamiliar with military and diplomatic protocol—looked at them in bewilderment, then advanced menacingly; herald and trumpeter beat a prudent retreat. When they moved forward again, the peasants, tiring of the byplay, bellowed: "*Vive le roi! Vive le clergé!*" "There was no doubt now," glumly concluded Colonel Boulard, commander of Marcé's advance guard, when he received their report, "that we were in the presence of an army of brigands."[19]

Dusk was falling. Marcé planned a dawn attack. But the "brigands" had no intention of waiting all night. Peasant sharpshooters took their positions behind trees and hedges, like the American farmers at Concord nineteen years before. Sighting over their long-barreled guns in the twilight, they picked out their targets and opened fire. It was like a shooting gallery. Every peasant with a gun seemed to have a target, while the Revolutionary soldiers did not even know where the enemy was. Firing wildly in all directions, mostly straight up in the air, they scattered in panic. The peasants pursued, shouting one of their favorite battle-cries, a guttural "*Rembarre! Rembarre!*" ("Go for them! Jump down their throats!") Rain began pouring down. Colonel Boulard and his horse fell into a ditch. From the end of the night all through the morning, drenched and panic-stricken Revolutionaries were staggering into the rear post of Saint Hermand. The commissioners from the Convention who were there deprived Marcé of his command, but could find nobody better to replace him than Boulard. By noon they had all concluded they had no choice but to order a general withdrawal to La Rochelle.

It was Tuesday, March 19, the feast day of St. Joseph the humble carpenter who was foster-father to the Incarnate God. In just one week since the rising began, the Catholic and Royal Army had liberated the whole department of the Vendée and half of Maine-et-Loire and Loire-Inférieure. At the Convention in Paris, members realized that it had been five days since any mail had come from Nantes. Gradually, bit by bit, the news trickled in, distorted by hatred and magnified by rumor: "the districts of St. Florent, Cholet, and Vihiers pillaged, ravaged, and burned, more than five hundred patriots slaughtered . . . two formidable columns of rebels led by experienced men are marching *en masse* on Saumur and Angers."[20] Jacobins and Girondins dropped their increasingly bitter feuding to unite against the common enemy, counterrevolution. On March 19 a deputy from Maine-et-Loire named Delaunay, supposedly representing the people who had risen in tens of thousands for their Faith and their King, moved the following decree in the Convention, which was immediately adopted:

> Priests, *ci-devant* nobles and seigneurs, or agents and servants of these people, foreigners and any person who has been employed, or who has exercised a public function under the former government or since the Revolution, found guilty of inciting or of supporting any rebels or their leaders, or of murder, arson and pillage, or of carrying arms, are to be handed over to a military tribunal and will be shot within twenty-four hours.[21]

War to the death had begun.

Most of the peasants of the Bocage returned to their homes for Holy Week, which ran that year from March 24 to 31; meanwhile General Berruyer, who had been sent down from Paris to take command of the army that was supposed to suppress the uprising, found that army frightened, near-mutinous, badly equipped and trained, in no condition to march immediately against anyone. The desertion of General Dumouriez to the Austrians in Belgium further discomfited the Convention, whose members—always inclined to see conspiracies everywhere—now debated and tried to act amidst a veritable blizzard of conspiracy theories, which, as always with this *genre* of speculation, were exciting and alarming but could never be made to agree with one another. On the whole the Mountain had the better of these confused debates, because the Girondin leaders, and also Danton, had been much friendlier with Dumouriez than the Jacobins. No one was able to develop a really plausible scenario linking Dumouriez's desertion with the rising in the Vendée, though it was not for lack of trying; almost two hundred years later some historians are still attempting to develop that link, though still without significant success.

Out of these days of boiling suspicion, fury, and hate in the Convention emerged two measures of supreme importance. The first was the abolition (on motion of Marat) of the special immunity of members of the Convention from legal prosecution. (Did anyone remember, when Marat introduced his motion, how they had disposed of the guarantee of personal inviolability to the King in the constitution of 1791?) If treason was everywhere, it could surely be within the Convention as well. The Girondin Biroteau supported Marat's motion, each side thinking that members of the other would be more likely to be prosecuted. In the trenchant words of Robert Christophe, "neither side realized that by endorsing the motion of Marat and Biroteau they had signed death warrants for a large proportion of their own membership."[22] The second measure was the creation of a new, supremely powerful executive that would work in secret: the Committee of Public Safety. These were its powers, granted April 6:

> This Committee will deliberate in secret. It will be charged with overseeing and speeding up the administrative action charged to the provisional Executive Council, whose decrees it may suspend, when it believes them contrary to the national interest, subject to the requirement of informing the Convention of such action without delay.
> It is authorized in urgent circumstances to take measures for the general defense both external and internal, and decrees, signed by the majority of its members (when two-thirds are not required), will be put into effect without delay by the provisional Executive Council....
> The national Treasury will be at the disposal of the Committee of Public Safety, up to 100,000 pounds [per month] for secret expenses, which will be disbursed by the Committee and paid on its orders which are signed as decrees.[23]

The Committee of Public Safety, thus chartered, had nine members. Those first chosen included Danton; the character and past records of the members made it certain that the committee would be under his domination. No Girondins and no leaders of the Mountain were included in the membership. The only really prominent member other than Danton was Barère of the Plain, who always went with the stronger side. Danton had dominated the Revolution for more than a year. Despite some slips and problems, he was still at the head of the pack. There is no sign whatever that his grief for Gabrielle and the circumstances of her death had affected in the slightest his commitment to the Revolution or his energy and ruthlessness in leading it.

Each member of the Committee of Public Safety took personal responsibility—which, under all the circumstances and in view of the language of the decree empowering the Committee, meant in the last analysis final authority—for one or more ministerial departments. Danton took the War Department and later, Foreign Affairs. This meant that he was now ultimately responsible for the suppression of the Catholic rising in the Vendée as well as for the prosecution of the war against all the great powers of Europe.

On April 11, despite many misgivings due to the poor quality and low morale of his troops, General Berruyer attacked the Vendeans at Chemillé, the town Cathelineau had so impressively taken almost a month before. The battle was a draw, but the Vendeans used up almost all their readily available ammunition and had to retreat. Disheartened by their first major reverse, many of these men—almost all untrained militia with only a few days' military experience—began to lose hope of victory. For the past two weeks young Henri, Marquis de la Rochejaquelein, who had been with Charette at the Tuileries seeking to save the King on August 10, and was a native of the Bocage, had been trying to raise more peasants in the area to fight for their Faith and their King. At first he had little success, probably because the more ardent spirits had already joined the uprising. But he was continuing this effort when the check at Chemillé occurred, and was able to rekindle the enthusiasm of the peasants just as the established leaders seemed for the moment incapable of doing so. Thousands gathered around the ardent young leader to hear him cry, on April 13:

> My friends, if my father were here, he would inspire you with confidence, but you scarcely know me, and I am still only a child [he was twenty years old]. I hope, at least, that by my conduct I will prove worthy to be your leader. If I advance, follow me; if I retreat, shoot me; if I am killed, avenge me.[24]

It was remembered as the greatest of all the speeches of the rising. With a mighty surge of enthusiasm his men followed him to the nearby town of Aubiers. It was the first of no less than twenty-five battles in which the young hero fought; before each one he prayed: "I ask God to take me to Himself—and if I should survive, to remain always with me."[25] At Aubiers he led a charge which carried all before it, even though most of the men making the attack had no ammunition and were armed only with clubs. The defenders fled, leaving behind two cannon and a large supply of the desperately needed ammunition. La Rochejaquelein promptly brought it to the main army, enabling it to regain possession of Cholet and Chemillé; Charette won a major victory at Legé near Machecoul on April 30, inflicting no less than 500 casualties on the Revolutionaries; by the beginning of May the Vendeans had once again driven their foes almost entirely out of the Bocage. The forces of Revolutionary General Quétineau retired from Bressuire in Deux-Sèvres department toward Thouars in such disorder that they forgot their Vendean prisoners being held in Bressuire and on the way fell into violent disputes on what road to take, entirely without regard to the orders of the general, that almost led to shooting among different factions of the Revolutionary army (whom the Vendeans always called the Blues, from the color of their uniforms).

Among the Vendean prisoners forgotten in Bressuire was the third of the would-be defenders of the King on August 10 whose fortunes that day we had occasion to follow: the Marquis de Lescure, 26, with his wife Marie-Louise Victoire, 20, who has left us the most vivid of all the memoirs of that struggle. Her description of the liberating army is much the best we have:

> Early in the morning I received a note from M. de Lescure [so Marie-Louise Victoire always refers to her husband in these memoirs, though everything else about them is the reverse of pompous], desiring me to expect him with Henri [de la Rochejaquelein] and twenty-four dragoons at Clisson. They brought with them the Chevalier de Beauvolliers, a young man of eighteen who had been enlisted by force at Loudun, and sent to Bressuire. In the evening on which the town was evacuated [by Quétineau], he found means of quitting his corps, and galloped full speed to carry the intelligence to the rebels.... He was full of bravery and gentleness, and became aide-de-camp and intimate friend of M. de Lescure. None of the other dragoons who came with these gentlemen had any military or very respectable appearance. Their horses were of all colors and sizes; some had pack-saddles, with ropes for stirrups; wooden shoes for boots, pistols at their girdles, with guns and sabers, suspended by pack-threads! Some had white cockades, others black or green! All of them, however, had a consecrated heart sewed upon their coats, and a chaplet hanging at their buttons. In contempt of the Blues, they had fastened to their horses' tails tri-colored cockades, and epaulettes taken from them....
>
> The soldiers sat down to breakfast; the peasants from the neighboring parishes crowded from all parts to join them. Women came with hatchets in their hands, after hav-

ing cut down the tree of liberty. The chateau was full of
people, who ate, drank, sung, and repeated with acclamations,
"Vive le Roi!" ["Long live the King!"] Meanwhile M. de Lescure informed us that he had been received with open arms
at Bressuire, that he was considered as the chief of all the
parishes in the canton, and appointed one of the council of
war. . . .

We went in a carriage escorted by armed servants, and
as we drew near the town, perceived the Vendéens. They
knew who we were, and began to call out "Vive le Roi!" We
repeated it with them, shedding tears of joy. I perceived
about fifty on their knees at the foot of a crucifix. Nothing
interrupted their devotion.

The town was occupied by about twenty thousand men,
of whom not more than six thousand had fire-arms. The rest
carried scythes fixed on handles (a frightful-looking weapon),
blades of knives, sickles fixed on sticks, spits, or great massy
clubs of knotted wood. All the peasants were intoxicated
with joy, and believed themselves invincible. The streets were
full, the bells rung, and they had made a bonfire in the
square with the tree of liberty and the papers of the administration.

The gentlemen went to seek the generals, and I walked
about the town with my maids. The peasants asked me if I
had been at Bressuire before. I told them of my having been
a prisoner there, and how they had delivered me. They were
all happy to have saved a lady. They told me the emigrants
were going to return, and assist them in restoring their king
and their religion. . . . In the evening I was both surprised
and edified to see all the soldiers who lodged in the same
house with us kneel and repeat a prayer, which one of them
read aloud. I understood they never failed to perform this
devotion three times a day.[26]

On May 5 the Vendeans followed Revolutionary General
Quétineau to Thouars, a walled city defended by more than five thousand men. The Catholic and Royal Army attacked at dawn and fought
all through the day. They literally dug breaches in the walls with their
bayonets, or climbed over them using bayonets as pitons. At the end
of the day someone raised a white flag (there was later an acrimonious
controversy over who did it). The city fell to the Vendeans, with 5,000
prisoners, 4,000 muskets, 12,000 pistols, 2,000 swords, 10 cannon and
100,000 pounds' worth of silver which had been stolen from churches.
Since the Vendeans had no means of caring for prisoners, most of
them were released "on condition that they gave their oath to remain
faithful to the religion of Louis XVII and never again to take up arms
against him or his armies."[27]

The tragic little boy in the Temple dungeon had not been forgotten after all.

The last major town held by the Revolutionary government in Vendée department was Fontenay in the rich plain south of the Bocage. An initial attack on this strongly held town failed with the loss of 32 cannon, including Marie-Jeanne. This attack had been insisted upon by Joseph-Louis, Sieur d'Elbée, another of the local nobility who had joined the group of commanders early in the uprising. Of limited military experience, small in stature and with a hesitating voice, rather vain, nicknamed by his troops "General Providence," it has never been quite clear why d'Elbée emerged as one of the principal generals of the Vendeans, since he never showed any unusual degree of military ability or leadership, though he was a competent soldier. The repulse at Fontenay has been attributed to his poor judgment.

Cathelineau, humble and self-effacing as always, did not attempt to override d'Elbée, but after his failure rallied the disheartened peasant soldiers to try again. On May 25 they carried the town in a tremendous hour's assault, though many of them were still armed only with clubs. Three thousand prisoners and large quantities of military stores were captured, of the greatest importance to the Vendeans since they included not only arms and ammunition, which they badly needed, but also shoes and clothing to replace theirs which had mostly never been adequate and were already beginning to wear out from two and a half months of marching and fighting. A box holding a million francs in Revolutionary paper money was found; the Vendean leaders endorsed the bills "Good, in the name of the King." However, the victors were distressed to learn that Marie-Jeanne was no longer in Fontenay. It (or should we say she?) was being dragged away by the retreating Revolutionaries on the road to Niort, further south beyond the departmental boundary of the Vendée. A detachment rushed off in hot pursuit and a furious hand-to-hand battle followed for possession of the famous cannon, which changed hands six times. At last the Vendeans secured it and brought it back to Fontenay, where they "crowned it with flowers and drank innumerable toasts to its long life."[28]

Two days later ten of the principal commanders of the Catholic and Royal Army, together with five priests (including the later famous Abbot Bernier who collaborated with Napoleon) met in Fontenay to form a Supreme Central Council for the uprising, to arrange for the administration of the substantial territories they now controlled, and to draw up a manifesto to the nation. The manifesto declared the objective of the rising to be "to recover and preserve forever our holy apostolic Roman Catholic religion . . . to have a king who serves as a father to all within [our country] and a protector from all without."[29] In keeping with this objective, the first action taken by the Council was to regularize the situation of the Church in the liberated region by restoring all the non-juring priests who were still there, and also accepting the services of all the priests who had taken the oath to the Revolutionary church who would now affirm the jurisdiction of the bishops recognized by the Pope. All Church property seized and sold by the Revolutionary government was ordered restored to the parishes from which it had been taken.

Upon receiving the news of the fall of Fontenay and the manifesto, Barère cried out in the Convention, in a moment of rare insight: "Nothing like this has been seen since the Crusades!"[30] There was now a growing confidence among the Catholic army that they would prevail, so that not only the leaders, but also the lesser officers and ordinary soldiers thought and talked from time to time of what they would do with a complete victory. Marie-Louise Victoire de Lescure heard them voicing their hopes, and she tells us:

> I know not what dreams of ambition may have been formed afterwards by some of the chiefs, but the views of the army, of the good peasants and their officers, were extremely humble.
> First, they meant to ask that the name of La Vendée, given by chance, should be preserved, and a province formed of the Bocage, with a distinct administration. It had long been a source of regret that a country united by manners, industry, and the nature of the soil, should be separated in three parts, each dependent on different provinces, whose administrations had always neglected the Bocage.
> Secondly, they would have solicited the King to honor for once that rude and remote country with his presence.
> Thirdly, they wished that, in memory of the war, the white flag might always be seen on the steeple of each parish, and that a corps of Vendéens should be admitted in the King's guard.[31]

Such were the war aims of the Catholic and Royal Army, facing the armies of the French Revolution whose leaders were committed to making over the whole world in their image.

NOTES

[1]E.L. Higgins, ed., *The French Revolution as Told by Contemporaries* (Boston, 1938), p. 274.
[2]Robert Christophe, *Danton* (London, n.d.), pp. 331-332.

[3]Arthur Bryant, *The Years of Endurance, 1793-1802* (London, 1942), pp. 76-77.

[4]Christophe, *Danton*, p. 337.

[5]Rupert Furneaux, *The Bourbon Tragedy* (London, 1968), p. 122.

[6]Stanley Loomis, *The Fatal Friendship; Marie Antoinette, Count Fersen, and the Flight to Varennes* (Garden City NY, 1972), p. 289.

[7]Christophe, *Danton*, p. 342.

[8]A. Billaud, *La Guerre de Vendée* (Fontenay, 1972), p. 17.

[9]*Ibid.*, p. 30. All quotations from this book are translated by the author.

[10]*Ibid.*, p. 32.

[11]*Ibid.*, p. 40.

[12]Michael Ross, *Banners of the King; the War of the Vendée, 1793-4* (New York, 1975), p. 67; Charles Tilly, *The Vendée* (Cambridge MA, 1964), p. 317.

[13]Billaud, *Guerre de Vendée*, p. 62.

[14]Ross, *Banners of the King*, p. 84.

[15]Michel de Saint Pierre, *Monsieur de Charette, Chevalier du Roi* (Paris, 1977), p. 13. Translation by the author.

[16]Ross, *Banners of the King*, p. 70.

[17]*Ibid.*, p. 91. Translation of the words of de Guerry to the congregation by the author. It is not clear why Ross left them untranslated while translating the rest of his text.

[18]Billaud, *Guerre de Vendée*, p. 43.

[19]Ross, *Banners of the King*, p. 97.

[20]Tilly, *The Vendée*, p. 315.

[21]*Ibid.*, p. 102.

[22]Christophe, *Danton*, p. 358.

[23]John Hardman, ed., *French Revolution Documents*, Volume II (1792-95) (Oxford, 1973), p. 90. Document in French, translated by the author.

[24]Ross, *Banners of the King*, p. 115.

[25]Saint-Pierre, *Charette*, p. 139. Translation by the author.

[26]Marchioness de la Rochejaquelein, *Memoirs* (tr. Sir Walter Scott) (Edinburgh, 1816), pp. 101-106. This courageous and vivacious lady survived the Revolution and the Napoleonic Wars that followed it. Her first husband, Marquis de Lescure, died of a mortal wound received in battle in the Bocage October 15, 1793; her second husband, the brother of Henri, first Marquis de la Rochejaquelein, died in battle against the troops of Napoleon, also in the Vendée, at another crisis of history, the eve of the Battle of Waterloo. Few women in history have known the love of two such heroes.

[27]Ross, *Banners of the King*, p. 121.

[28]*Ibid.*, p. 128.

[29]*Ibid.*, p. 129. French text translated by the author.

[30]Billaud, *Guerre de Vendée*, p. 64.

[31]Marchioness de la Rochejaquelein, *Memoirs*, pp. 124-125.

VI.

The Assassin, the Penitent, and the Martyr
(May 27-September 6, 1793)

The French Revolution was like a series of earthquakes, each one altering the political landscape almost beyond recognition, and toppling any person or group seeking to remain in the same place, into the abyss.

In the beginning, which might have been a century ago but actually was just four years, when in May 1789 the Estates-General had met, the conservatives stood with the King, the center wanted a national legislature that would be to a significant degree independent of the King, and the radicals wanted a constitution that would sharply limit the powers of the King. After the Tennis Court oath in June 1789, the conservatives wanted the constitution, the center wanted a constitution with a major share in the government, and the radicals wanted full control of the government with the King reduced to a figurehead. After the storming of the Bastille in July 1789, the conservatives wanted a constitution with a major share in the government, the center wanted full control of the government with the King reduced to a figurehead, and the radicals wanted the King imprisoned. After the storming of Versailles and the imprisonment of the King in October 1789, the conservatives wanted full control of the government with the King a figurehead but eventually freed, the center wanted the helpless King as a prisoner, and the radicals began to look to a republic. After the King's flight to Varennes and recapture in June 1791, the conservatives wanted to keep the King but as a prisoner, the center wanted him removed but not just yet, and the radicals wanted him removed immediately. After August 10, 1792 the conservatives wanted to remove the King but to send him into exile rather than kill him; the center was satisfied to see him dead but wanted cabinet-style government with an orderly, dignified legislature and some rights of local self-government; and the radicals wanted to execute him without even a trial and go on to impose their total ideology on every corner of France and then all the rest of the world. After the execution of the King the conservatives still sought orderly government and local rights, the center cried for more centralization of governmental power, and the radicals decided the time had come to visit the fate of Louis XVI upon the now-conservatives who still sought orderly government and local rights.

These newly targeted victims in the spring of 1793, most of whom have come to be known to history as the Girondins (though this was little used as a party name at the time), were more bewildered than anyone by finding themselves, relativistically speaking, conservatives. Nothing had been further from their intention or expectation. As recently as early 1792 most of them had been regarded, and regarded themselves, as flaming revolutionaries; many had been among the most active members of the Jacobin clubs. Now they were assailed as counterrevolutionaries and traitors, even "royalists." Such madness had descended upon Paris that Pierre Vergniaud, who had voted to kill his King just four months before, could now be publicly, and without irony, called a royalist.

Generations of historians have expressed profound sympathy and admiration for the Girondin victims. No compassionate man can withhold sympathy from anyone caught in the toils of the death machine of the French Revolution. A Joseph Stalin would have deserved better of civilization than the appalling travesty of "justice" meted out by "Strike-Hard" Maillard and Fouquier-Tinville. But, in true justice, it is important to keep in mind how much these men had done to create the monster, in the comfortable assurance that its claws would never touch them—and how none of their leaders ever publicly expressed regret for what he had done.

On May 27, 1793—the very day the leaders of the crusaders for Faith and King in the Vendée met to set their government in order and draw up their manifesto committing them "to recover and preserve forever our holy apostolic Roman Catholic religion"[1]—the bell began to toll for the Girondins.

Three days before, a special Commission of Twelve, appointed by the Convention at the request of the Girondins to investigate the efforts of the Paris Commune to gain control of the Convention by

physical force, had arrested Jacques-René Hébert, the vicious and vehemently atheist journalist who, with Marat, was constantly inciting
the Parisian mob to demand the heads of the Girondin leaders, and
had recently become Deputy Procurator of the Commune. (They had
already tried arresting Marat, back in April, only to see him promptly
acquitted by the Revolutionary Tribunal.) Twenty-eight of the 48
"sections" or wards of Paris demanded Hébert's immediate release.
They were supported by Minister of Justice Garat and Minister of
War Pache. More and more vociferous and threatening supporters of
the Mountain pushed their way into the theater of the Tuileries
Palace where the Convention, having finally left the Riding School,
now met. Eventually Girondin deputy Maximin Isnard, who was president that day, reached the end of his patience and endurance. He
cried:

> Listen to what I am about to tell you. If in one of the
> insurrections which have recurred perpetually since March
> 10, and of which the magistrates have never warned the As-
> sembly, any attack were made on the representatives of the
> Nation, I declare to you, in the name of the whole of France,
> that *Paris would be destroyed: yes! the whole of France would
> avenge the outrage, and men would soon be wondering on which
> bank of the Seine Paris had stood!*[2]

The French Revolution had reached the point where one of its
leaders—and a leader of what had become the "conservative" faction—was threatening the destruction of the nation's capital city.

Isnard's cry was taken as (and was probably intended to be) a
declaration of war. But whatever else they were, the Girondins were
not, any of them, men of war. They were orators and writers. Most of
them seem hardly to have known one end of a gun from the other.
They had virtually no following in the army. They had virtually no
following in the National Guard. They had virtually no following in
the countryside. Only in a few of the larger cities of France, outside
Paris, did they have enough support even to make it possible to think
realistically of raising a local militia on their behalf. For them to talk
of destroying Paris so completely that no one would know on which
bank of the Seine it had stood, was pure unadulterated fantasy.

Their opponents, on the other hand, had the power to destroy a
city that completely, and were to exercise much of it during the coming months.

At three o'clock in the morning of May 31, 1793 the tocsin
sounded again in Paris. Drums beat, alarm guns boomed, the National
Guard and the people were called to arms. This time there was no

faithful Mandat to be killed; the brewer Santerre, who had been appointed chief of the National Guard in his stead, had been sent west to fight the Vendeans. (They knew who he was, and that he had stood guard over the execution of the King; they swore to capture him and put him in an iron cage.) The revolutionary army of Paris needed a new commander. The man the Commune chose is the weirdest of all the figures of the French Revolution, so wildly improbable a history-maker that one gets the impression that many historians cannot quite bring themselves to believe that he existed. Unfortunately, he was all too real. His name was François Hanriot and he was, not to put too fine a point on it, a drunken bum. At one time or another in his very checkered past he had been a clerk, a footman, a brandy seller, and a police spy. He had come to the attention of the Paris Commune by leading a group in the attack on the Tuileries August 10, 1792. A police report described him as "a coarse and irascible man who never opened his lips without bawling . . . remarkable for a harsh and grimacing countenance."[3] Almost as deficient in intelligence as in military experience, he could be wound up and pointed in the direction of the target like a glorified toy soldier (provided he was more or less sober), but was totally incapable of handling any unexpected situation or problem. In none of all their actions did the Jacobins and the Mountain display such withering contempt for their opponents as in appointing Hanriot commander of the National Guard on May 31, 1793. Those who chose some of the greatest soldiers of all time to fight on France's frontiers and against the Catholic and Royal Army in the Vendée were satisfied that Hanriot was good enough to handle the Girondins in the Convention. And he was.

The scenes in the Convention during the next three days beggar the imagination. Except for the few who were orchestrating the purge, the once glorified members of that body were like sheets of paper in the Cave of the Winds. Almost all who report these events mention repeatedly the almost continuous, deafening noise. On May 31, the day the tocsin was rung, Hanriot surrounded the Tuileries Theater where the Convention was now meeting with no less than 30,000 men; as many as possible crowded inside to shout for the spokesmen of the Mountain and to shout down the Girondins. Early in the day War Minister Pache swaggered to the tribune and "vowed everything was quiet, and that as long as he lived nobody 'would dare' to set a match to a cannon. Before the words were out of his mouth, the cannon had begun to roar. Hanriot had 'dared.' "[4]

Hanriot was not actually shooting at anything. It is not altogether clear that at this point he knew how; after all, it was his first day on the job. But periodically through the day a discharge of cannon would remind the deputies that he was just outside.

By dawn of June 2 no less than 80,000 men and sixty cannon surrounded the Tuileries, and drunken men and women filled the floor as well as the galleries of the theater where the Convention met. Hooting as though from a forest full of owls filled the chamber whenever one of the Girondins rose to speak. Twenty-two of their leaders, including Vergniaud, had been marked by the Mountain weeks before for arrest and death; but so far the Mountain had been unable to persuade the Convention to order their arrest. Now this became the inevitable order of the day. One of the twenty-two, Lanjuinais, roared out to the terrified Convention, over the howling and the hooting: "You have done nothing; you have permitted everything; you have given way to all that was required of you. An insurrectional committee meets. It prepares a revolt. It appoints commanders to lead it. And you do *nothing* to prevent it."[5] These brave words were followed by a wrestling match at the tribune, with several of Hanriot's bullies trying to drag Lanjuinais away from it while he hung on desperately. After a last demand that the Commune's Insurrectionary Committee be disbanded, Lanjuinais finally stepped down, to be followed by the Commune's "petitioners." "The crimes of the factious members of the Convention [the twenty-two] are known to you!" the spokesmen for the Paris Commune shouted. *"We have come to accuse them before you for the last time!"* Then their followers rushed to the doors, flung them open, and cried: *"Let us save the fatherland! To arms!"*[6]

At this point several deputies tried to leave the hall, but were driven back by a vigorous application of musket-butts. They then pointed out to their colleagues that all of them were now prisoners. Barère went to the tribune. How would he stay on the right side of everybody this time? He thought he had found a way.

"Let us prove that we are free!" he cried. "I propose that the Convention shall proceed to hold its deliberations in the midst of the armed forces which, no doubt, will protect it!"[7]

Some three hundred deputies responded, marching ceremoniously to the main entrance behind their decorative, dandified president, Hérault de Séchelles. The door led to Carrousel Square where the assault force and guns had been massed against the royal family last August 10. Now a line of cannon stood wheel to wheel across the square, in front of them a little man on horseback grotesquely outfitted in an enormous hat with nodding white plumes. It was Hanriot.

"What does the people want?" Hérault de Séchelles inquired politely of this apparition. "The Convention only desires its happiness."

"Hérault," said Hanriot, "the people has not risen to listen to empty talk: it demands that twenty-four guilty men shall be handed over to it." (He had the wrong number, but that was hardly surprising for Hanriot.) "Hand us all over!" some of the deputies shouted back, seeking safety in togetherness.

Hanriot yanked the reins, turning his horse, and with "a yell that would have reduced a fortress to silence," bellowed: *"Gunners! To your guns!"*[8]

The three hundred deputies slunk back through the door; Hanriot slammed it behind them. Then, as Louis Madelin tells us:

> The unhappy band began to wander round and round the prison in which it as shut up: through courtyards and gardens it went, seeking some outlet, under the scornful eyes of the troops, who shouted, *"Long live the Mountain! To the guillotine with the Girondins."* At the swing bridge they found Marat, at the head of some soldiers. He flew at them, screaming, "I call on you to return to the posts you have abandoned like cowards!" and back to their posts they went, with Marat snarling at their heels. The troops were all jeering at them: the "Giant Assembly" was a laughing-stock.[9]

The arrest of the twenty-two Girondins was decreed. Within a year, nearly all of them had died either by their own hands, or by the guillotine.

What role had Danton played in all this? Probably not a leading role; it is not clear even yet who all the principal organizers of the purge of the Girondins were, but they undoubtedly included Robespierre and Marat, both of whom had been denouncing the 22 Girondin victims in the most violent terms for some time, and particularly during the climactic three days. Danton had also denounced them, but without demanding their death; his recorded words during the three days of tumult do not suggest that he was enjoying the proceedings as he had so clearly enjoyed those of August 10, 1792. He continued to appear regularly at the Jacobin Club, and was still a leading member of the Committee of Public Safety. It is said that he was much involved during this period in secret foreign negotiations to try to break up the international coalition making war on France. But his mind seemed to be elsewhere, not altogether focused on public affairs.

It is now June; the fifth summer of the Revolution is about to begin. That June in France is unusually warm and fair. Brilliantly clear days follow one after another. Flowers bloom in profusion. The agony through which France has already passed, the greater agony through which she is about to pass, find no echo at this point in nature. But those agonies echo in the realm of the spirit. On the battlegrounds of salvation, the ultimate powers that shape history are taking position: the power of Heaven; the power of Hell; the power and freedom of the human will to choose between them. A trinity of turning points in the immense drama of the French Revolution is at hand. Only one of them becomes visible immediately. A second is soon to be revealed. The third remains half-guessed, half-understood, its full scope known only to God; but we know and can deduce enough, through the Christian view of history, to see the starlit trail of its glory.

The twenty days from the 9th to the 29th of June 1793 in France encompass the critical decisions of an assassin, a penitent, and a martyr. The assassin: one of history's most famous and perhaps history's most extraordinary, Charlotte Corday; the penitent: none other than Georges-Jacques Danton; the martyr: Jacques Cathelineau, the "saint of Angers," poor peddler and inspired general, who had been ready from the beginning of the great Catholic rising in the west to give his life for his faith, and now was called upon to do so.

Charlotte Corday came of an impoverished branch of a noble Norman family whose ancestry can be traced back to 1077. She was brought up as a child on a farm called Ferme au Bois; at the age of twelve her father moved to Caen, one of the principal towns of Normandy. She was the great-granddaughter of the famous seventeenth-century French dramatist Corneille. She received her education at the convent school of Abbaye-aux-Dames, where in the choir of the church, under a slab of black marble, rested the mortal remains of Matilda, the bold and passionate queen of William the Conqueror, whose home country this was. Masses for the repose of Matilda's soul were still said daily in the church.

Charlotte had been a student at the Abbaye-aux-Dames from 1785 until it was closed by decree of the Revolution in 1791. Her intellect was exceptional and her willingness to speak her mind frankly even more so. She was difficult to educate in the Faith because she questioned so much; but she listened to the answers, and came to accept them. She was devout and chaste, calm and resolute. She matured into a tall, graceful woman of extraordinary beauty, with a low musical voice whose timbre and loveliness were unforgettable. She was twenty-five years old in June 1793.

She read very widely, especially in ancient history and in the works of Rousseau and the Encyclopedists. At the beginning of the Revolution she was enthusiastic for it. She took the most lofty perorations of its advocates about virtue at face value. She despised weakness in high places. When asked why she would not drink, with her family, to the health of the "virtuous" King after the failure of his flight to Varennes, she replied: "I believe that he is a good king; but how can a weak king be virtuous? A weak king can only bring misfortune to his people."[10] But she was shocked by his execution, writing to a friend: "You have heard the frightful news, and your heart like mine must be quivering with indignation. Poor France, at the mercy of these wretches who have already done us so much harm! God only knows where all this will end."[11] She had been even more shocked by the massacres of September, for which she was convinced that Marat was responsible.

Gradually she came to believe that the Girondins stood for the virtue she so admired, particularly as they were more and more threatened by the Mountain. She ignored, if she ever realized, the fact that so many of them did not share her faith; for Charlotte Corday was that rare supporter of the Revolution who remained a strongly believing Catholic. Then came the purge of June 2 and the flight of those Girondin deputies able to get out of Paris. A number of them followed Buzot, one of the twenty-two marked for death, to Normandy, since he was a Norman and assured them that they would find much support in that region. There was not in fact very much support for them there; what there was gathered in Caen, where the fugitives stayed at the Hôtel de l'Intendance, visible from Charlotte Corday's bedroom. All during the week of June 9 Girondins and Girondin sympathizers circulated about the hotel, declaiming in the streets to anyone who would listen to them. But it may well soon have become apparent to Charlotte Corday's piercing intellect that they were going nowhere; they were not men of decision. (She would certainly have known it if she could have beheld the ugly comedy at the Convention from May 31 to June 2, which would have revolted her heroic soul.) Later it was remembered that a friend of her aunt's had cried out in her presence: "How is it that these excesses are tolerated? How is it that these monsters are endured? Are there no men left in France?"[12]

By June 20, when she went to the Hôtel de l'Intendance to meet personally with Charles Barbaroux, another of the proscribed twenty-two, to ask him to provide her with a letter of introduction to a member of the Convention in Paris, she had made up her mind what she was going to do. She had answered the question which she had embroidered on a bit of silk left behind in her room: Shall I or shall I not? She was already putting her affairs in order, returning everything that she had borrowed—she returned a book of lace designs to a certain Madame Paisan, saying "I shall have no more need of lace," and a book on the history of the Knights of Malta to the former abbess of

Abbaye-aux-Dames. She burned her political literature. Once her aunt found her weeping, and asked the reason.

"Who would not weep, dear Aunt, in such times as these?" she replied. "Who knows who may be struck down next? Which of us is safe so long as Marat lives?"[13]

Charlotte Corday had decided to assassinate Jean-Paul Marat, who had become for her the incarnation of all the evil in the Revolution, by stabbing him to death.

Tyrannicide is an age-old Catholic doctrine, though it has always made many people uneasy. A woman as intelligent and well-read as Charlotte Corday probably knew this Catholic doctrine, along with the then very familiar and fashionable tales of tyrannicides in classical antiquity. If it is clear that one man rules outside the law; that he rules by terror and killing which will continue indefinitely if he is not removed; that there is no peaceful or political or judicial way of removing him; and that there is good reason to believe that his removal will bring the regime of tyranny and oppression to an end, then it is moral to kill that man by any means available. Klaus von Stauffenberg, the profoundly Catholic hero who came closest of all to killing Adolf Hitler in July 1944, which could well have changed the whole course of the history of Europe if not of the world for the remainder of the twentieth century, examined these moral issues for months before deciding to go through with his plan. Hitler's case stands as the best real-life example of what would have been justified tyrannicide.

But the Second World War was a time of heroes; the French Revolution, except in the Vendée, by and large was not. It seems that Charlotte Corday sensed that, and was trying to make up for it. She was seeking by one splendid dramatic act to break the spell that held her country in thrall. But killing Marat would not do that. He was no Hitler. He did not rule absolutely. The French Revolution was far bigger than he. It could easily go on without him. And it is said (though Charlotte could hardly have known this) that his complex of repulsive diseases had already made him a dying man.

History shows us few more evil men than Jean-Paul Marat. But his case did not meet the Catholic moral requirements for tyrannicide. For him, therefore, the Catholic was called only to remember: "Vengeance is mine, says the Lord."

Since St. Joan of Arc, France has produced no more heroic spirit than Charlotte Corday. But her heroism was misdirected. She might have become a leader like St. Joan, and a martyr like her. She had all the qualities for both. One almost dares to think that God may have given her those qualities precisely so that she might use them at this critical moment, in the words of de Guerry of the Vendée, to "drive the devils right back into Hell." But her decision was to become an assassin, to kill a man whose death now would change nothing.

The Church of Christ comes above all to bring life, not death. Tyrannicide can be, for the well instructed Catholic, a moral act; but penance is a sacrament.

In the darkening days of her fourth and last pregnancy, under the shadow of her bitter knowledge of her husband's responsibility for the September massacres, Gabrielle Danton had drawn closer and closer to the much younger girl who had become her best friend, Louise Gély. Louise was very young—in June 1793 she had not yet reached her sixteenth birthday—but astonishingly mature for her age. She was highly intelligent, calm, reserved, discreet, strong-willed, deeply compassionate. No woman in history has kept her counsel more carefully, disproved more completely the ancient stereotype of woman as gossip, than Louise Gély. It may be that few have ever carried a more tremendous secret all through a long life to the grave; Louise lived until 1856 without ever speaking, to anyone who recorded her words, of Georges-Jacques Danton in the year of the Terror. Of her appearance, we are told that "she had quick, bright eyes, a heart-shaped face, and fine chestnut hair."[14]

After Gabrielle's death, Louise and her parents cared for Danton's children, while he was off in Belgium or tied up in the day-and-night sessions of the Convention. When he was at home, Danton spent much time in her company. She conversed freely with him, her precocious mind and serene spirit refusing to be overpowered by the mighty torrent of his words and his will. The scene captivates the imagination: the gigantic, barrel-chested revolution-maker of thirty-three, the gladiator of audacity, the terror of kings, in animated conversation with a fifteen-year-old girl who gives back as good as she gets.

Did she know what he had done? She must have; she had been Gabrielle's best friend. Did she reject him because of it? No; her friend had loved him; his children needed her. Did she think of Christ's words about searching for the lost sheep? We shall never know in this world, for Louise Gély kept her silence through all the years of her life that were to come.

Some time late in that beautiful spring of 1793 Georges-Jacques Danton asked Louise Gély to marry him. We do not know when he asked her; but we do know that by June 12 she had accepted. The thought leaps immediately to mind, remembering Danton's curious and uncharacteristic vagueness and air of distraction during the purge of the Girondins two weeks before, that this may have been when he was waiting for her answer—or had received it, and was trying to decide how he would respond to it.

For Louise Gély said yes to Danton's proposal, on two firm conditions: that he should first go to confession before a priest in communion with the Pope; and that they should be married by such a priest, who would bless their marriage in the name of the Holy Roman Catholic Church. And by June 12 Danton had accepted both conditions.

Well might a famous French historian of the Revolution say: "Of all the startling spectacles that the chronicle of the Revolution has bequeathed to posterity, Danton's confession is assuredly one of the most unexpected."[15] And, the Catholic historian must add, potentially one of the most significant.

Where might a non-juring priest, a priest who had never accepted the "constitutional" church and was still in communion with Rome, be found in the Paris of June 1793? Louise's parents knew. They were in contact with a former Sulpician priest named Kéravénan. He had been imprisoned in the old Carmelite monastery in September 1792, where almost all the priests and religious were slaughtered by Maillard's hired killers; but Father Kéravénan survived to write his memoirs. When the massacre began he was in the lavatory. He managed to climb up the wall, move a loose board in the ceiling, and squeeze into a hiding-place under the roof, where he lay immobile for a full twenty-four hours. Then he climbed down and made his escape. Ever since then he had lived in Paris as an outlaw, moving repeatedly to avoid discovery, but continuing his ministrations as a priest wherever he went. And so, one day that June, in some hidden attic whose location has never been revealed, Father Kéravénan came face to face with the man who had given the orders which should have killed him in September of the preceding year.[16] He has left us a description of how Danton appeared to him at that moment:

> His face was pitted with smallpox. There was a wrinkle denoting bad temper between his eyebrows. The crease of good nature was at the corner of his mouth. He had thick lips, big teeth, a hand like that of a street porter, and a piercing eye.[17]

Danton fell to his knees. "Bless me, Father, for I have sinned . . ."

No man on earth will ever know what Danton said to Father Kéravénan that day, in his confession. The few historians who mention it generally seem to assume that Danton was simply going through the motions to fulfill his promise to Louise. That is of course possible. But it is not easy to believe that even Danton would have made a false or frivolous confession to a priest he had once sought to kill. And the ultimate test of a good confession is the amends or restitution that are made, the change in behavior that results. By that standard, through the few months that remained to him, the quality of the confession Danton made to Father Kéravénan may be judged.

Louise then came to the priest's hiding place; she and Danton spoke the ancient words of the Catholic marriage service; and Father Kéravénan blessed their union in the name of the Church which has guarded and glorified matrimony as no other institution, society, or doctrine on earth ever has or ever will.

We do not know the exact date of Danton's confession and his marriage with Louise before Father Kéravénan; but it was within a few days of the middle of the month of June, very soon after the marriage contract was signed June 12. The chronology of Danton's public life yields at once a fascinating fact, the first bearing on the question of the quality of the confession which Louise had insisted that he make. On June 7, about a week before his confession, Danton appeared, as he had so often, at a meeting of the Paris Jacobin Club, center of revolutionary planning and activity. It was his last appearance there for a long time. He did not attend another meeting of the Jacobin Club until December 3, when he had begun his great effort to end the Terror and had to be ready to defend himself against the Club.

Nor did he even attend another session of the Convention or meeting of the Committee of Public Safety until July 6. He spent the intervening three weeks in the country with Louise. His sudden and complete disappearance was the subject of much comment. When on July 10 the Convention, guided by Robespierre, reduced the membership of the Committee of Public Safety from sixteen to nine and called for a new election of its members, Danton was not one of those selected. He made no protest. On July 27 Robespierre, after having waited a bit with his habitual caution to make sure the risk was minimal and the coast clear, finally joined the Committee himself.

Meanwhile Jacques Cathelineau's time of decision had come.

On June 9, the same day that the Girondin refugees and their knot of supporters began to gather in Caen, impelling Charlotte Corday toward her grim decision, the Catholic and Royal Army had taken the strongly fortified city of Saumur on the Loire River in another of their splendid assaults. (The city's defenses had been scouted a day or two before by La Rochejaquelein disguised as a peasant.) They were steadily gaining strength, and after the victory at Saumur were joined by a substantial number of the troops from its garrison, especially those of the German legion which had been stationed there; many of the legionaries volunteered to serve under Stofflet, the Vendean commander who spoke their language. They had also now been joined by some 120 Swiss, a company which had originally been part of the Swiss Guard which was mostly stationed at the Tuileries to protect the King; this company had been sent to Normandy and so had escaped the massacre of August 10. But it loomed large in their memories; they fought fiercely and relentlessly against the Revolution.

The victory at Saumur had a tremendous impact on the surrounding region of central France, beyond the Bocage where the great Catholic rising had begun. Towns in that region began surrendering without a fight to the first Vendeans to approach them. Strategically located, Saumur was a base from which the Catholic and Royal Army could move northeast toward Paris, 150 miles away; north toward Normandy, about 100 miles away; or northwest into Brittany. On June 10 Charette took Machecoul and gained full control of the Pays de Retz adjoining the mouth of the Loire, downstream from the great port of Nantes which was still held by the Revolution. The fact that at this time the fugitive Girondin deputies from the Convention were attempting, with some success, to encourage uprisings against the authority of the purged Convention in Normandy (Caen and Rouen), Bordeaux (home of several of the Girondin leaders), Lyons, and Marseilles gave the Catholic and Royal Army a greater opportunity for victory by fragmenting the potential military response of the Revolution to the rising in the west, though there was never any question of collaboration between the Vendeans and the Girondins. The Vendeans well knew that many of the Girondins had voted to kill King Louis XVI and that all of them had voted to depose and convict him. The Girondins knew that the Vendeans were committed to the restoration of the monarchy and the elimination of the Revolution.

Enormously important strategic decisions had to be made immediately, upon which the whole fate of the Catholic rising in the west might well depend—as, in the end, it did. It is to the highest credit of the many and varied leaders of the Catholic and Royal Army that they saw at once the overriding necessity of unity of command. As Lescure put it, writing from his bed where he was recovering from a wound in the shoulder suffered at the storming of Saumur: "The insurrection has now become so important, and our successes so promising, that we ought to appoint a general in chief ... I give my vote for Cathelineau."[18]

So did all the other commanders. Cathelineau was chosen unanimously. His commission as commander-in-chief of the Catholic and Royal Army was signed by its fourteen principal generals. So noble was Cathelineau's character and so humble were his origins that none of his fellow commanders felt jealous of him; and all outside accusations of conspiracy and manipulation in the western rising, then and since, fall into embarrassed silence before the transparent sincerity of the peddler of Le Pin-en-Mauges.

As commander-in-chief, Cathelineau's first and vital duty was to decide where the Catholic and Royal Army should march, and what its basic strategy should be for winning the war. There was never a moment's doubt in Cathelineau's clear direct mind that they must win it. There was no peace to be made with the Revolution. So long as the Revolutionary, regicide government existed it would never accept the freedom of the Catholic west any more than it would accept the restoration of the monarchy. They could not simply dig in where they were; the Revolution, despite its troubles, had more than enough power and energy to destroy them if they merely presented a standing target. They must maintain the offensive. Once again Cathelineau was to show the truth of Napoleon's encomium, that he possessed the primary quality of a man of war, that of never resting, whether on the laurels of victory or the ashes of defeat.

On June 15 he called a council of war in Saumur. It was the hour of decision. Stofflet and La Rochejaquelein called for the boldest move: an immediate march on Paris. "Anarchy," cried La Rochejaquelein (was he thinking of that day of horror he had witnessed at the Tuileries August 10?), "is a monster which can be killed only by striking at its heart!" "The road to the capital is open to us," Stofflet said. "Let us go to Paris, find our little king, and crown him at Cholet!"[19]

Commenting later on the war in the Vendée, no less an authority than Napoleon agreed with Stofflet and La Rochejaquelein:

> If, profiting from their astonishing success, Charette and Cathelineau had drawn together all their forces in order to march on the capital after the affair [taking] of Machecoul, the Republic would have been finished; nothing could have stopped the triumphant march of the Royal Army. The white flag would have flown over the towers of Notre Dame before it would have been possible for the armies of the Rhine to come to the aid of their government.[20]

But a different and also bold and promising proposal had been submitted by Charette and was supported by the Marquis de Donnis-

san, the father of Lescure's wife Marie-Louise Victoire, author of the
striking memoirs of the war in the Vendée. This proposal was for an
attack on Nantes. This port city was the only remaining large and
well-defended Revolutionary stronghold in the west. Unless and until
it were taken, the Vendeans had no port close to their heartland from
which supplies could be received in quantity from England, where
they probably knew that Edmund Burke, the man who with unerring
vision had seen and exposed to the English-speaking world the truth
about the French Revolution when it was scarcely a year old, was calling ceaselessly for aid to be sent to them. With Nantes in their hands,
a firm alliance with strongly Catholic Brittany, stretching northwest
from the limits of that city, could easily be forged. Brittany had lacked
only organization and leadership to rise; there was no question that
royalist sympathy was very widespread there. Charette's troops were
ready and in position. He was himself a native of Nantes and knew
just how the city might be successfully attacked.

The decision was Cathelineau's. For the first time the limitations
of his background showed. He had never been to Paris; it seemed very
far away. He knew Nantes and its importance. He loved and respected
Charette. He knew that his peasant soldiers would be very reluctant to
march 150 miles from home, even if it might mean final victory. The
arguments for the attack on Nantes had real force. He made his decision:

> We cannot go to Paris; it is too far. We should not re-
> main inactive here; it would be dangerous. Let us take the
> middle way: let us march on Nantes. We will offer thereby
> our hand to our brothers in Brittany. The attack, well led,
> ought to succeed: Monsieur Charette will approach by the
> left bank; we will arrive on the other side. And afterwards,
> by the grace of God . . .[21]

He did not finish, because he was not sure what would come afterwards. But on leaving the council of war, he encountered
Quétineau, the Revolutionary general whom he had captured at
Thouars, and again at Saumur, whom he and his men respected for his
courage and frankness, though he had firmly refused to abandon his
support of the Revolution. "Your soldiers," Quétineau said to him,
"fight like lions; you are all heroes! But alone against the Republic,
you will not always win. And then?" "Then," Cathelineau replied quietly, "we shall die."[22]

So it was to be. But it might, just possibly, have been different,
had there been in Jacques Cathelineau only a little more of *toujours
l'audace.*

The attack on Nantes took place June 29. Within a week of the summer solstice, in the high latitudes of northern Europe, there was very little night; Charette launched his assault at two-thirty in the morning. But many of the people of Nantes were still fired by the initial enthusiasm of the Revolution; their mayor, Baco de la Chapelle, as brave as any of the Vendeans, had vowed to defend his city to the last man; their general, the Alsatian Beysser, was a merciless killer who, when he had captured Machecoul, had ordered its chief defender Souchu slain at once upon his capture by an axe to the head. (The fact that Souchu himself, unlike most of the Vendeans up to this point, had been guilty of atrocities still did not justify such disposition of a defenseless prisoner.) Consequently Beysser did not feel he was in any position to risk capture by the Catholic and Royal Army, and would also fight to the death.

Charette's attack was therefore strongly resisted, and he became more and more disturbed as the hours passed and the dawn brightened into a clear summer morning and there was still no sign of the main army approaching from the north and east, that was supposed to have joined him in the assault at five o'clock. They had been held up at the Erdre River northeast of Nantes by a Revolutionary battalion at Nort, which fought too stubbornly to be dislodged; outflanking it and finding another river crossing took hours. The division of Bonchamps, which had been waiting for the main army to get past this obstacle, finally attacked at eight o'clock, when Cathelineau was known to be approaching at last, though still not in sight. But Bonchamps himself was not with his division, due to the effects of the two wounds he had suffered in the course of the spring campaigns; without his personal leadership to fire it, the attack was not pressed home. Charette was isolated to the south, exchanging cannonades with the defenders but no longer in a position to help much, when Cathelineau finally arrived at ten o'clock at the head of 10,000 fresh men. His force alone was almost equal in size to the Nantes garrison of 12,000.

The peddler of Le Pin-en-Mauges waved his sword high in the air, and a surge of peasant soldiers crashed like Cape Horn surf upon the defenders in the earthworks on the heights of Baroin at the edge of the city of Nantes. Through the trenches and upon the ramparts men grappled hand-to-hand, with bayonet, sword, long knife, and club. Ringing cries of *"Vive la religion!"* (Long live the Faith!), *"Vive le Roi!"* (Long live the King!), and *"En avant!"* (Forward!) mingled with the familiar rumbling growl of *"Rembarre! Rembarre!"* Unable to withstand the mighty shock, the Revolutionaries retreated; but it was a fighting retreat. Mayor Baco was in the ranks, calling out to his Nantais to fight on, until he fell wounded and had to be carried off in a cart. "Comrades," roared the terrible Beysser, "if we must die, let us die gloriously with weapons in our hands!"[23] The Prince of Talmont, a recent recruit to the Catholic and Royal Army, opened fire with two cannon. The relentless pressure of the men who wore the emblems of the Cross and the Sacred Heart carried the advance into the heart of the city, to their objective, Viarme Square. Still the Revolutionaries fought.

It is one of the critical moments in the military history of Christendom. Victory at Nantes by the Catholic and Royal Army June 29, 1793 might well have defeated the French Revolution, either by its own direct effects or by persuading Cathelineau that Paris and total victory should now become his objective; if it had, the history of the world for the past two hundred years would have unfolded without the seduction and the shadow the French Revolution has cast—and quite possibly without its heir, the Communist Revolution.

But men make history, not strategy and tactics, nor guns and ammunition, nor ideologies and economic systems. Because of that, there are times when the course of history for a century and more can be shaped by how straight one man shoots.

In an upper story of a building facing Viarme Square in the heart of Nantes at that supreme moment of crisis and decision stood an unknown marksman, his name lost to history. Tradition says that he was a shoemaker of the city. As the battling host of crusaders surged into the square, with the Revolutionaries retreating before them, he thrust his gun through a window, sighted down the long barrel, and put a bullet through the lungs of Jacques Cathelineau.

In those days before antiseptics and anesthetics, the dark ages of medicine, a bullet in the chest cavity was invariably fatal, though it usually took the victim some time to die.

In a flash of anguish even more mental than physical—for Cathelineau's heart and soul were in his cause and, though too humble to realize how indispensable he was, he knew what defeat at Nantes would mean to that cause, and how likely it was that his wounding would bring about that defeat—he cried out: "Leave me! Leave me! Do your duty." But his men would not leave him; the attack ground to a halt, as all about rose the sorrowing cry: "Cathelineau is wounded! Cathelineau is dead!"[24]

The irresolute d'Elbée took command, but only after the attack had long since ceased. It was left to him only to order the withdrawal. The moment of opportunity had passed. There had been no march on Paris and no taking of Nantes. During July and August the Vendeans confined themselves entirely to attempting to secure and consolidate their hold on the territory they had already occupied and to repel Revolutionary forays against it. In these months they launched no less than three separate attacks against the town of Luçon near the southern border of the Vendée, which the Revolutionaries now held, and all three attacks failed. Meanwhile the troops of the international coalition against Revolutionary France had forced the surrender of ten thousand of the best soldiers of the Republic in the German city of Mainz. In accordance with a widely used military custom of that time when large prison camps were unavailable, the garrison of Mainz was allowed to return to France on the pledge of its commanders and the Revolutionary government that none of these troops would be used again against the coalition. But the coalition did not include the Catholic and Royal Army, of which its leaders had scarcely heard; therefore the army of Mainz could be used against them. It was commanded by Jean-Baptiste Kléber, later Napoleon's second-in-command in Egypt, a brilliant soldier, of relentless perseverance and ingenious resource. On September 5, Kléber arrived in never-captured Nantes with the army of Mainz.

Meanwhile, on July 14, Cathelineau was dying at Saint-Florent-le-Vieil, the first town he had taken on the day he went to war for his Lord, his Faith, and his King, March 13. Thousands knelt outside the building where he lay, offering their prayers for him. Though in great pain, he did not cry out. He was anointed. He bade farewell to his wife and his children, and to those who still lived of the twenty men who had first followed him out of Le Pin-en-Mauges, to the crusade. In the evening his cousin, Jean Blon, came out to the people and said: "The good Cathelineau has rendered up his soul to Him who gave it to him to defend His glory."[25]

Perhaps, indeed, the French Revolution was too great an evil to be overcome by arms alone, even in the hands of crusaders. Perhaps in the end it could be defeated only by prayer.

By the world's standards, the martyr had failed; now it was the turn of the assassin. On July 9—the day before Danton the penitent was removed from the Committee of Public Safety—Charlotte Corday left Caen for Paris, travelling on a one-way ticket. She arrived July 11 and spent the next day writing an "address to the French people" pointing to the chaos and tyranny into which France had fallen and declaring "that Marat was condemned by the universe and that his bloody deeds had placed him outside the law."[26] On July 13 she rose at six o'clock in the morning and made her way to a shopping arcade in the Palais Royal market, where she bought a kitchen knife with an

ebony handle and a six-inch blade, soon after the shops opened at
seven. At nine she hailed a cab and asked to be taken to the residence
of Marat, which was at 30 Cordeliers Street. Refused admittance by
Marat's wife and her sister, she sent him a note at noon, saying that
she had a report on the plotting at Caen. At seven-thirty in the
evening she returned again to Marat's dwelling, and was able to slip
inside when two men connected with the printing and distribution of
his newspaper were admitted. She asked again to see Marat. Overhear-
ing the argument that followed, Marat called out that she could come
in. He was in the bath in which he soaked himself for many hours
each day in a largely futile effort to combat his skin disease.

Stanley Loomis vividly describes the scene:

> Marat sat in his bathtub, a curious portable contraption
> shaped like a stub-nosed, high-backed shoe. It covered his
> shrivelled body to a line high above his waist. A bandanna
> soaked in vinegar was wrapped around his forehead and a
> bathrobe slung over his shoulders. His chest was bare. A long
> board, on which were placed an ink bottle, a quill and some
> paper, lay across the front of the bathtub; here he was able
> to correct proof and compose copy. . . .
> Two crossed pistols hung on one wall, and beneath
> them, written on an enormous cardboard poster, were the sin-
> ister and significant words LA MORT [death]. The room was
> lit by a single window directly behind Marat's bathtub, which
> shed an amber light over the aquarium-like chamber. The
> stage on which she found herself was far from any described
> in the dramas of her ancestor Corneille.[27]

Charlotte told Marat, as she had told him earlier in her letter,
that she had information about the Girondins in Caen. He was planning to report at length in the next issue of his paper on the situation
in Normandy and the activities of his target Girondins there. So he
urged her to give him all the information she had. She gave him the
names of four of the proscribed 22 Girondin leaders who were in
Caen. Marat copied their names, his pen scratching on the writing
board across the tub. When he had written them all down, he raised
his head and gave her his death's-head grin.

"Excellent!" he said; we may imagine him licking his lips and
glancing at the huge poster on the wall that said "DEATH." "In a few
days' time I shall have them all guillotined in Paris."[28]

Rarely has a man died at a more appropriate moment. No
sooner were the words out of his mouth than Charlotte Corday pulled
the long knife from her bodice and out of its sheath and drove it
straight through his aorta, the great blood vessel that leads out of the

heart. A fountain of blood rose into the air. In less than five minutes the author of the September massacres was dead.

Charlotte was stopped on her way out the door by Marat's newspaper distributor, arrested, and interrogated. Her interrogators were the ex-priest Chabot, who had demanded that the royal family not sit with the Assembly on August 10, 1792; Legendre, the butcher who had done much to help carry out the September massacres; and Drouet, the former postmaster who had stopped the royal family on their flight to Varennes in 1791. She caught Chabot stealing her gold watch, and stopped him with: "Have you forgotten that the Capuchins take a vow of poverty?" When Legendre insinuated that she might have been planning to kill him too, she said icily: "A man such as you is not big enough to be a tyrant. It would not be worth the trouble to kill you. I never had the intention of striking anyone but Marat."[29] After midnight, Drouet took her to the Abbaye prison, where the massacres of September had begun. "I have done my duty," she said when she arrived. "Now let others do theirs."[30]

It was that day, the day after the assassination of Marat, that Cathelineau died in Saint-Florent-le-Vieil.

On July 16 an immense and blasphemous public funeral was held for Marat. A huge procession followed his already decomposing body, with many chanting "O heart of Jesus; O sacred heart of Marat!"[31] His body was buried in the garden of the Cordeliers Club, the springboard of the Revolution that had propelled Danton to power; his heart was cut out and placed in a porphyry urn suspended from the ceiling of the Club. During the rest of the Terror, every meeting of the Cordeliers Club was held under Marat's heart.

On July 17 Fouquier-Tinville put Charlotte Corday on trial before the Revolutionary Tribunal. For once there was no doubt that the defendant was guilty as charged. At six o'clock they took her to the guillotine. Her courage never wavered. Sanson the executioner said that in the whole course of the Terror he never saw anything like it. She even examined the killing machine with interest. It is obvious from all the accounts that every Revolutionary who dealt with her was abashed, even afraid.

In the heat of a late summer afternoon the great crashing knife struck off Charlotte Corday's head. The martyr and the assassin were dead. The Revolution went on. The penitent remained. But he was far from clearly understanding yet what he should do. Much of the time during July and August, when he spoke, he sounded like the old Danton. From July 25 to August 7 he served the usual two-week term as president of the Convention, declaring at one point during that period:

"I demand that every day some aristocrat, some enemy of the people, expiate his crimes on the guillotine!"[32] One confession alone, however good and honest and however dramatic its circumstances, rarely if ever totally transforms a man's life. Continuing prayers are needed. We may be morally certain that Louise Danton provided them.

Meanwhile the Committee of Public Safety, from the time that Robespierre was added to its membership, took on a new and fearsome energy.

It became the Revolutionary executive, the real government of France. In a single year more than ten thousand decrees flowed out of the famous green room in the Tuileries, with its large oval table covered with green cloth, matching the green paper on the walls, where the Committee met, working far into almost every night. The designated cabinet ministers of the so-called provisional government soon became mere lackeys of the Committee. It was the Committee that made the decision, on August 1, to send Kléber's army of Mainz to the Vendée. On the same day it ordered the destruction of the tombs of the kings of France at the church of Saint Denis near Paris; whatever remained of the bodies of Louis XIV and Louis XV and even the exiled James II of England was thrown into a common grave and devoured by lime. Another part of the same savage decree linked the living with the dead: Marie Antoinette, already separated from her son who had been given into the custody of the cobbler Antoine Simon to be raised as a "sans-culotte," was now separated from her daughter and her sister-in-law as well, and put into solitary confinement in the grim prison called the Conciergerie. The order for the separation and the transfer was given to her at two o'clock in the morning of August 2 by the inimitable Hanriot. We are hardly surprised to hear in the memoirs of Marie-Thérèse, the King's daughter and only survivor of the royal family, that his "manners were rough and he used bad language."[33] As Marie Antoinette left the Temple, on her way down the stairs, she struck her head on the low lintel of the door. A guard asked: "Did you hurt yourself?" The former Queen answered: "No. Nothing can hurt me now."[34]

There was one last attempt to rescue her, the Plot of the Carnation. An old friend, the chevalier de Rougeville, arranged to visit her in her cell and left notes for her inside two carnations. One of the police commissioners charged with guarding her, Michonis, had taken pity on her and, like Toulan before him, was willing to risk his life to help her. (Both Toulan and Michonis died by the guillotine for their generosity.) Two guards were bribed. At eleven o'clock in the evening of September 2 Michonis arrived claiming orders to transfer the "widow Capet" back to the Temple. Rougeville was waiting outside in a carriage. The two guards opened her cell and began passing through the series of gates barring the corridors leading from her cell to the outside door. They had actually reached the outside door when one of the guards refused to proceed further, and took Marie Antoinette back to her cell. Why he went this far, without being willing to let her go in the end, has never been clearly explained. It was probably simple fear—once again, the shadow of the guillotine.

Three days later, on September 5, there was a new march on the Convention by the Paris mob, led as usual by representatives of the Commune and the Jacobin Club, with a new slogan and demand: "Make terror the order of the day!"[35] Robespierre was at that time holding the two-week presidency of the Convention. He was considerably embarrassed by the demonstration, which had the appearance of a challenge to his leadership, since he had clearly dominated the Convention at least from the time he joined the Committee of Public Safety July 27. Robespierre and Barère, in response, promised to step up the Terror. The Revolutionary Tribunal was expanded and divided into four sections with sixteen judges instead of ten, and Fouquier-Tinville was given five assistants.

The next day the Committee of Public Safety recommended to the Convention the addition of more members to its number. It nominated two, Billaud-Varenne[36] and Collot d'Herbois, who had been among the leaders in promoting the march on the Convention the previous day. They had used it, in effect, as a lever to pry themselves onto the all-powerful Committee that now really ran the Revolution.

The Convention accepted these nominees of the Committee of Public Safety. But then they surprised Robespierre and Barère. They added one more member whom the Committee had not recommended, who had not even sought the appointment. They appointed Danton. Someone said that he had a good "revolutionary head."[37]

Danton got to his feet. His great voice thundered through the hall as of old.

"I swear by the liberty of my country that I will never accept a place on that Committee!"[38]

The penitent remained. The hour was drawing near when Georges-Jacques Danton, titan of the French Revolution, would go forth, like Frankenstein against his monster, to grapple to the death with the hideous thing he had created.

NOTES

[1]Michael Ross, *Banners of the King; the War of the Vendée 1793-4* (New York, 1975), p. 129.

[2]Louis Madelin, *The French Revolution* (New York, 1925), p. 338.

[3]C. Hibbert, *The Days of the French Revolution* (NY 1980), p. 198.

[4]Madelin, *French Revolution*, p. 340.

[5]Hibbert, *Days of the French Revolution*, p. 199.

[6]Madelin, *French Revolution*, p. 342.

[7]*Ibid.*, p. 343.

[8]*Ibid.*, pp. 343-344.

[9]*Ibid.*, p. 344.

[10]Stanley Loomis, *Paris in the Terror, June 1793-July 1794* (Philadelphia, 1964), p. 68.

[11]*Ibid.*, p. 103.

[12]*Ibid.*, p. 107.

[13]*Ibid.*, p. 111.

[14]Christophe, *Danton*, p. 367.

[15]Loomis, *Paris in the Terror*, p. 249.

[16]Christophe, *Danton*, pp. 371-372.

[17]Loomis, *Paris in the Terror*, p. 249.

[18]Marchioness de la Rochejaquelein, *Memoirs* (tr. Sir Walter Scott) (Edinburgh, 1816), p. 167.

[19]A. Billaud, *La Guerre de Vendée* (Fontenay, 1972), p. 69. All translations from this book by the author.

[20]Michel de Saint Pierre, *Monsieur de Charette, Chevalier du Roi* (Paris, 1977), p. 132. Translation by the author.

[21]Billaud, *Guerre de Vendée*, p. 71.

[22]*Ibid.*, p. 72.

[23]Ross, *Banners of the King*, p. 164.

[24]*Ibid.*

[25]Billaud, *Guerre de Vendée*, p. 81.

[26]Loomis, *Paris in the Terror*, p. 121.

[27]*Ibid.*, pp. 128-129.

[28]*Ibid.*, p. 130.

[29]*Ibid.*, pp. 133-134.

[30]*Ibid.*, p. 136.

[31]*Ibid.*, p. 142.

[32]Christophe, *Danton*, p. 381.

[33]Rupert Furneaux, *The Bourbon Tragedy* (London, 1968), p. 140.

[34]Stanley Loomis, *The Fatal Friendship; Marie Antoinette, Count Fersen, and the Flight to Varennes* (Garden City NY, 1972), p. 305.

[35]R.R. Palmer, *Twelve Who Ruled; the Year of Terror in the French Revolution* (Princeton, 1941, 1969), p. 52.

[36]An eager participant in the September massacres, see Ch.2.

[37]Palmer, *Twelve Who Ruled*, p. 54.

[38]Christophe, *Danton*, p. 387.

VII.
The Abolition of Christianity
(September 6-November 30, 1793)

The Committee of Public Safety now ruled France and the Revolution. Robespierre did not yet totally dominate the Committee; his influence was temporarily somewhat weakened by the addition to its membership of Billaud-Varenne and Collot d'Herbois from the leaders of the September 5 riots, known as Hébertists for the man generally regarded as their mentor: the scurrilous, malevolent journalist Jacques Hébert, editor and publisher of the obscenity-spotted daily newspaper *Pére Duchesne*, a little weasel of a man, the son of a ruined goldsmith, a leader of the Paris Commune at the time of the rising of August 10, 1792, a vehement atheist married to a former nun. Robespierre disliked Hébert, who rarely bothered to talk about the "republican virtue" which Robespierre constantly claimed as his sole inspiration; but at the moment he could not dispense with him. The engine of revolution was running almost out of control. To keep it from destroying the armed forces and thereby ensuring the triumph of the Revolution's enemies was the most Robespierre and his supporters could manage in the fall of 1793. Its other victims they were quite willing to see sacrificed, while seeking to use its destructive power for their own ends.

"Terror," everyone kept saying, was "the order of the day."[1] To help make it so, and more efficiently administered, on September 17 the Convention passed the Law of Suspects. This law for the first time gave legal standing to the local revolutionary vigilante groups known as committees of surveillance, or revolutionary committees, which were most active in the Sections of Paris, but were also to be found in many of the cities and departments of the rest of the country. These were now authorized to issue certificates of "good citizenship," without which any person would automatically be a suspect liable to arrest at any time. Other parts of the law stated that all were suspect "who, by their conduct, relations, or language spoken or written, have shown themselves partisans of tyranny or federalism and enemies of liberty;"[2] "who could not give a satisfactory account of their means of support or their discharge of civic obligations since the preceding March 21;"[3] and, with the black humor of nightmare, those "who, though they have done nothing against liberty, have also done nothing for it."[4] The local revolutionary committees were to be the judges of who met these vague but exceedingly comprehensive criteria, by granting or refusing to grant certificates of good citizenship. The opportunities given for corruption, for the buying and selling of the certificates, and for the satisfaction of personal hatreds and grudges were virtually unlimited.

During September, as a result of the passage of the Law of Suspects, the number of prisoners in Paris rose by approximately 50 per cent, from 1,607 to 2,365. Many more than this number were included among the legal suspects, but there were simply not enough secure places of confinement in Paris to put all or most of them in jail. Collot d'Herbois, finding it difficult to reconcile himself to this physical limitation upon his desire to act against the suspects, proposed that they be put into mined houses which would then be blown up, killing them all. The Committee of Public Safety did not feel that the time was yet quite ripe for this. Collot also demanded that merchants who raised their prices should become another class of arrestable "suspects."

The Committee did not agree to that either, but on September 29 voted full price and wage control, the so-called "General Maximum." Ceiling prices were decreed for a long list of commodities: "fresh and salted meat, salted fish, butter and oil; wine, brandy, vinegar, cider and beer; coal, charcoal, candles and soap; salt, soda, sugar and honey; leather, iron, steel, lead, and copper; paper, wool, and various cloths; shoes and tobacco."[5] Price control is almost invariably attempted early in the history of totalitarian regimes; each new totalitarian feels that he has finally found the answer to the failure of all his predecessors to make such edicts work. But of course the result in France in 1793 was the same as it always is: the goods with controlled prices disappear or become exceedingly scarce in the legitimate market and are largely diverted to the illegal or "black" market, where many of them are bought up by the price controllers themselves, individually or in small conspiratorial groups.[6] As always, the ordinary people, without the means to buy much in the "black" market or in many cases the secret knowledge to find it, suffer most. Shortages of basic commodities in Paris remained a constant feature of the Revolutionary regime throughout the next six years, until the advent of Napoleon.

On October 10, on motion of Saint-Just, the Committee of Public Safety sealed its domination of the Revolution by decreeing its own continuation for the duration of the war—a war which the Committee could evidently make last as long as it wished. (Saint-Just himself responded to one Austrian request for negotiations with the following language, hardly calculated to reduce the duration of the war: "The French Republic receives from its enemies and sends them in return naught but lead."[7])

Three days later Danton, claiming illness, obtained leave of absence from the Convention and returned to his native village of Arcis-sur-l'Aube, Arcis on the River of Dawn. He told his friends he wanted "a breathing space away from his fellow men."[8] He took with him only Louise, his two children by Gabrielle, a maid, and a valet. In the town he met with his childhood friends, and with the former parish priest, now no longer exercising his duties officially. He tended his black mares and saw to the raising of his pigs. He pruned his trees and worked in his garden. He spent whole afternoons fishing on the River of Dawn. And we may be sure that he talked much with Louise, for he had always particularly enjoyed doing that.

Danton left Paris October 13. At least until he left, we may presume that he kept himself well informed on the course of public events. He would have known of the great victory of the Catholic and Royal Army over the whole of Kléber's crack army of Mainz at Torfou in the Vendée September 19, though perhaps not of all the extraordinary details: Charette carried away by retreat, facing disaster, crying: "If you desert me, I alone will win or die! Those of you who love me will follow me!" and turning back the rout while six bullets pierced his clothes but did not touch him; Lescure shouting as he launched a critical counterattack: "Are there four hundred men brave enough to die with me?"; Bonchamps, severely wounded, leaping from his stretcher to lead his own counterattack; Colonel Chevardin, commanding the Saône-et-Loire battalion for the Revolution, holding a critical bridge at Boussaye to save the army of Mainz from the Vendeans as the counterattack rolled on, his battalion dying to the last man, and he with it; finally Kléber, later one of Napoleon's great commanders, turning to a representative of the Committee of Public Safety who reproached him for having retreated, with the words: "It's easy for you to talk, but those devils in wooden shoes fight as well as we do and shoot better."[9]

Just before leaving Paris Danton would have heard, as did the whole Convention, that the Revolutionary troops had taken Lyons from the last of the Girondin rebels October 9 after a siege of two months, with Georges Couthon from the Committee of Public Safety directing operations; and he would most certainly have known of the Convention's stark decree of October 12 relating to this city:

> The city of Lyons shall be destroyed. Every habitation of the rich shall be demolished; there shall remain only the homes of the poor, the houses of patriots who have been led astray or proscribed, the buildings employed in industry and the monuments devoted to humanity and public instruction.
> The name of Lyons shall be effaced from the list of cities of the Republic. . . . On the ruins of Lyons shall be raised a column attesting to posterity the crimes and the punishment of the royalists of the city, with this inscription: "Lyons made war on Liberty. Lyons is no more."[10]

Finally, he would probably have known, not only that the Convention on October 3 had ordered Fouquier-Tinville to prepare the case for prosecution of Marie Antoinette, but that Hébert himself in the following days had persuaded her son, now in the custody of the cobbler Simon, to sign his name to a document alleging that his own mother had encouraged him in unnatural sexual vices and joined in them with him. And it is quite possible—even likely, for Danton's connections throughout revolutionary Paris were extensive and his sources of information excellent—that he knew what had happened to Marie Antoinette the night before he left for the River of Dawn, the night following the day on which the Convention decreed the obliteration of Lyons. She had been brought after dark to the former Grand Chamber of the *Parlement*, the chief law court of Paris under the old regime, which adjoined the Conciergerie prison where she was held, and was now the seat of the Revolutionary Tribunal. It was a huge Gothic hall with a floor made up of alternating squares of black and white marble. A Crucifixion scene had been removed; in its place was a bust of Marat. Fouquier-Tinville sat at the examining table with one of his examiners, Nicolas Hermann. Both men were dressed all in black, even to the plumes on their hats. There were only two candles in the room—no other light. There were other people present, but Marie Antoinette could see only Fouquier-Tinville, Hermann, and a stenographer. The fugitive gleams from the candles must have seemed swallowed up in the black clothing of the two men and the black squares of marble on the floor. The stenographer noted that she was "alarmed." It must have looked to her like the gates of Hell.

Yet she answered all Hermann's thirty-five questions steadily and intelligently. No, she had sent no money to foreign powers. No, she had not dominated her husband or advised him to veto bills (which he had a right to do in any case, under the original constitution) or to leave France. No, she had not trampled on the tricolor. She and her family had always wished only happiness for France.

Fouquier-Tinville offered to provide her with defense counsel: Chauveau-Lagarde, who had "defended" Charlotte Corday. She agreed, and was sent back to her cell.

All that night Fouquier-Tinville labored (with virtually no reference to the testimony that had been taken from her) to produce her indictment. It began: "Like Messalina, Brunehaut, Frédégonde, and the Médicis, once called Queens of France, whose names are forever odious, Marie Antoinette, the widow of Louis Capet, since her arrival in France has been the curse and the leech of the French people."[11] In its rambling course, it accused her not only of the standard charges of aiding France's enemies, supporting counterrevolution, and forcing her husband to make legal vetoes, but of somehow fomenting the events of August 10, 1792 "by keeping the Swiss guards continually drunk" and "herself biting shut their cartridges" and of having pamphlets slandering her printed "so as to arouse pity abroad."[12] Rarely if ever in all of history has a leading figure of a nation given a public trial before execution been charged with such malignant madness. And the indictment concluded: "Finally, the Widow Capet, immoral in every way and a new Agrippina, is so perverted and so familiar with every crime that, forgetting her position as mother and the line drawn by the laws of nature, she did not recoil from indulging with Louis-Charles Capet, her son, as confessed by the latter, in indecencies the mere idea and mention of which arouse a shudder of horror."[13] By the next afternoon the indictment was ready, and delivered to Chauveau-Lagarde as Danton was already riding for the River of Dawn.

It may, of course, all be only coincidence. So many things happened so quickly during the French Revolution that there is a natural clustering of pivotal events. Yet it is, at least, worthy of comment and reflection that Danton's departure from Paris for the long stay at his home village which was to send him back to the Revolutionary arena a profoundly changed man, took place the very day after the decree for the destruction of Lyons, the nocturnal interrogation of Marie Antoinette, and the preparation of her indictment whose final charge plumbed depths below any that even the Revolution had yet penetrated. If he knew of all those things, they may well have moved him a long step toward the decision he was about to make regarding his own future in the Revolution.

The next day the trial of Marie Antoinette began, at eight o'clock in the morning.

There was a tribunal of five judges, all carefully selected by Fouquier-Tinville, with his colleague in the night examination of October 12, Nicolas Hermann, presiding. There were twelve jurors, hand-picked by Fouquier-Tinville, all considered dependable revolutionaries. One of them, Trinchard, described the accused in a letter to his brother as "the ferocious beast who has devoured a great part of the Republic."[14] The galleries were packed with others like them. But an audible gasp came from the audience when Marie Antoinette appeared. They had been expecting someone who at least resembled the Queen they remembered. What they saw was a victim who might have come from the rack. She was desperately thin, especially in her legs, so that she could scarcely stand. Her hair was completely white. She was going blind. Yet still she entered the courtroom with quiet dignity, which some of the most hostile still called pride.

Fouquier-Tinville had assembled 41 witnesses, but had not had time to coach them all. Nineteen of them therefore declared from the stand that they knew nothing of any of the offenses with which Marie Antoinette had been charged in the indictment. The first who would testify against her described "feasts and orgies" while she and her family still lived in the palace at Versailles; the second witness said he had found wine bottles under her bed in the Tuileries, proving that she had been making the Swiss Guard drunk. The fourth witness was Hébert, who repeated in open court the abominable charge regarding her relations with her son.

She had not seen it before. Either Fouquier-Tinville had left it out of her copy of the indictment or her lawyer, Chauveau-Lagarde, had removed it before showing it to her. Both possibilities seem unlikely, but one must be the truth, and it is more likely the latter. Chauveau-Lagarde would certainly not have wanted his client to be surprised. Perhaps he hoped for a last-minute resuscitation of common humanity in her accusers; perhaps he simply could not bear to be the one to tell her about it first.

At first she simply denied the hideous charge. When a juror pressed it, she rose and addressed the violently hostile gallery, which included many of the revolutionary harridans of Paris who knitted at the foot of the guillotine and had screamed for her blood at the storming of Versailles in 1789.

"Nature refuses to answer such a charge against a mother. I appeal to all mothers in this room."[15] For just a moment, there was an emotional reaction in her favor.

The trial went on until eleven o'clock, fifteen hours. On the next day, October 15, it was resumed at nine o'clock on a cold rainy morning with a high wind. The first witness was a former admiral of the old regime who testified that her intrigues had once caused him to lose a promotion—an action so despicable and so petty that it seems likely that this former aristocrat was forced to testify thus by threats against his family or himself. Later the former War Minister, La Tour du Pin, also testified against her. But before testifying he recognized her by a bow, in the manner of the old court. For this he was later guillotined.

At four-thirty the trial was recessed, and Marie Antoinette was given a cup of soup. Meanwhile, two hundred miles to the west in the Vendée, Kléber with the revolutionary army, recovered from his defeat at Torfou a month before, was marching on the town of Cholet which had become the principal base and headquarters of the Catholic and Royal Army. Hurrying to cut him off, the man who had tried so hard to reach the royal family in the Tuileries that fateful August 10 in order to offer his sword for their protection, Marquis de Lescure, received a mortal wound in the head in a small-scale action. Lescure lived until November 4, long enough to hear of the fate of his Queen, crying out: "The monsters have then killed her! I fought to deliver her! If I live, it will be to revenge her."[16]

Also on that day Danton and his family, coming from Paris, reached his home at Arcis on the River of Dawn.

When the court session resumed, after dark, Fouquier-Tinville himself took charge of the questioning of the witnesses. When he was finally finished with them, after midnight, he called on the defense to present its case. Marie Antoinette's attorney, Chauveau-Lagarde, spoke on her behalf for two hours, pointing out that there was no specific evidence against her. When he had finished speaking, Fouquier-Tinville, angered, arrested him. His associate counsel for the defense, Tronson du Coudray, then made his plea; as soon as he sat down, he too was arrested. At three o'clock in the morning the jury retired. Marie Antoinette asked for a glass of water; she had had nothing to eat or drink for eighteen hours except the cup of soup at four-thirty in the afternoon. One of her guards, de Busne, found water for her. It was very cold now.

At four o'clock in the morning the jury returned. Marie Antoinette was convicted on every count. Fouquier-Tinville ordered that she be executed that very day; until it was time for it, she would be sent back to the Conciergerie, along with her two attorneys who were now also to be confined there.

Descending the stairs on the way, ill-lit by a single candle, she suddenly stopped. "I can no longer see," she said. "I can go no farther."[17] The guard de Busne gave her his arm. For that, and for giving her the glass of water earlier, he was denounced by another guard, arrested that morning, and sent to join Marie Antoinette and her two lawyers in the Conciergerie. At four-thirty in the morning, in her cell, she wrote her last letter, to her sister-in-law Elizabeth. The original, which has been preserved, still shows the stains of her tears.

> I die in the Catholic, Apostolic, and Roman religion, that of my fathers in which I was raised and which I have always professed, having no expectation of spiritual solace and not even knowing if there are any priests of that religion here and in any case the place where I am would expose them to too much danger if they should enter. I sincerely beg pardon of God for all the wrong I have done during my lifetime. I hope that in His goodness He will receive my soul in His mercy and goodness. I ask pardon of all whom I know and of you in particular, sister, for all the distress that, without wishing, I may have caused. I forgive my enemies the harm that they have done me. I say farewell here to my aunts and to all my brothers and sisters. I had friends. The idea of being separated from them forever and of their grief is one of my greatest regrets in dying. May they know at least that my thoughts were with them until the last moment.
>
> Farewell, my good and loving sister. May this letter reach you! Think of me always. I embrace you with all my heart, together with those poor, dear children. Oh God, what anguish it is to leave them forever! Adieu! Adieu! From this moment I shall occupy myself only with my spiritual duties.[18]

The letter was not allowed to reach Elizabeth. Marie Antoinette's jailer gave it to Fouquier-Tinville, who gave it to Robespierre. It was found among his papers.

Thirty thousand people watched Marie Antoinette hauled through the streets of Paris for a full hour in a manure cart drawn by two plow-horses. A priest accompanied her, but she would not ask him for the last sacraments, because he had defied the Pope and accepted the Revolutionary church. Her white hair was cut jaggedly to expose the back of her neck where the guillotine would fall; her hands were tied behind her. Her face was pale as a wisp of cloud, except for two burning red spots on her cheeks. Her eyes were red, downcast, almost sightless. But she climbed the wooden stairs to the guillotine unaided, seeming almost to hurry to the end. The huge knife fell with its steely thud.

The next day Hébert wrote in his newspaper: "The greatest joy of all the joys experienced by Père Duchesne came after seeing with his own eyes the head of the female VETO separated from her [obscenity] crane's neck."[19] That same day, in the evening, Robespierre, Saint-Just and Barère, now the three principal leaders of the Revolution—Hébert was never really in this category—met for dinner at a well-known restaurant. Another man, Vilate, was also present, and later described the meeting and conversation. They spoke of the trial and execution of Marie Antoinette. Robespierre deplored Hébert's obscene charge, as likely to create some sympathy for the ex-Queen. But Saint-Just was inflexible: "Morals will gain by this act of national justice," he said. They went on to speak of the Revolution's many enemies, in which Barère included all priests. Saint-Just urged his program of confiscating the property of all suspects. Barère then commented: "The vessel of the Revolution cannot arrive at port except upon a sea reddened with waves of blood." Saint-Just responded: "That is true. A nation regenerates itself only upon heaps of corpses."[20]

That day the Revolutionary army under Jourdan defeated the Austrians and the British at Wattignies in Belgium. The next day, October 17, in a furious, swaying combat outside Cholet that lasted all day and far into the night, Kléber gained revenge for Torfou by out-generalling the Catholic and Royal Army, finally driving it into a trap where it was swept by a deadly hail of grapeshot in the night. D'Elbée, the supreme commander, was seriously wounded and the heroic Marquis de Bonchamp mortally wounded by a grapeshot in the stomach. The Vendée was lost. La Rochejaquelein covered the retreat as best he could. Marquis Donnissan, the father of Marie-Louise Victoire, Lescure's wife, took command. The next day nearly 100,000 Vendeans—men, women, and children—began crossing the Loire River to plunge into northern France, away from the army that had beaten them, but with no clear strategy, direction, or purpose. They still held six thousand revolutionary prisoners and it was proposed to slaughter them all. The dying Bonchamp heard of it, and issued his last order:

> Comrades, until today, which is my last, you have always obeyed me. As your commander, I order you to pardon my prisoners. If the orders of a dying leader have no longer any significance to you, then I beg you in the name of humanity and in the name of God, for Whom you are fighting, to spare their lives. Comrades, if you disregard my orders and my prayers, I declare that I will have myself borne into the

midst of my prisoners and that your first bullets will strike me."[21]

The six thousand lived, and Bonchamp died. He received viaticum from a loyal priest accompanying the army, and said: "I trust in the mercy of God. I have never fought for human glory. If I have not been able to restore the altars and the throne, at least I have defended them. I have served my God, my king, my country."[22]

Just one week later the Convention, after discussions which had lasted through most of the month of October, abolished the Christian era. No longer were years to be dated from the Incarnation of Our Lord and Savior Jesus Christ. No longer were the festivals of the Christian year to be celebrated; even the days on which they had been commemorated were gone. The months were changed; they were given different names and put in places in the year which in no way corresponded to the months that had been used. The weeks were changed; no longer were they to consist of seven days, but of ten. Sunday was abolished; the day of rest would be the *décadi*, the tenth day of the new week. The new Revolutionary era began with the date of the overthrow of the monarchy, September 22, 1792; the year that followed was the Year One of Liberty, and it was now the Year Two. The official abolition of Christianity was underway.

But before it could be completed, there was one last item of unfinished prior public business. It was time for the Girondin leaders arrested in the purge of the Convention in early June and languishing in jail ever since, to follow Marie Antoinette, whom they had done so much to help destroy, to the guillotine.

Their trial began on the very day—October 24—that the Christian era was officially abolished in France. (Not that it would have mattered much to most of them, for nearly all of the group had long since repudiated the Catholic faith into which they had been born; only one, the former priest Claude Fauchet, returned to it as he faced the Judgment.) The defendants numbered twenty-one, including Vergniaud and Brissot. Their defense attorney was the indomitable Chauveau-Legarde, let out of the Conciergerie when Fouquier-Tinville's anger cooled. Since many of the defenders were themselves lawyers and brilliant orators, there was at least a theoretical prospect that some of them might save themselves from the guillotine. But it does not appear that any of them ever had a real chance.

The trial was held in the same gloomy room of the Palace of Justice where Marie Antoinette had been first questioned, and finally found guilty. The Revolutionary Tribunal, with Hermann again presiding, remained partial to night sessions; the lighting of the room had

not improved. Fouquier-Tinville was present throughout. Many accounts speak of his macabre and obscene joking with the defendants;
he took care to tell them each day how many people were scheduled
to die under the guillotine the following day. There was another hand-
picked hanging jury; its foreman was an aristocrat, the former Marquis d'Antonelle, who felt that because of his birth he constantly had
to prove his loyalty to the Revolution by doing whatever its leaders
wanted. Outside, Hanriot had been wound up and put into action
again: the streets around the Palace of Justice swarmed with National
Guardsmen, cannon, and men in gaudy uniforms riding or sauntering
about brandishing sabers.

The Chauveau-Lagarde rose to point out that neither he nor any of
the defendants had yet seen any of the documents to be used in evidence against them, only the bare indictments. Fouquier-Tinville
replied blandly that several of the documents had "not yet arrived"
while others were "still under seal." The trial would proceed as
planned. In good time the defense would be shown the documents. As
Robespierre's newspaper put it that day: "This tribunal . . . does not
seek the guilty. It would like to find all the accused innocent. It fur-
nishes them with all the means of justifying themselves."[23]

The witnesses included Hébert the atheist; Pierre Chaumette,
who had openly defended the September massacres and been a leader
in the mob attack on the Convention at the end of May that purged
the Girondins now on trial, and was violently hostile to the Catholic
Faith; and Chabot, the unfrocked priest. (Seeing Chabot swagger into
the courtroom, one of the defendants, Ducos, remarked: "We will now
hear a sermon from the devil.")[24]

On the second day of the trial Chaumette attacked Vergniaud
for his most decent act during the Revolution—the pledge of protection for the King and his family which he had given in the name of
the old Legislative Assembly on August 10, 1792, but had long since
dishonored. There was not a trace of human feeling in Chaumette's
big flat face under a mop of roughly dressed black hair, as he took
Vergniaud to task for attempting this act of mercy. "To show sorrow
under the circumstances," Chaumette declared, "was enough to show
that one was criminal."[25]

By the fifth day of the trial (October 28 by the Christian calendar, 7 Brumaire by the Revolutionary) the one real ability the defendants had—their impressive power of oratory—and the flagrantly un-
fair character of the proceedings were beginning to produce some reaction against the Terrorists, even among the highly partisan spectators. Fouquier-Tinville sensed the change in atmosphere. He wrote to

the Convention asking that the defense be silenced. His letter has been preserved. It stands as a monument to totalitarian injustice matching the worst examples from our own time.

> We are impeded in our work by the forms prescribed by the law. The trial of the deputies whom you have accused began five days ago, and only nine witnesses have been heard. . . . Why should we have witnesses? The Convention—the whole of France—accuses these men. Proofs of their crimes are evident, and everyone is convinced they are guilty. The Tribunal can do nothing by itself—it is obliged to follow the law; it rests with the Convention to do away with all formalities which impede its work.[26]

The next day Robespierre's organ, the newspaper *The Anti-Federalist*, echoed Fouquier-Tinville:

> Should the Revolutionary Tribunal be subjected to forms good for ordinary tribunals? To judge the accused, would not the act of the accusation be sufficient? Does it not contain the faithful history of the conspiracy and the crimes of its chiefs? Does not this chain of proofs against them carry conviction to the souls of the jurors? The mode of judgment is injurious to the people. . . . Why do not the jurors have the right to declare to the judges, when they think it apropos, that their opinion is formed? Why is this law not instantly added to the decree relative to the organization of the Revolutionary Tribunal? Brave members of the Mountain, it is up to you to have this salutary measure decreed.[27]

Decreed it was, that very day. The final manuscript draft of the decree still exists, in Robespierre's own handwriting.

> If the judgment of a case brought to the Revolutionary Tribunal has been prolonged three days, the president will open the following session by asking the members of the jury if their conscience is sufficiently enlightened, and if the jury answers yes, it will pass immediately to judgment. The president will suffer no interpolations or incident contrary to the disposition of this decree.[28]

The next day, October 30, as proceedings began at nine o'clock in the morning, Fouquier-Tinville read this decree to the jury and asked them if their consciences had been sufficiently enlightened. The jury retired for a brief deliberation. Their foreman, the ex-Marquis d'Antonelle, reported that they wished further enlightenment, which they proceeded to receive in the form of "testimony" for the prosecution that was little more than a series of vitriolic speeches denouncing the defendants. At two o'clock the proceedings were recessed; at six the Tribunal reconvened, and d'Antonelle announced that, despite having heard no direct testimony whatsoever from any defendant, but only their rebuttals to prosecution testimony, and no summation or concluding plea from any of them, the jury's consciences had now been sufficiently enlightened. At ten-thirty, once again in the gloom of night with guttering candles, the jury returned. Every defendant was convicted on every count. Hermann asked them if they had anything to say.

They had everything to say. Pandemonium broke loose, with most of them shouting at once. Some of them actually threw into the crowd the notes and drafts of the evidence and summations they had prepared for their defense. Only Vergniaud remained silent and calm; the most intelligent and coldly realistic of the group, he had long since known that nothing could save any of them from the guillotine. Beside him Valazé, whose house in Paris had been one of the original meeting places of the Girondins, plunged a dagger into his heart. Vergniaud turned to another defendant, a physician. "Doctor, sacrifice a cock to Aesculapius; one of your patients is already cured."[29]

Other doctors were called and pronounced Valazé dead. Fouquier-Tinville demanded that his corpse be sent to the guillotine anyway, to have its head cut off with the rest. Even Hermann protested at this. The two men compromised by ordering the corpse sent to the guillotine but not decapitated, and then taken from there for burial with the other bodies after they had lost their heads.

The surviving Girondin leaders went to the guillotine singing the Marseillaise, unrepentant to the last—except for Fauchet—for what they had said and done. Vergniaud and Brissot explicitly refused confession and anointing. The rolling drums drowned out their last attempts to speak.

It was still only pleasantly cool in the quiet fields and woods around Arcis on the River of Dawn, with the falling leaves of autumn rustling underfoot. On November 2 Danton was out walking with a friend and neighbor named Doulet. Another man came running up to them with a newspaper, crying, "Good news! The Girondists have been condemned and executed!"

Tears rose in Danton's eyes, and the mighty thundering voice which had once led the Revolution roared out again.

"Do you call *that* good news, you wretch? *Good news* that some Girondists are dead?"

"Well," his informant ventured, "they were factionaries, weren't they?"

"*Factionaries!*" Danton bellowed. "Aren't we all factionaries, every one of us? If the Girondists deserved to die, so do we all. And we shall; one after another, we shall suffer the same fate as they did."[30]

On November 8 Madame Roland was executed, without having been allowed to be heard in her own defense; noticing a statue of Liberty next to the guillotine as she approached it, she said: "O Liberty, what crimes are committed in thy name!"[31] When her husband, hiding in a back alley in Rouen, heard of her execution, he at once committed suicide.

The previous day the "constitutional" archbishop of Paris, Jean-Baptiste Gobel, an Alsatian priest who had been one of the clerical deputies in the Estates-General at the beginning of the Revolution, had been brought to the Convention by the Hébertists as a sort of human trophy in a procession which included mocking young men wearing plundered vestments and drinking common wine out of plundered chalices, to declare that he would no longer exercise the functions of a priest. He at least refused to renounce his faith, but made no protest when Laloi, who was presiding, declared that since the Supreme Being "desired no worship other than the worship of Reason, that should in the future be the national religion."[32] Gobel took off his cassock, donned a red cap of liberty, and laid his episcopal cross and ring (to which he had never had any right in the Catholic Church, being in schism from the Pope) before the Convention. He was followed by a cowed succession of three bishops, numerous priests, and even some Protestant ministers, all eager to renounce their Christian vocation.

November 10 (20 Brumaire) was a Sunday. The Commune of Paris had decreed, at the urging of Chaumette, that a festival of Reason should be held then "before the image of that divinity, in the edifice which was formerly the church of the metropolis."[33] That meant the cathedral of Notre Dame; the language of the decree was the most explicit yet in an official document, pointing to the abolition of Christianity. If the cathedral of Notre Dame, for centuries the symbol of French Catholicity, was no longer a church, what had it become? The "Temple of Reason" was the answer; it was to mark its transformation from Catholic cathedral into temple of Reason that the blasphemous ceremonies of November 10 were intended.

In the nave of this lovely, hallowed building, bathed in the soft shimmering light which almost all its visitors down through the centuries have particularly noticed and remembered, workmen of the Revolution had during the past two days erected a strange angular structure of wood and cardboard intended to represent a mountain.

On top of it was a small imitation Greek temple dedicated "to philosophy." A burning torch cast flickering gleams and shadows on the busts of three men: Voltaire, Rousseau, and Benjamin Franklin. Outside, it was raining again; it had been a very wet autumn. Through the rain, at ten o'clock in the morning, came a procession of Commune officials, musicians, singers, and actresses. The streets were lined with people, though the crowd does not seem to have been nearly as large as the organizers of the "festival" had hoped, and the Convention was not even officially represented at that time. Mademoiselle Aubry, one of the actresses, played the goddess Reason. Clad in a flowing tricolor gown, she climbed the "mountain" and received the plaudits of the crowd from the imitation Greek temple at the top.³⁴

Shortly after three o'clock in the afternoon the procession of blasphemers made its way from Notre Dame to the Tuileries where the Convention sat, quite close by. Chabot moved that the cathedral be officially renamed the Temple of Reason; the motion passed. Laloi, the president, embraced first the pathetic Gobel, then Mademoiselle Aubry. Some of the Convention members then went to Notre Dame, where the "ceremonies" of the morning at the "mountain" were re-enacted.

The next day more "constitutional" priests renounced their priesthood, many churches were officially closed, and the Paris Section of the Rights of Man formally repudiated the Catholic Faith and ordered its practice to cease in the part of Paris this Section governed. On November 12 Chaumette carried in the Convention a decree for the destruction of the statues on the porch of Notre Dame, but when it actually came to destroying them, even the revolutionaries held back; in the end they compromised by covering the statues with wood. On November 14 the Convention decreed the deification of Marat side by side with Reason. It is hard to imagine a more ill-assorted pair.

The next day five more Paris sections renounced the Faith and ordered all churches in their territory permanently closed; one of them, the Section of Montmartre, named for what had been one of Paris' most revered shrines, changed its name to Mont-Marat. Meanwhile, during that week, in many other parts of France dechristianization was going forward. Two members of the Convention on mission to Alsace ordered all Catholic practice in Strasbourg stopped. In conquered Lyons a festival was held for its slain Revolutionary leader Chalier, at which a Gospel and crucifix were burned, a donkey drank out of a chalice, and consecrated Hosts were trampled. Others of France's most famous cathedrals—at Chartres, Reims, Metz, Bordeaux, and Tours—were treated as Notre Dame of Paris had been.

On Sunday, November 17, one week after Notre Dame had been made into the "Temple of Reason," the Commune forbade all religious funerals in Paris. Most of the churches in the city were already closed. Hanriot with an armed force expelled worshippers from the Church of Saint-Gervais and turned it over to the mob for drinking and dancing far into the night; soon afterward it was declared to be the Temple of Youth. During much of the day there were immense crowds at the successive Masses said in the church of Saint-Nicolas-du-Chardonnet, one of the few still open to the faithful, and by mid-afternoon some of those present at this church were calling for a petition to the Convention to allow the continued free practice of the Catholic religion. Within an hour the local revolutionary committee closed the church.

At Arcis on the River of Dawn that Sunday, Danton and Louise and a few friends had just finished lunch together when a man came riding hard through the woods to their door: Danton's nephew Mergez. He had come straight from Paris, and asked to speak to Danton privately. Danton told him to speak without hesitation in front of his wife and his friends.

> "Fabre and Desmoulins want you to come back now, as fast as you can. Robespierre and his followers are really out to get you—"
> "You mean they want my head? They'd never dare—"
> "Don't be too sure of that. Come back with me now; there's no time to lose."
> Raising his great voice as though he were on the rostrum, Danton replied: "Go back and tell Robespierre that I'll be there in plenty of time to crush him, and his accomplices with him!"[35]

Danton did not hurry. This man once so impulsive, so headlong in speech and action, was now much more reflective and deliberate. He thought over what his nephew had said and what he had said in reply. Did he consult with Louise? It seems very likely. We would give much to have even a hint of what passed in their conversation. He knew there was danger; he had been explicitly warned of it. But Danton had the heart of a lion; danger would never deter him. Some might wonder that he took Louise back to Paris with him. One who does, has not yet understood either Danton or Louise, since their marriage. They were inseparable. He could not have kept her away unless he locked her up.

Danton was neither a fool nor foolhardy. He knew the Revolution, no man better; he had done more than anyone else to create it. There is good reason to believe that up to the moment that Mergez came riding through the poplar trees to give him the message from Paris, he had hoped somehow to withdraw from active participation in the Revolution, to retire from its arena and keep his head. But now he knew he could not do that, and must have wondered why he had ever thought he could. The hour of decision was upon him. He had essentially three choices: (1) to rejoin the Revolution under its present leadership, perhaps hoping to guide it to a different course while still sharing in its direction; (2) to flee the country, becoming another émigré like Lafayette; (3) to challenge the beast in the arena and battle it to the death.

In the twenty-four silent hours from his receipt of Mergez's message to his departure for Paris, Danton must have considered all three alternatives, in their essence and their variations. His pride and ambition would have drawn him to the first; his love for his family and for life and freedom would have drawn him to the second; but, Danton being what he was, there was probably never much real doubt in his mind that he would choose the third, the alternative of *toujours l'audace*. Threatened, he would neither conciliate his enemies nor flee. And if he were a sincere penitent, if his confession in June and his marriage to Louise and her prayers and example had meant to him what much that was soon to happen so strongly suggests that they did mean, he would have been impelled even more forcibly to the third alternative. He had let Satan into the house of his homeland. If he had come to understand that, it was not in Georges-Jacques Danton to go in and sup with him, even with the proverbial long spoon, nor to walk away and leave the house in his possession. He would stay and fight.

Whether he prayed for aid we cannot know. Very likely he had not yet come that far, depending still too much on himself and his mighty talents. But we may be sure that Louise prayed for him; and we have already seen the power of her prayers.

Georges-Jacques and Louise Gély Danton and his two little sons by Gabrielle set out for Paris from Arcis on the River of Dawn toward the end of the day Monday, November 18. Travelling by a roundabout route, they reached their apartment on the rue des Cordeliers on the evening of the 20th. They found that since their departure, the street had been renamed for Marat.

On that day in the Convention Fayau, a deputy from the Vendée, introduced a motion for the total destruction of his own homeland: that "the whole territory must be so utterly consumed by fire that, for at least a year, no man or beast will be able to find sustenance."[36]

The next day, November 21, on the Place de Grève where the assault force had assembled for the attack on the royal family in the Tuileries August 10, 1792, the relics of Saint Geneviève, beloved patron of Paris, more than a thousand years old, torn from their treasury and dumped into a plain wooden box, were thrown upon a pile of wood and burned "in order to expiate the crime of having served to propagate error and to foster luxury among so many idlers."[37]

On Sunday, November 24 (4 Frimaire in the Revolutionary calendar) the final step was taken in the abolition of Christianity by the French Revolution. The Commune ordered every church in Paris closed, including those recently redesignated as "temples." Whoever asked to have them opened would be immediately liable to arrest as a "suspect." Within twenty days 2,436 churches throughout France, in addition to all those in Paris, had been forbidden for use in the practice of the Catholic religion.

During all these apocalyptic events of November 1793, striking at the very heart of the centuries-old faith of the people of France, so long honored as "the eldest daughter of the Church," no one had lifted a hand to stop them. Many were uncomfortable with what was being done; even Robespierre found it imprudent and in bad taste, and spoke against it. But nothing was done to stop it. It seemed the Church had no true defenders left, except for the dying Catholic and Royal Army, from the Vendée but no longer in it.

Yet the Church of Jesus Christ rises up on wings of eagles and changes the hearts of men. On November 26 Georges-Jacques Danton strode to the bar of the Convention, for the first time in more than two months. He condemned the "religious masquerades" of the Hébertists. Then he challenged the Terror itself. "Perhaps the Terror once served a purpose," he said, "but it ought not to strike at innocent people. No one wishes to see an individual treated as a guilty person because he doesn't happen to have sufficient revolutionary vigor."[38]

Many had wished to see exactly that, and Danton must have known it. Perhaps, with all the talk about deifying reason, he had some hope that a reasonable argument might prevail. But it was surely fleeting.

Much more significant was a conversation among Danton, Camille Desmoulins, and a doctor named Souberbielle as they were returning from the Convention one evening, most probably at this time, the end of November. They were walking beside the Seine. The rays of a huge, brilliant setting sun painted the waters red. Dr. Souberbielle, who was a member of the Revolutionary Tribunal, mentioned that this day fifteen had been executed by the guillotine and 27 were scheduled for the guillotine tomorrow.

Danton gazed down at the lovely curving river of Paris.

"Look at the Seine," he said. "It's flowing blood."

The doctor expressed his uneasiness and his fear, and murmured: "Ah, if only I were Danton—"

"Danton is returning to the fray. He has slept too long." The giant turned to Desmoulins. "There has been too much blood spilled. Camille, take up your pen again. Appeal to them to be more merciful. I'll back you up." He thrust out his mighty hand, which Father Kéravénan had called "the hand of a street porter." "You can see my hand; you know its strength . . ."[39]

Danton's expiation had begun.

NOTES

[1]The slogan of the mob which had marched on the Convention September 5. See R.R. Palmer, *Twelve Who Ruled; the Year of Terror in the French Revolution* (Princeton, 1941, 1969), p. 52.

[2]Palmer, *Twelve Who Ruled*, p. 67.

[3]Stanley Loomis, *Paris in the Terror, June 1793-July 1794* (Philadelphia, 1964), p. 255.

[4]Robert Christophe, *Danton* (London, n.d.), p. 383.

[5]Palmer, *Twelve Who Ruled*, p. 69.

[6]The process remains basically the same in free societies which attempt price controls. They will work in such societies to a significant degree (though never very well) only during a relatively brief period of generally recognized and appreciated national emergency; and when they break down, there tends to be less participation of government officials in the black market than in totalitarian societies.

[7]Eugene N. Curtis, *Saint-Just, Colleague of Robespierre* (New York, 1935, 1973), p. 154.

[8]Christophe, *Danton*, p. 390.

[9]Michael Ross, *Banners of the King; the War of the Vendée, 1793-4* (New York, 1975), pp. 213-214.

[10]Palmer, *Twelve Who Ruled*, p. 156.

[11]Stanley Loomis, *The Fatal Friendship* (Garden City NY, 1972), p. 319.

[12]Vincent Cronin, *Louis and Antoinette* (New York, 1975), p. 386.

[13]Loomis, *Fatal Friendship*, pp. 319-320.

[14]Cronin, *Louis and Antoinette*, p. 385.

[15]*Ibid.*, p. 387.

[16]Marchioness de La Rochejaquelein, *Memoirs* (tr. Sir Walter Scott) (Edinburgh, 1816), p. 313.

[17]Loomis, *Fatal Friendship*, p. 330.

[18]*Ibid.*, p. 332.

[19]Cronin, *Louis and Antoinette*, p. 392.

[20]Curtis, *Saint-Just*, pp. 235-236.

[21]Ross, *Banners of the King*, p. 228.

[22]A. Billaud, *La Guerre de Vendée* (Fontenay, 1972), p. 129. Translation by the writer.

[23]Claude G. Bowers, *Pierre Vergniaud, Voice of the French Revolution* (New York, 1950), pp. 466, 470.

[24]*Ibid.*, p. 467.

[25]*Ibid.*, p. 471.

[26]*Ibid.*, p. 481.

[27]*Ibid.*, pp. 482-483.

[28]*Ibid.*, p. 485.

[29]*Ibid.*, p. 490.

[30]Christophe, *Danton*, pp. 391-392.

[31]Louis Madelin, *The French Revolution* (New York, 1925), p. 372.

[32]*Ibid.*, p. 388.

[33]*Ibid.*

[34]Pierre de la Gorce, *Histoire religieuse de la Révolution* (Paris, 1912-23; New York, 1969), III, 98-100. Legend has embellished these events, which are revealing enough without needing embellishment. Mademoiselle Aubry was neither naked nor a professional prostitute, whatever her personal morals may have been, and she did not go upon the high altar, but only up the newly built "mountain." Indeed, the revolutionaries seem to have carefully avoided the altar and the sanctuary. Perhaps the cathedral of Notre Dame had not yet altogether forfeited the protection of the Mother of God to whom it was dedicated.

[35]Christophe, *Danton*, p. 394.

[36]Ross, *Banners of the King*, p. 302.

[37]Jacques Hérissay, *La Vie religieuse à Paris sous la Terreur (1792-1794)* (Paris, 1952), p. 163. Translation by the writer.

[38]Loomis, *Paris in the Terror*, p. 281.

[39]Christophe, *Danton*, p. 402.

VIII.
Danton's Expiation
(December 1, 1793-April 5, 1794)

On the first day of December Danton took the next step in his attack on the Terror. Most significantly, he took it in defense of the Catholic rebels of the west, in a speech before the Convention denouncing the rampant cruelty of its commissioners in the Vendée.

The significance of this choice of theme and target can hardly be exaggerated, though it has been overlooked by most historians. It was clear even to the most vehemently revolutionary leaders of the Convention, convinced as they were that the people were with them, that the revolt in the Vendée had been a genuine popular rising not just protesting the abuses of the Revolution, like the Girondin uprisings in Lyons and Bordeaux, but the Revolution itself. It had been strong and widespread enough to pose a serious threat to the whole Revolutionary regime. The Convention's hostility toward it was consequently savage. If Danton's primary goal had been to restore his position of leadership in that regime, even while perhaps hoping to incline it away from the Terror, he would surely have chosen—at least initially—less provocative objects of the mercy he now advocated.

But if he was inspired primarily by a new sense of his Christian duty, the people of the Vendée clearly had first claim on him. The Catholic and Royal Army, including most of their able-bodied young men of military age, had been driven away to the north, leaving mostly women and children and old people behind, defenseless against the occupying armies of the Revolution and the commissioners from the Convention. Merciless destruction and slaughter had already begun. The Revolution's man in charge at Nantes was the sadistic Jean-Baptiste Carrier, a lawyer from Auvergne elected for the first time to national office as a deputy to the Convention during the September massacres, who "talked incessantly of killing and while doing so would often slash his sword through the air in the gesture of a man cutting off heads." He had a special hatred of children, whom he said should be "butchered without mercy."[1] Regarding the guillotine as too slow, he had developed a new method of execution known as the *noyades*, in which the victims were pushed out into the Loire River on large rafts with a plug in their bottoms; then the plug would be removed and all the victims would drown. More than six thousand people, including many priests, religious, women, and children, died in Carrier's *noyades*. The first of them took place November 17; among the victims were 90 priests.[2]

The response to Danton's unexpected intervention was immediate. Two days later the Hébertists took him to task at the Jacobin Club for opposing tax-money subsidies for the Club from the government. At this time Robespierre saw Hébert and Danton as equally dangerous challengers to his authority, with Hébert somewhat the more dangerous of the two. He therefore defended Danton, but in a way which clearly hinted his intention to turn on him later. He listed all the "crimes" of action and thought which his enemies had imputed to Danton, and then declared:

> I may be mistaken about Danton, but I have seen him in his family circle; his conduct there deserves nothing but praise. In his political attitudes too I have observed him very closely. It is true that he was slow to hate Brissot and to suspect Dumouriez, but if I did not always agree with him, who am I to conclude that he has betrayed his country? He has always *seemed* to be serving it zealously.[3]

On the following day in Lyons, Collot d'Herbois of the Committee of Public Safety and Joseph Fouché, a teacher educated at the Oratorian College at Nantes who had become a vehement atheist and assisted in the suppression of the Vendeans before being sent to Lyons, ordered the first mass executions in reprisal for that city's support of the Girondin rebellion. The guillotine was already cutting off twenty heads a day in Lyons, but Collot and Fouché considered this much too slow. The system they used was to line up the victims among the open ditches which would be their graves, mow them down with grapeshot, have the survivors sabered by cavalrymen, and then dump the bodies in the ditches with earth thrown over them. On December 5, 209 people were killed in this manner in Lyons.[4] Whole sections of the city were demolished, including the Place Bellecourt, admired throughout Europe for the beauty of its architecture. But these proceedings also were condemned as too slow: "The demolitions in this abominable city are going too slowly. Republican impatience demands more rapid methods. Nothing but the explosion of mines and the use of fire can give full expression to the omnipotence of the People."[5]

December 5 was also the day when the first issue of a new newspaper appeared in Paris: the "Old Cordelier," edited by Camille Desmoulins. Back in 1792 the Cordeliers Club had been the base from which Danton had risen to power; although the Club was now controlled by the Hébertists, its name had an ineradicable association with Danton. In the first issue of the "Old Cordelier" Desmoulins sang Danton's praises and strongly attacked the Law of Suspects. "Open the prisons!" Desmoulins cried. "Release the two hundred thousand suspects who are in them! In the Declaration of Man's Rights there is no house of suspicion. There are only houses of arrest."[6]

Desmoulins had taken the precaution of submitting the proofs of his first issue to Robespierre before publication; he did the same with the second, published December 10 (they were published at five-day intervals, that is to say, twice a week in the ten-day week of the Revolutionary calendar). He also praised Robespierre in the first issue for having "held out his hand in friendship" to Danton at the Jacobin Club meeting December 3 when the Hébertists attacked him. These actions and statements give us a glimpse of Danton's strategy, and provide an occasion for some reflection on the immense difficulties he faced.

If Danton had decided that he was morally obligated to try to change fundamentally the course of the Revolution, using all his immense prestige with the Revolutionaries to help him do so, he certainly could not come out openly in the beginning and declare this to be his objective. He would at once have been condemned, arrested, and executed as a traitor. If, on the other hand, he simply wanted to restore his once high position in the counsels of the leaders of the Revolution and perhaps moderate the worst of its excesses, he would not have taken the risks involved in seeming to defend the hated Vendean Catholic royalists and in challenging directly the Law of Suspects which gave local revolutionary committees life-and-death power over their fellow-men. Realistically speaking, he could not be fully frank about his intentions, if his intentions were to bring France back toward Christian morality; yet morally speaking, he could not stand by while the worst of the atrocities went forward. He would have to condemn the atrocities and the oppression while still giving lip service to the Revolution, seeking to restore enough moral sense in enough of the Revolution's leaders and creatures to cause them to re-

ject the atrocities and the oppression on the moral grounds they had
heretofore ignored or scornfully dismissed, without being rejected as
counterrevolutionary.

It was a night walk along a cliff's edge. Few men but Danton
would have thought they could manage it. Danton did. His confidence
in himself was unbounded. When he began this fight he was quite
sure he could win. Up to the very end he never saw himself as a sacrifice. It was both his strength and his weakness.

The response to the "Old Cordelier" among the terrorized people
of Paris was immensely enthusiastic. Fifty thousand copies of the second issue were sold. It made Robespierre very uneasy. His uneasiness
increased when on December 12 Bourdon de l'Oise, a deputy who was
a friend of Danton, rose in the Convention to propose a requirement
of periodic re-election for the members of the Committee of Public
Safety. That showed Robespierre that the challenge to the Terror was
going beyond criticism of the worst excesses of the Hébertists and beginning to strike home on the men in the Committee of Public Safety
who were actually directing the Revolution and bore the ultimate responsibility for all the horrors being committed in its name. Although
no action was taken at the time on Bourdon's motion, Robespierre had
his warning.

Then came the third issue of the "Old Cordelier," on December
15. This issue was not submitted to Robespierre's inspection before
publication. It reminded readers of the oppression in ancient Rome
under Emperors Gaius Caligula and Nero, when denunciation by an
informer, regardless of his reputation or motives, often destroyed a
man's life and career. That situation in ancient Rome was explicitly
compared to the situation in France under the Law of Suspects. In this
issue of the "Old Cordelier" Desmoulins directly asked the Committee
of Public Safety: "Do you really think that these helpless women,
these old men, these poor laggards of the Revolution whom you have
shut up are dangerous?"[7]

The entire printing of this issue was sold out in Paris before the
end of the day it appeared. A large crowd assembled at the hall where
the Convention met to call for the release of the imprisoned suspects.
Inside, Danton was reminding the Convention that none of the arguments used earlier to justify the Terror still applied. The country and
the Revolution were no longer in acute danger. All the Girondin uprisings had been suppressed, and that of the Vendée was rapidly approaching its end (the Vendean army which had crossed the Loire and
marched north was finally destroyed at the Battle of Savenay December 23). The British holding Toulon were tightly besieged (Captain

Napoleone Buonaparte was about to place the artillery which drove
them out December 19) and the Austrians in Alsace were at a stand-
still. There was no longer a military crisis. The Terror should cease
and the Committee of Public Safety give up its dictatorial powers.

On December 20 a delegation of citizens from Lyons came before the Convention to beg that the Terror might be lifted from their
city. The Convention referred their plea to the Committee of Public
Safety. However, one of its most ruthless members, Collot d'Herbois,
had been the principal architect of the Terror in Lyons. Knowing that
the delegation was on its way, he had hurried back to Paris to arrive
ahead of them. He defended the mass executions in Lyons on the basis
of a tissue of imaginary conspiracies and the alleged benefits of holding speedy trials and executions outdoors "under the vault of nature"
instead of in stuffy courtrooms with slow court procedures. The victims were not truly of the people, he said; they deserved no considera-
tion. Speaking to the Jacobin Club that night, he further condemned
the people of Lyons, including the women, "plunged madly into adul-
tery and prostitution." Within a day or two he had a letter from
Fouché: "We have only one way of celebrating victory. This evening
we send two hundred and thirteen rebels under the fire of the light-
ning-bolt."[8]

At this same moment, from December 22 to 25, more than 1,700
people—men, women, and children—were being drowned by order of
Carrier in the fourth, fifth, sixth, and seventh of the *noyades* of
Nantes.[9]

The day that had been the joyous anniversary of the birth of the
Savior came to Paris without official notice that year. Though Robespierre, in what seems to have been a conciliatory gesture to Danton
on December 6, had carried a bill in the Convention guaranteeing religious freedom to Catholics, in most of the capital city the guarantee
was not observed; that year, for the first time in countless centuries in
the history of Paris which had remained faithfully Catholic even
through the Calvinist (Huguenot) uprisings of the sixteenth century,
no public midnight Masses were offered as Christmas day began. But
there was another issue of the "Old Cordelier," in which Camille
Desmoulins addressed Robespierre directly and personally:

> Companion of my school days, whose eloquent
> speeches will be read by generations yet unborn, remember
> the lessons which history and philosophy teach us: that love
> is stronger and more enduring than fear. . . . Release from
> prison those 200,000 citizens you describe as "suspects"; in the
> Declaration of Rights there is no clause providing for im-
> prisonment on suspicion. . . . You are determined to extermi-

nate all opposition by means of the guillotine. Yet could any undertaking be more nonsensical? You cannot destroy one opponent on the scaffold without making ten more enemies from among his family and friends. . . . Believe me, freedom would be more firmly established, and Europe would be brought to her knees, if you had a "Committee of Mercy."[10]

This issue sold out even faster than its predecessor. Long lines formed in front of the office of its publisher; many who bought it resold it at a large profit. Originally priced at two sous, within a day or two a copy, if obtainable at all, cost 20 francs. Not only the Terror, but its ultimate author and master, Robespierre, had been challenged.

Robespierre knew that he and the Terror were inseparable. His differences with the Hébertists were purely tactical and personal; he thought their attack on the Catholic Faith excessive and vulgar and saw in them a political threat to his ascendancy. But on the Terror itself there was no difference between him and them. On this Christmas day he presented a report to the Convention in the name of the Committee of Public Safety on the principles of Revolutionary government, in which he declared: "In times of peace the springs of popular government are in virtue; but in times of revolution, they are both in virtue and in terror."[11]

Others were still more outspoken. "Camille is skirting very close to the guillotine," said Nicolas, official printer to the Revolutionary government and a member of the Revolutionary Tribunal which sent men to the guillotine. Barère of the Committee of Public Safety declared, in obvious reference to Desmoulins: "The man who complains about everything that happens during a revolution is a suspect."[12]

It was still too soon to attack Danton, with his enormous prestige among the people, directly. But Desmoulins was on the firing line.

With more courage than he is generally given credit for, Desmoulins fired back, not only at Hébert but also at the still more powerful Barère, and Collot d'Herbois as well, in the fifth issue of the "Old Cordelier" published January 5, 1794. Meanwhile Robespierre—encouraged by Saint-Just, returned from Alsace December 31—had forced Hérault de Séchelles, Danton's one strong supporter in the Committee of Public Safety, off that committee and had denounced Fabre d'Eglantine, another leading supporter of Danton's, for corruption. On January 7 Desmoulins came under strong attack at a meeting of the Jacobin Club; Robespierre went to the rostrum to pronounce his verdict.

Camille, who sits there all puffed up over the prodigious sale of his newspaper and by the perfidious praise

which the aristocrats have showered on him, has not left the
path of error. His writings are dangerous. They give hope to
our enemies and they stir up public malignity. . . . Camille is
a spoiled child who once had good inclinations, but who is
now led astray by bad companions. We must use severity towards his paper, which even Brissot would not have dared
acknowledge; yet we must keep Camille among us.[13]

Then Robespierre paused. After a long silence he raised his
glasses to his brow, the almost hypnotic gaze of his strange green eyes
sweeping the room and everyone in it as though searching for prey.

"I demand," he said at length, "that the offensive issues of this
journal be burned in the hall of the Society!"

That searching look of Robespierre's usually paralyzed the will
of prospective opponents; but Desmoulins had Danton behind him,
and actually there with him at the Jacobin Club that night. This may
well have given him a courage not his by nature.

"To burn is not to answer," he shot back, quoting Rousseau.

Robespierre almost never showed emotion. He showed it now.
His pale bilious face turned red.

"Know this, Camille," he said. "If you were not Camille, the
amount of indulgence shown you here would be unthinkable. Your attitude proves to me that your intentions are dishonest. . . . A man who
so stubbornly defends such perfidious writings is worse perhaps than a
mere laggard."[14]

Robespierre frightened most men. He did not frighten Danton.

"Citizens!" Danton declared. "Let all your decisions be made
calmly, and in accordance with the dictates of justice! When you pass
judgment on Desmoulins, take care lest you strike a deadly blow at the
freedom of the press!"[15]

Either just before or just after this pivotal meeting of the Jacobin Club, Danton went personally to Robespierre to urge him to
support an end to the Terror in which the innocent were perishing
with the guilty. "Who told you, pray?" Robespierre asked him icily,
"that a single innocent person had been put to death?" Danton looked
at Robespierre as he might have looked at some loathsome reptile.
"What do you say? Not one innocent person has perished!"[16] Danton
turned on his heel and left the room.

The duel to the death had now truly begun.

Robespierre's strategy was to strike first at Danton's more
prominent and vulnerable supporters, particularly Fabre d'Eglantine
and Hérault de Séchelles, who had already been denounced. Fabre was
arrested on January 12 and Hérault on January 17. Both were charged
with corruption, of which they were almost surely guilty—as were

many other Revolutionary leaders (though not Robespierre, who took great pride in being "the Incorruptible") who were not arrested. The two arrests were clearly moves against Danton.

One day as he was leaving the Convention, Danton saw Vadier, a member of the General Security Committee, point to him and overheard him say: "We're going to gut that fat porpoise." Danton turned to the men beside him and said: "Somebody tell that villain over there that if ever I have reason to fear for my life I'll become worse than a cannibal: I'll eat his brains."[17] Historians have mocked Danton for such apparently wild statements; but it was essential for him to show those who now clearly intended to have him killed that he did not fear them, for Robespierre ruled by the aura of fear he cast.

In this atmosphere of spreading fear, of charge and countercharge, of arrest and blackmail—an atmosphere in which every man prominently involved knew himself to be guilty of crimes that in any normal time would have made him liable to capital punishment—one of the most mysterious events in all of modern history took place. Thousands of hours of study and analysis by dozens of writers and researchers have not elucidated it. It has been called the last great historical mystery, and is probably insoluble, though the mass of written data on the French Revolution and the people involved in it is so great that there remains a faint possibility that the explanation may still come to light some day. The mystery is that of the fate of the eight-year-old boy whom French royalists still regarded as their rightful king, Louis XVII. It cannot be treated at length here, for it is not directly relevant to our story of the guillotine and the Cross during the Terror; but its critical event happened at this point, in the midst of one of the most dramatic parts of that story.

On January 18 Georges Couthon, member of the Committee of Public Safety and close associate of Robespierre, declared to the Convention: "An infamous plot has been discovered, the original object of which was to murder all the deputies of the Mountain, and then proclaim the boy Capet king. The number of accomplices is immense, and over 4,000 persons have already been arrested."[18] There is not the slightest reliable historical evidence of the reality of any such plot; but it is hard to believe there was no connection between this extraordinary announcement by the highly placed Couthon and the fact that on the following day, January 19, the cobbler Simon was abruptly relieved of his duties as guardian of young Louis, and moved all his belongings out of the Temple. A boy continued to live in one of the rooms of the Temple, but he was alone and remained completely alone, as he had never been before. Although sounds carried well in the Temple, and his sister and aunt were still kept in rooms where they could easily have heard him if he cried out in solitary confinement, for months upon months they heard no sound from him, only occasional movements. Never again, not even at the time of his alleged death and burial in 1795, was his sister permitted to see the boy or identify him. These facts, and others derived from a substantial body of later testimony including the explicit avowal of Mrs. Simon and the firm assertion in later life of his sister, now become Duchess of Angoulême, that "my brother did not die," form the basis for the conclusion that the son of Louis XVI and Marie Antoinette was removed from the Temple January 19 and another boy—probably deaf and dumb—substituted. The body of the boy pronounced dead June 8, 1795 has been three times exhumed and examined by physicians, who have been unable to agree on whether the body could have been that of a child of the age that Louis XVII would then have been. Naturally there were later pretenders; none of their stories stands up well under close examination. No one knows what happened to the tragic boy, and probably no one ever will know.[19] The contending Revolutionary factions at this point were obviously capable of any crime, and it is quite possible that one of them spirited him away and killed him to prevent one of the others from using him against them. But there is evidence that Robespierre did not know what had happened to him; it is most unlikely that Danton knew; and it is hard to imagine the Hébertists—never notable for intelligence or craft—managing so successful an abduction and then covering their tracks so perfectly. The mystery remains.

On January 19 General Turreau in the Vendée prepared orders dividing the Revolutionary army into 24 columns sent out to burn and destroy everything in their path and to kill many of the people—almost all of them noncombatants—in order to terrorize them into total submission. These "infernal columns" ranged the Vendean countryside through the remainder of January, all of February and into March, devastating, killing, mutilating. One example of their work will suffice—if it is clearly remembered that it is only one example of many. About two hundred peasants—men, women, and children—were assembled in a field. Their noses, ears, and fingers were cut off and their tongues torn out; their cries could be heard for more than a mile. Afterwards, that field was known as "the meadow of the howling."[20]

The principal Vendean army had been shattered at Savenay December 23; but in the face of such atrocities a desperate, hopeless resistance continued all through the countryside, for surely it was better to die fighting than at the hands of the torturers. On January 6 d'Elbée was captured and shot; the dashing, heroic La Rochejaquelein died fighting January 29; Stofflet and Charette survived, fighting a guerrilla war with a series of hairsbreadth escapes, until at last both were captured and executed in 1796. But all hope of victory in the Vendée was gone.

The Christian's ultimate weapon remained; and it was time to unsheath it.

At two o'clock in the morning of January 30 the Carmelite sisters of Grenelle Street, who had been detained for several weeks, were brought before the Revolutionary Tribunal. The interrogator, speaking for the Terror, confronted Sister Vitasse, thirty-two years old. She was not terrified.

"I am a judge of the Revolutionary Tribunal. It is necessary that you know that this tribunal is established to judge and to condemn to death all those who are against the Revolution."

She met his eyes. It would seem that she must have smiled.

"*C'est bon!* Very well!"

That must have startled him; but he quickly recollected himself.

"Have you taken the oath?" He meant the oath to accept the Civil Constitution of the Clergy, the Revolutionary law creating a schismatic church in France.

"No."

"Why not?"

"Because it is contrary to my conscience and my vows."

A few moments later he asked her:

"Does your religion permit you to lie?"

"No."

"Well then: did priests come to Cassette Street?"

"We have friends who come sometimes to see us."

"I did not ask if friends came to see you; I asked you specifically if priests came!" bellowed the infuriated interrogator. "Answer me! Did priests come to see you?"

"Sometimes."

"Often?"

"No."

"Their names?"

"I will not tell you."

"Why not?"

"Because I do not wish to tell you."

"If you do not name them, it will go badly for you."

"Only what God permits, will happen."

"It is not God who judges you," roared the interrogator, "it is I, and all the judges of the tribunal."

"It is God Who permits the judgment you render to me." They were, almost exactly, Christ's words to Pilate.

"What stubbornness! You wish to expose yourself to death for them and you would not do that for your own father!"

"Pardon me; I would certainly give my life to save that of my father, and I would do the same for you."

"It is not true! You would not do that for me."

"Pardon me; I would not wish to save my life at the expense of yours."

"You will not name them, then?"

"No."[21]

On February 4 the Revolutionary Tribunal indicted the Carmelites of Grenelle Street for "fanaticism," for illegally continuing to live in community, for receiving refractory priests (meaning those who would not swear the oath to obey the Civil Constitution of the Clergy), and for inciting civil war and conspiracy against the Republic. On February 7 they were imprisoned in the Conciergerie, where Marie Antoinette had spent her last weeks. In the course of further questioning the Tribunal determined that Father Kéravénan, the priest to whom Danton had made his confession, was one of those who had visited the community at Grenelle Street in recent months, though they continued to be unsuccessful in apprehending him. Perhaps surprisingly, the Carmelites of Grenelle Street were not sentenced to death, only to deportation. But they were not in fact deported, remaining in jail—and therefore constantly in danger of death—until the end of the Terror. Others of their order, following the road they had been ready to travel, were soon to be martyred by the guillotine.

On February 19 Louis Antoine Saint-Just began his turn at being president of the Convention for fifteen days. (From its original convening until the end of the Terror, the Convention rigorously followed its rule of changing presidents every fifteen days.) He was its youngest member, but his prestige was very high; he stood at the right hand of Robespierre, and never had the slightest doubt of where he was going. Terror, more terror, and still more terror was his prescription for meeting whatever dangers and problems the Revolution faced or might face. In presenting a bill providing for the seizure and sale of all the property of persons confined as suspects—even the Revolution had previously done this only in the case of those who had fled the country—Saint-Just declared: "Destroy the rebel party; make liberty hard as steel; avenge the patriot victims of intrigue." He scorned those "who wish to destroy the scaffold because they fear to mount it themselves."[22] There could hardly be a more explicit threat to Danton, Desmoulins, and all who supported them.

But Saint-Just was resolved to crush the Hébertists as well; he regarded them as irresponsible fanatics whose inconstancy and incompetence seriously endangered the Revolution for different reasons. Using his position as president of the Convention to denounce "factions" and "foreign plots," he encouraged Robespierre to strike both the Hébertists and the followers of Danton and Desmoulins. Himself a member of the Committee of Public Safety, Saint-Just was able to use this position to secure the support of the two members of the Committee originally associated with the Hébertists, Collot d'Herbois and Billaud-Varenne, for the suppression of their former companions. The Hébertists played into his hands by attempting March 4 to stir up another mob demonstration, such as they had conducted with Robespierre's approval against the Girondins early in June of the previous year, and again, without Robespierre's approval, on September 5 when thereby they forced the Committee of Public Safety to add Collot and Billaud to its membership. But Collot and Billaud were now co-opted, and the attempted Hébertist mob action of March 4 became the occasion for their downfall. Saint-Just's brief term of office as president of the Convention ended March 6, but his prestige had now risen so high that he was able to carry the whole Convention with him, without a dissenting voice, in the destruction of the Hébertists.

"Every party is then criminal," he declared March 13, "because it is a form of isolation from the people and the popular societies, a form of independence from the government. Every faction is then criminal, because it tends to divide the citizens; every faction is criminal because it neutralizes the power of public virtue."[23] He went on to define the Revolutionary Republic explicitly in terms of its destructive power and killing action. "What constitutes the Republic is the destruction of everything opposed to it. A man is guilty against the Republic when he takes pity on prisoners; he is guilty because he has no desire for virtue; he is guilty because he is opposed to the Terror."[24] After thus proclaiming the full totalitarian creed, Saint-Just called for the arrest of the Hébertist "conspirators," the broadening of the law of treason, and the creation of six new commissions to judge suspects. Instead of letting suspects go when there was no solid evidence against them, as Danton and Desmoulins had been urging since the beginning of December, the scales of justice were to be weighted even more against them.

Yet the first to suffer the weight of the new laws would be the Hébertists—a move of diabolical political cleverness, which distracted people's attention from Danton as the real target and even made it seem that his efforts were prevailing, while preparing the groundwork for his destruction and eliminating another source of potential opposition to the dictatorship of Robespierre. On the night following Saint-Just's speech, Hébert and four of his principal associates were arrested; fifteen more were put behind bars in the next few days. All but one were condemned; on March 24 they were executed. Hébert, who had hounded so many to their doom, died a coward's death, alternately whimpering and screaming.

On March 19 Danton urged reconciliation and unity upon the Convention, and on March 22 he went to Robespierre in his rooms to recommend this to him personally. Robespierre was powdering his hair, with a kind of apron over his green-striped coat to keep the powder off. Danton wore, as usual, a simple open-necked shirt.

"Let us forget our differences," Danton pleaded, "and look at nothing but our country and her needs. Once the Republic is respected outside our borders she will become beloved within them, even by men who now show their enmity against her."

Robespierre's answer suggests that he sensed something of where Danton's new attitude was coming from.

"With your principles and your morals," he said (had anyone before thought of Danton as having "principles" and "morals," except those called Revolutionary which were in fact, and were explicitly declared to be, contrary to all conventional morality?), "nobody would ever find any criminals to punish."

"Would you regret that?" Danton asked him. "Would you be sorry not to find any criminals to punish?"

Danton specifically urged mercy for 73 Convention deputies who had been imprisoned since the preceding summer for criticizing the methods used in the overthrow of the Girondins.

"The only way to establish liberty is to cut off the heads of such criminals," Robespierre said.

Tears rose in Danton's eyes. Robespierre saw them, and despised them for showing what he thought to be weakness. Danton warned him that in the long run France would repudiate the Terror. He begged him, for the last time, to show mercy. He tried to embrace Robespierre, who pulled away, "cold as marble."[25]

Many now knew that Robespierre was plotting Danton's destruction, and that his arrest was impending. Danton received at least two advance warnings after the decree of arrest had actually been voted by the Committee of Public Safety (by 18 to 2) on the evening of March 30. Some of Danton's friends urged him to strike first; others urged him to flee. Some felt him to be "lackadaisical"—some historians still accuse him of it—for refusing to do either. His answer to the proponents of a counter-stroke through the Revolutionary regime was: "Better, a hundred times better, to suffer the guillotine than to inflict it on others!" And his answer to those who urged him to flee was: "Can a man take his country with him on the soles of his shoes?"[26]

It is true that the first of these answers does not fit the old Danton, though the second does. But if there had been a rebirth of the Catholic Faith in him, the first answer fits perfectly. More than any other man, he had loosed the guillotine on France. He who had risen to power by the bloody blade of its great gleaming knife would not save his life by continuing to use it. He would stand before it and condemn it. And he would never flee; his calling was now to fight to the end, but with the weapons of words and of truth, not of death and destruction.

He was arrested just before sunrise on March 31 by the old calendar, 11 Germinal by the new. He tried to reassure Louise, who was weeping, telling her that he would soon be back. He was still confident that his last stand would turn the tide.

He was taken to Luxembourg Prison (formerly a palace) along with Desmoulins, Philippeaux, and others of his friends. The prisoners there gathered in astonishment to behold the leader and architect of the Revolution joining them in confinement. Danton faced them, perhaps with a wry grin.

"Gentlemen," he said, "I had hoped to get you all out of this place. Unfortunately I'm now shut up in it with you. . . . If reason doesn't soon return to this poor country, what you have seen so far will be a bed of roses compared to what will follow."[27]

In the Convention that morning the butcher Legendre, one of the leaders in the September massacres, tried to protest Danton's arrest and defend him. But it was too late in the day for Legendre to discover mercy. He moved that the Convention allow Danton to appear before it to defend himself. Before the motion could be put to a vote, Robespierre arrived, wearing his familiar, ominous green-tinted glasses. The big, busy room fell silent as the hooded gaze of the little lawyer from Arras passed over it.

"Legendre has mentioned Danton," Robespierre said, venomously. "He seems to believe that some privilege attaches to his name. But has Danton any claim to privilege? Is he in any respect better than the rest of his fellow citizens? No! We will have no more privileges here! And we will have no more idols either!" He raised his glasses to his brow and turned his unblinking gray-green stare directly upon Legendre. "The man who trembles at my words is guilty," he said. "Innocence has never feared public scrutiny."

Legendre paled. "If Robespierre thinks that I am capable of sacrificing liberty to an individual, he mistook my intention. Those who have the proof in their hands realize better than we do the guilt of the men who have been arrested."[28]

Saint-Just read and explained the indictment—long, vicious, and fanciful to the point of paranoia. As he spoke, he kept making a chopping gesture with his left hand which suggested to some observers the fall of the guillotine's knife. When he had finished, the indictment was endorsed unanimously. Legendre voted for it along with all the others present and voting.

On the night of April 1, Danton and those who had been arrested with him were moved to the Conciergerie. One wonders how far away from their cells were those occupied by Sister Vitasse and the other Carmelite nun prisoners from Grenelle Street—and how far away was the one which had been occupied by Marie Antoinette.

Danton had not lost any of his splendid, defiant courage. Confronted that morning by Fouquier-Tinville with the question whether he had conspired to restore the monarchy and destroy Republican government, he had replied with a scornful shrug of his massive shoulders. Asked if he had a defense attorney, he had replied that he could and most certainly would defend himself. Of his judges-to-be, the Revolutionary Tribunal, he said: "We shall see what kind of a figure they cut when they appear before us."[29] After his arrival at the Conciergerie, he spoke more profoundly and memorably of that blood-stained body: "A year ago I established the Revolutionary Tribunal. I ask pardon of God and men. I did it to prevent a renewal of the September massacres, not to be the scourge of humanity." Then, more significantly still: "It is better to be a poor fisherman than a ruler of men."[30] Why, specifically, a fisherman? Danton was not a fisherman (except, occasionally, for recreation); he had been a farmer. But once there had been a poor fisherman in a far land across the sea—a fisherman who found the Messiah, and became the Vicar of Christ.

The "trial" began the morning of April 2. Just as at the trial of Marie Antoinette, Nicolas Hermann presided and Fouquier-Tinville prosecuted. Both men knew that the Committee of Public Safety had already drafted and signed warrants for their arrest, to be instantly executed if they should fail to secure the conviction of the defendants. The Committee had sent two special assistants to be at Fouquier-

Tinville's side to make sure that he did what was expected of him. They had not forgotten that Fouquier-Tinville originally owed his position to Danton. But they need not have worried. Antoine Quentin Fouquier-Tinville did not know the meaning of personal loyalty. He was the perfect bureaucrat, always doing exactly as he was told by his superiors in the government in power. He would have made a superb clerk at Auschwitz.

It was his Fouquier-Tinville's task to pick a jury that would assuredly condemn Danton to death. The beginning of the trial was delayed between two and three hours while he did his best to make sure of his men. In the end he chose only seven jurors, though the law required twelve. One of them was a former aristocrat, once Marquis Leroy de Montflobert. His Revolutionary name was "Leroy-dix-août," Leroy of the Tenth of August.

The fourteen defendants were called to the bar, the jurors swore "to administer justice impartially," and the reading of Saint-Just's lengthy indictment began. During its reading three Convention deputies arrived, slipping in behind Hermann and whispering to him. They included Couthon of the Committee of Public Safety and Amar, a deputy who had once urged the whole Convention to go to watch the working of the guillotine: "Let us go to the foot of the great altar and attend the celebration of the red Mass!"[31]

Danton rose to his feet: "I demand permission to write to the Convention and have a commission appointed to hear my denunciation, and that of Desmoulins, against dictatorial practices in the Committees of Public Safety and Security!"

Shouts of approval rose from the crowd. So great was the tumult that the terrified Hermann immediately adjourned that day's session of the tribunal.

"The bastards wouldn't let me finish," Danton growled, as they led him back to his cell in the Conciergerie. "Never mind, I'll make mincemeat of the judges tomorrow."[32]

He still believed that his last stand would prevail.

The next morning two new defendants were added to the group—one of them, ironically, being General Westermann, the commander of the attack on the Swiss Guard August 10, 1792. Hermann refused even to interrogate him for the record as to why he was there. When Danton joined in Westermann's protests, Hermann called him to order.

"We have the right to be heard in this place!" bellowed Danton. "I was responsible for creating this Tribunal; I know its rules of procedure better than anyone!"

Uproar followed. Hermann began frantically ringing his bell for order. When this had no effect, he shouted at Danton: "Didn't you hear my bell?"

"A man fighting for his life pays no attention to bells!" Danton shouted back.[33]

Later on that day, April 3, Danton was finally permitted by the Tribunal to speak in his own defense. His mighty voice could be heard not only all through the courtroom but for blocks around in the streets outside and, it is said, even across the Seine. He scorned the contrived conspiratorial fantasies of his indictment and demanded that his actual accusers confront him. "I summon my accusers to come forth," he cried. "I demand the right to pit my strength against theirs. Let them show themselves, the vile impostors, and I'll tear away the mask that protects them from public chastisement!"[34]

He could not attack the Revolution directly, even yet, for that would have seemed to confirm the charges against him. His task was to show the malicious absurdity of the proceedings, the extent to which they had become an utter travesty of justice; this he did magnificently. So effective were his denunciations and so overwhelming was the power of his oratory that when that day's session ended it appeared that, by his opening statement alone, he was building up so much popular sentiment in his favor that the Tribunal might not dare to convict him. And then he had a long list of witnesses to call on his behalf, including even Robert Lindet, one of the two members of the Committee of Public Safety who had refused to sign the document indicting him.

That evening Fouquier-Tinville wrote a request to the Committee of Public Safety. Once again he sought a dispensation from legal requirements protecting the rights of defendants. When the Terror was over, this written request of Fouquier-Tinville was the principal exhibit in evidence that brought him to the guillotine.

> A fearful storm has been raging since the session began. The accused are behaving like madmen and are frantically demanding the summoning of their witnesses. They are denouncing to the people what they say is the rejection of their demand. In spite of the firmness of the President [Hermann] and the entire court, their repeated requests are disrupting the session. They say that, short of a decree, they will not be quiet until their witnesses have been heard. We ask you what to do about their demand since our judicial powers give us no authority for rejecting it.[35]

This letter was a bit too much even for Saint-Just to reveal word for word to the Convention. So he paraphrased it, declaring that "the

Public Prosecutor has just informed us that the revolt of the guilty men has forced him to suspend their trial until the Convention shall have taken measures. . . . No further proofs are needed. The very resistance of these wretches is an acknowledgment of their guilt!" He then produced a letter to Robespierre from a prisoner in the Luxembourg claiming that a plot had been hatched for a prison breakout taking advantage of the excitement created by Danton's trial and aided by money offered by Desmoulins' wife. Whether this letter was forged, obtained by bribery, or simply an attempt by a terrified prisoner in danger of death to curry favor from the men in the Committee of Public Safety who held the power of life and death, no one knows. Saint-Just demanded that the Convention immediately decree that "every accused person who resisted or insulted the national justice should be forbidden to plead."[36]

Paralyzed by fear, the Convention approved this law. Amar hurried from the Tuileries where the Convention met to the Palace of Justice to give the text to Fouquier-Tinville.

"This should make the job easier for you," he told him after having him called out of the courtroom to hand it to him.

"Indeed we needed it," Fouquier-Tinville said. He went back into the courtroom and read the decree there.

Amar was now sitting in the courtroom, along with Vadier who had declared his intention to "gut" Danton weeks before, and David the painter, erstwhile friend of Danton now become his enemy in order to curry favor with the present masters of the Revolution. All three were members of the Committee of General Security. Danton looked at them, knowing exactly what they were and what they stood for and who their real ruler was. He rose to his full height with a roar that shook the walls.

"You are murderers!" he cried. "Murderers! Look at them! They have hounded us to our deaths! Vile Robespierre! You too will go to the scaffold. You will follow me, Robespierre!"[37]

The next morning, April 5, Fouquier-Tinville announced the end of the trial, under the authority of the law passed the day before. But one obstacle still remained before Danton's head could be put under the knife. The jury had to vote him guilty—the hanging jury that Fouquier-Tinville had so carefully picked. And for some time that jury would not do so.

As the hours passed without a conviction, Fouquier-Tinville and Hermann became first impatient, then alarmed. Finally they simply walked into the jury room to remind the jurors what they were supposed to do. When the jurors still would not do it, Amar and Vadier of the Committee of General Security arrived to add their pressure and threats. They produced a document of some kind—possibly a compromising letter found when Danton's home was searched at the time of his arrest—which allegedly convinced the jurors of his guilt. In view of all the circumstances it would seem a good deal more likely that it was the shadow of the guillotine for themselves that convinced the jurors. At any rate, they finally voted Danton's conviction and the death penalty.

Within a few minutes of the sentence the preparation for the death of the condemned men began. Desmoulins, sobbing and sometimes screaming, had to be tied to his bench. Danton, alternately joking and serious, expressed his contempt for his destroyers, his mockery of the madness which now held Paris in its grip, and his hopes for a change that had not been realized: "I have the consolation of believing," he said as he stepped into the cart that was to take him to the guillotine, "that the man who died as leader of the Indulgents will be treated mercifully by posterity."[38]

Three carts carried the men condemned with Danton. Slowly they crept through Paris toward Revolution Square where the guillotine loomed. The crowds along the way were vast but silent. All eyes were on Danton, but he would not speak now, except occasionally to those with him in the cart. But his eyes kept ranging the scene—the familiar streets, the sea of upturned faces. About halfway in the long slow course of that procession to death, on St. Honoré Street, Danton suddenly gazed fixedly at a man wearing a red hat and carmagnole who had kept pace with his cart all the way from the Palace of Justice. Dressed as he was, this man looked like any other revolutionary; but at length, on St. Honoré Street, Danton recognized him.

He was Father Kéravénan. Louise had asked him especially to be there; but we may be sure that he would have come even without her entreaty.

He had been reciting the prayers for the dying. When Danton met his eyes and recognized him, he bowed his head. From the roadside, Father Kéravénan gave him conditional absolution.

There were fifteen men to be killed that pale filmy late afternoon of earliest spring in Paris. Danton was the last. One by one he watched the heads fall, and a red stain spread on the planks of the platform of the Revolution's death machine. Like a rock he stood outlined against its monstrous bulk in the fading sunshine. An eyewitness tells us: "In the dying light of day the great leader seemed to be rising out of his tomb as much as preparing to descend into it. Never was anything more bold than that athlete's countenance, never anything more formidable than the look of that profile which seemed to defy the knife."

When at last it was his turn, for just a moment his control faltered as a vision of Louise, his good angel, came before his eyes.

"Oh my beloved," he said. "Shall I never see you again?"

Then: "Come, come, Danton. There must be no weakness."

He turned to Sanson the executioner, holding up his head with a last gesture of defiance.

"You must show my head to the people," he said. "It is worth it."[39]

The great knife fell. Georges-Jacques Danton, architect and leader of the French Revolution, was slain by its hand at the age of thirty-four.

Danton was dead; the Revolution and the Terror went on. We have good reason to hope that repentance and expiation had saved his soul. But in the end, on the last battlefield of the spirit, the guillotine could only be defeated by the Cross. It was Sister Vitasse of the Carmelites of Grenelle Street, not the gladiator of audacity, who had revealed what was in truth the only road to victory over an evil so great.

NOTES

[1]Stanley Loomis, *Paris in the Terror, June 1793-July 1794* (Philadelphia, 1964), p. 288.

[2]*Ibid.,* pp. 288-289; A. Billaud, *La Guerre de Vendée* (Fontenay, 1972), pp. 171-172.

[3]Loomis, *Paris in the Terror*, p. 282.

[4]R. R. Palmer, *Twelve Who Ruled; the Year of the Terror in the French Revolution* (Princeton, 1941, 1969), pp. 169-170.

[5]Loomis, *Paris in the Terror*, p. 361.

[6]Loomis, *Paris in the Terror*, p. 283.

[7]*Ibid.,* p. 288.

[8]Palmer, *Twelve Who Ruled*, pp. 174-175.

[9]Billaud, *Guerre de Vendée*, p. 172.

[10]Robert Christophe, *Danton* (London, n.d.), p. 405.

[11]Louis Madelin, *The French Revolution* (New York, 1925), p. 366.

[12]Loomis, *Paris in the Terror*, p. 292.

[13]*Ibid.,* p. 293.

[14]*Ibid.,* p. 294.

[15]Christophe, *Danton*, p. 413.

[16]Madelin, *French Revolution*, p. 393.

[17]Loomis, *Paris in the Terror*, p. 296.

[18]Madelin, *French Revolution*, p. 366.

[19]See Rupert Furneaux, *The Bourbon Tragedy* (London, 1968), pp. 159-181, 197-215 for a good and sober summary of the available evidence on the fate of Louis XVII.

[20]Michel de Saint Pierre, *Monsieur Charette, chevalier du Roi* (Paris, 1977), p. 14.

[21]Jacques Hérissay, *La Vie religieuse à Paris sous la Terreur (1792-1794)* (Paris, 1952), pp. 206-207. Translation by the writer.

[22]Eugene Curtis, *Saint-Just, Colleague of Robespierre* (New York, 1935, 1973), pp. 191, 189.

[23]Palmer, *Twelve Who Ruled*, p. 291.

[24]Madelin, *French Revolution*, p. 394.

[25]Loomis, *Paris in the Terror*, pp. 298-299.

[26]Christophe, *Danton*, p. 418.

[27]Loomis, *Paris in the Terror*, p. 307.

[28]*Ibid.*, p. 306.

[29]Christophe, *Danton*, p. 429.

[30]Loomis, *Paris in the Terror*, p. 308.

[31]Madelin, *French Revolution*, p. 367.

[32]Christophe, *Danton*, p. 433.

[33]*Ibid.*, p. 434.

[34]Loomis, *Paris in the Terror*, p. 311.

[35]Christopher Hibbert, *The Days of the French Revolution* (New York, 1980), p. 242.

[36]Loomis, *Paris in the Terror*, pp. 314-315.

[37]*Ibid.*, p. 315.

[38]*Ibid.*, p. 317.

[39]*Ibid.*, pp. 319-320.

IX.

Rally of the Martyrs
(April 6-July 17, 1793)

For nearly four months Paris, famous as the City of Light, stood in the heart of darkness.

"I saw Paris in those days of crime and mourning," Joseph Broz, then 19, later a member of the French Academy, recalled. "From the stupefied expression on people's faces you would have said that it was a city desolated by a plague. The laughter of a few cannibals alone interrupted the deadly silence."[1]

The death machine seemed to have acquired a life of its own. Robespierre used it, and controlled it if anyone did; members of the Committee of Public Safety and the Committee of General Security signed its decrees; Fouquier-Tinville pulled its levers; but all through these ghastly months they give the impression of serving it almost blindly, as though mesmerized by the daily downward swoop of the guillotine's great shining blade. At one nightmarish moment Fouquier-Tinville was crossing the New Bridge over the Seine in the evening when suddenly he reeled and stumbled, nearly falling into the river. "I am not well," he said to his companion. "Sometimes I imagine that I see the shadows of the dead following me."[2] Stanley Loomis, the most evocative historian of the Terror, says: "It is impossible to read of this period without the impression that one is here confronted with forces more powerful than those controlled by men."[3] The much more prosaic and restrained R. R. Palmer, in many respects an apologist for the Revolution, writing from no detectable Catholic or Christian perspective, says in a startling moment of truth: "Even reasonable men now succumbed to the contagion. A spirit was abroad which contemporary conservatives truly described as satanic."[4]

In the two months from Danton's execution to the passage of the law of 22 Prairial (June 10), which for the first time authorized executions by order of the Revolutionary Tribunal with no trial at all, more than five hundred men and women were guillotined in Paris alone—an average of ten a day. From June 10 until July 27, when the overthrow of Robespierre ended the Terror, 1,366 men and women were guillotined—an average of thirty a day. More than seven thousand others had already been condemned to death and were awaiting execution by July 27 in Paris alone—nearly a hundred thousand throughout the country. Though we have concentrated here on the executions in Paris, the guillotine was almost as active in many other cities throughout France. On July 27 three thousand prisoners were awaiting execution in Strasbourg, 1,500 at Toulouse, and one thousand in Arras. And there were no less than 300,000 additional officially designated "suspects" liable at any moment to arrest, indictment, and execution without trial under the law of 22 Prairial.[5]

Since by this time no active armed opposition to the Revolution remained in France except among a few scattered guerrilla bands in Brittany and in the Vendée, which had been reduced to a tiny fraction of their earlier strength, virtually all of these victims were seized when helpless and almost none had ever borne arms against the government.

It was time, indeed, for the rally of the martyrs; for only martyrdom can triumph over a tyranny like this. Their ranks were to be augmented by a decree of April 11 which made the giving of any hospitality, food, or shelter to a non-juring priest an offense punishable by death.

The next day was the next to last on earth for Jean-Baptiste Gobel, the sometime schismatic Archbishop of Paris who had renounced his priesthood in the "dechristianization" of November. Now he faced the guillotine, with shattering irony, as a Hébertist; but he died repentant, in the faith which was his by grace of baptism, confirmation, ordination, and the Eucharist. On April 12 he wrote to the old episcopal vicar Lothringer, one of the three clerics openly carrying out their duties in Paris who had refused to follow him in rejecting the priesthood:

> I am on the eve of my death; I send you my confession in writing. In a few days I will expiate, by the mercy of God, all my crimes and my scandals against His holy religion. In my heart I have always applauded your principles. Forgive me, dear abbé, if I have tempted you to error. I beg you not to refuse me the last help of your ministry, by coming to the gate of the Conciergerie, without compromising yourself, and, when I come out, giving me absolution from my sins,

without forgetting the first words, "from all the chains of excommunication" (*ab omni vinculo excommunicationis*). Farewell, my dear abbé; pray to God for my soul that it may find mercy before Him.[6]

Father Lothringer did as he was asked, at the risk of his life. Bishop Gobel rode to the guillotine April 13 in the same cart with Chaumette, the architect of "dechristianization," who shouted and raved in incoherent rage, while Gobel sat quietly, with lowered eyes, silent except for the constant murmur of his prayers for the dying. But before the guillotine he raised his head high and his voice rang out in one last cry: *"Vive Jesus Christ!"*[7]

It was Palm Sunday, eight days after Danton's execution. Both men had been given the absolution for the dying by priests at the roadside as they passed in the death carts.

On that same Palm Sunday the beautiful Lucile Desmoulins had been condemned to death for having tried to save her husband's life. Horace, the baby son born of her marriage to Camille, was left an orphan. Robespierre was Horace's godfather. The letter Lucile's distraught mother wrote to Robespierre speaks for all his victims:

> It is not enough for you to have murdered your best friend; you must have his wife's blood as well. Your monster Fouquier-Tinville has just ordered Lucile to be taken to the scaffold. In less than two hours' time she will be dead. If you aren't a human tiger, if Camille's blood hasn't driven you mad, if you are still able to remember the happy evenings you once spent before our fire fondling our Horace, spare an innocent victim. If not—then hurry and take us all, Horace, myself and my other daughter Adèle. Hurry and tear us apart with your claws that still drip with Camille's blood . . . hurry, hurry so that we can all sleep in the same grave.[8]

Lucile went to the guillotine in a cart behind the one that carried Gobel and Chaumette, with a cool courage that belied her reputation as a flighty, flirtatious girl. Dressed with "uncommon attention and taste," she mounted the steps to the guillotine unhesitatingly and "received the fatal blow without appearing to notice what the executioner was doing."[9]

On the night of the tocsin, August 10, 1792, when the climax of the French Revolution began, three women had spent the night in Danton's apartment, under his protection. Now two of them were dead; and so was Danton.

On April 15, in a major speech before the Convention, Saint-Just demanded still more severity:

It is necessary to avenge our fathers and to bury under
its debris that monarchy, immense sepulcher of so many en-
slaved, unhappy generations . . . You must therefore direct
your attention to the policing of the state and exercise a very
rigid censorship upon the enemies of the Revolution and
upon the public authorities. Encourage the judges to render
justice bravely, protect them, make them respected too, but if
they depart from your decrees, punish them severely.[10]

To this end, Saint-Just presented a bill in 18 articles, which the
Convention expanded to 26 and passed the next day. Nobles and for-
eigners were no longer to be allowed to live in Paris at all. As many as
possible of those accused of conspiracy anywhere in France should be
brought to Paris for trial by the Revolutionary Tribunal. Anyone who
complained about the Revolution, if he had no "definite occupation"
and was under sixty and reasonably healthy, was to be transported to
Guiana. A new commission was established "to draw up a body of civil
institutions for the conservation of morals and the spirit of liberty."[11]

On April 28 the guillotine took 32 victims, including the former
Marquise de Montbrun and her sister whose sole crime, other than
their aristocratic lineage, was having harbored five Ursuline nuns.
Early in May Princess Elizabeth, sister of Louis XVI and the only
surviving adult member of the royal family in captivity, was guillotined along with the famous scientist Lavoisier.

On May 6 Robespierre created a considerable sensation by an-
nouncing to the Committee of Public Safety that he had decided that
the French Republic should officially recognize the existence of God.

Not the God of the Catholic Faith. The priests were still regarded as inveterate enemies of the Revolution. Robespierre never
mentioned Christ at all. The God for whose existence he was demanding official government recognition was that comfortable deist abstraction that gave immortality to the soul but never intervened in
human affairs; his only title was "Supreme Being."

This declaration, the speech to the Convention on this subject
which followed the next day, and above all the extraordinary "festival
of the Supreme Being" which took place a month later, are all discussed by most historians, even Catholic historians, with a seriousness
which under all the circumstances they hardly seem to deserve. Whatever it was that Robespierre was talking about was very far removed
from the God of the martyrs of the Revolution and the God before
whom Danton and Gobel had abased themselves in repentance. It was
a "god" who seems to have borne a rather close resemblance to Maximilien Robespierre himself. At the "festival of the Supreme Being"
he hailed this god from an enormous pasteboard mountain which he

had run ahead of the formal procession to be assured of climbing first. From its summit, dressed in a robin's-egg blue coat and jonquil-colored breeches, he addressed an enormous throng through clouds of incense. In honor of the occasion, the guillotine was draped in velvet that day and did not strike off a single head.

The next day, before putting the guillotine back in action, they moved it from Revolution Square to the square where the Bastille had stood. The main reason for doing this was an unexpected problem which had developed: the animals which drew the death carts would no longer enter the square. The blood-saturated ground offended their noses and frightened them; an animal knows as well as a man what blood means and can smell it better. They would not set foot upon it; and all the decrees of the Committee of Public Safety would not change that.

During the week of May 11, a 66-year-old lady named Geneviève Goyon was guillotined along with two Dominican nuns she had sheltered, and with them three priests who had remained loyal to the Pope; Father Lartigue, former pastor of Fontenay-aux-Roses parish in Paris, was guillotined for his fidelity, as was Father Rougane of Auvergne the next day for the same reason. Nor were all the martyrs priests and religious and those who helped them. Pierre Mauclaire was a humble shopkeeper, a dealer in second-hand goods. He was arrested for speaking against the attempt to eliminate the practice of the Catholic Faith in Paris. From Luxembourg prison on May 15 he wrote:

> Is there not reason to say that we have been under open persecution for four years, beginning with the priests, by which a vast number of Christians have perished and are perishing every day? . . . How many innocent victims suffer in the prisons of this unhappy France, and await the end of these evils, secure in their conscience. They raise cries full of tears to their God, for Whom they suffer. . . . Convert us, Lord, in order that we return to You and do penance for so much heinous crime . . . Give us, by Your mercy, a very Christian king, in order to change the pitiable state of France, to raise up with zeal Your temples, Your altars, and the relics of Your saints, which have been profaned with such fury. Give us, Lord, holy priests in order to teach the true religion, in order to offer to God thrice holy the only Victim able to appease Your anger . . . Give peace to France.[12]

Pierre Mauclaire died by the guillotine May 24. In his last letter, written May 21, he declared his faith and his hope, his confidence that God would give him strength in sustaining before the Revolutionary judges his faith "which was established and cemented by the Blood of God and the blood of millions of martyrs."[13]

During these weeks, when the armed resistance against the Revolution in France had declined to mere scattered skirmishes, the war against the other European powers continued in the pattern begun with the day of strange battle at Valmy. The Austrian generals had already decided it was hopeless to try to regain Belgium from the Revolutionary government and army when on June 26, in the Battle of Fleurus, French rule over Belgium was confirmed by a complete military victory there. Even on the sea, Great Britain's own element, the Revolutionary navy mounted a sufficient challenge to require a maximum effort by the main British battle fleet under Admiral "Black Dick" Howe; and while the British prevailed in a five-day encounter ending June 1, a large French convoy with an essential cargo of wheat from America made port safely though it had been Howe's mission to prevent that from happening. There would be no foreign rescue from the Revolution—not, at least, for a long time.

On June 10 Georges Couthon, in the name of the Committee of Public Safety, presented to the Convention the law of 22 Prairial, which provided for the first time for ordering executions routinely without trial, immediately following indictment by the Revolutionary Tribunal. This law was Robespierre's idea; its purpose, he said, was to enable the Tribunal to complete action on every case and person before it in less than twenty-four hours. (He was catching up to the execution speed of "Strike-Hard" Maillard, guillotined as a Hébertist several months before.) Robespierre demanded passage of the new law by the Convention that very day. Although some members of the Committee of Public Safety later claimed that it had been introduced without consultation with them, at the time none of them challenged Couthon's presentation of it as a Committee measure. It was a mere "prejudice of the old regime," Couthon declared, that "evidence could not rightfully establish conviction without witnesses or written testimony."[14] This appalling legislation, a virtual blueprint for modern totalitarianism, deserves quotation at length:

> The revolutionary tribunal is instituted for the punishment of the enemies of the people. The enemies of the people are those who seek to destroy public liberty, either by force or by intrigue. The following shall be considered enemies of the people:
> Those who shall have promoted the re-establishment of royalty or have sought to discredit or dissolve the National Convention and the revolutionary and republican government, whose nucleus it is;

Those who shall have betrayed the Republic while in command of fortresses and armies, or while fulfilling any other military function, who shall have held communication with the enemies of the Republic, or who shall have sought to bring about a shortage of supplies or men;

Those who shall have sought to prevent the provisioning of Paris, or cause famine in the Republic;

Those who shall have seconded the projects of France's enemies by concealing and sheltering conspirators and aristocrats, by persecuting and slandering the patriots, by corrupting the representatives of the people, or by abusing the principles of the Revolution, the law, and the government through false and perfidious applications;

Those who shall have deceived the people or the representatives of the people to induce them to actions contrary to the interests of liberty;

Those who shall have sought to spread discouragement in order to forward the enterprises of the tyrants leagued against the Republic;

Those who shall have disseminated false news in order to divide and trouble the people;

Those who shall have sought to mislead public opinion, prevent the enlightenment of the people, deprave morals, corrupt the national conscience, and impair the strength and purity of the revolutionary and republican principles, or arrest their progress, either by insidious, counter-revolutionary writings, or some other machination;

Those who compromise the safety of the Republic by dishonest contracts and squanderings of the public wealth, other than those comprised in the provisions of the law of the 7th Frimaire;

Those who, being charged with public functions, abuse them to aid the enemies of the Revolution, annoy the patriots, and oppress the people;

And finally, all those who are designated in previous laws relative to the punishment of conspirators and counter-revolutionists, and who by any means or under any guise shall have made attacks against the liberty, unity, or safety of the Republic, or sought to hinder their advancement.

The penalty for all crimes whose investigation appertains to the Revolutionary Tribunal is death. The proof necessary to condemn the enemies of the people is any kind of document, material, moral, verbal, or written, which would naturally influence any just and reasonable mind.[15]

Well might Convention delegate Ruamps, hearing this language read, cry: "If this law passes I may as well blow out my brains at once! I ask for an adjournment." But Robespierre replied, in his thin cold voice: "For a long time the Convention has been debating and voting decrees, because for a long time it has been ruled entirely by the power of factions. I propose that the Convention shall not notice the motion for adjournment and shall continue, if necessary, to discuss the proposal submitted to it till eight o'clock tonight!"[16] The Convention did attempt, feebly, at least to exempt its own members from the operation of the law. But Robespierre would not have it; cowed, terrified, they succumbed. The law was passed that very day, just as he had demanded. The next day the Convention reaffirmed that it must approve the arrest of any of its members, though once arrested any member could still be executed without trial under the law passed the previous day. The distinction was not at the time significant, due to Robespierre's almost absolute domination of the Convention.

He was also in full control of the Paris Commune, that engine of revolution; but the fact that harsh disputes began to break out in the Committee of Public Safety almost immediately after the passage of the law of 22 Prairial suggests that it may have been true that most of its members were not consulted in advance about that law. Also, on June 6 Robespierre had been taken entirely by surprise by the election of Joseph Fouché as president of the Paris Jacobin Club. Fouché had gained the fierce enmity of the Jacobins in Lyons when he had been one of the leaders of the Terror there, but had not wished to share power with them; on April 6, the day after Danton's execution, he had arrived in Paris on Robespierre's summons to find the capital city firmly in Robespierre's grip.

Joseph Fouché, descendant of a long line of Breton seamen, was of all the men drawn up from the deeps by the tornado of the Revolution probably the most devious, the most indestructible, and the most completely amoral. The man followed no star, not even his own. He knew no cause or principle greater than himself; but neither was he ambitious as Napoleon was. His goals were ancient and basic: power, money, and survival with both. He recognized no moral limitations whatsoever on how he secured them. They were not easy to attain and keep during the French Revolution. He attained and kept them.

This revolutionary who had voted the death of his king and ordered the massacre of thousands at Lyons held high office in six different regimes in France in direct succession, each one of which he helped to build up and then helped to destroy at substantial profit to himself. He died in his bed, as the Duke of Otranto, honored counsellor to Louis XVIII. His cynicism corroded everything and everyone it touched; "I know men well," he said, "and am quite familiar with the base passions that motivate them."[17] When Napoleon had the Duke d'Enghien, prominent young member of the royal family (the only son of the last prince of Bourbon-Condé) treacherously seized and shot, to a storm of criticism throughout Europe, Fouché (then Napoleon's chief of police) commented: "It was worse than a crime; it was a blun-

der." When the French Revolution and Napoleon were at last defeated
and the monarchy restored, and Fouché was reminded by Louis XVIII
of his vote to execute his brother, he responded: "It was the first service I was able to render Your Majesty."[18] This reply reduced Louis
XVIII to silence; there was just enough truth in it to cut the moral
ground out from under him.

As Stanley Loomis well says: "Fouché was to survive all the men
of the Revolution, as he survived most of those of the Directory and
of the Consulate. One did not cross swords lightly with Joseph Fouché.
Robespierre did not live to profit from this lesson, which others who
followed him were to learn to their cost."[19]

The adroit maneuver by which he had himself elected president
of the Paris Jacobin Club, where Robespierre had long taken his control for granted, was the first step in Fouché's campaign to save himself from the guillotine for which he was quite sure that Robespierre
had destined him. Fouché had known Robespierre in Arras when for
a time he had acted as administrator of the Oratorian seminary at that
town; in fact, he had jilted Robespierre's sister Charlotte, proposing
marriage to her and then breaking the engagement. There was never
any love lost between the two men. Fouché had underestimated Robespierre at first, as many people did (including Danton); but he had
learned better very quickly.

The day after the passage of the law of 22 Prairial Robespierre
appeared before the Paris Jacobin Club to denounce Fouché. However, as president of the Club, Fouché had the authority to close debate. He exercised it and departed. The Club met again the next
evening, but Fouché was not there. Robespierre had him summoned.
He responded by letter, requesting the Club to withhold action on
Robespierre's complaint against him until he had responded in writing.
Robespierre then declared him to be "the ringleader of a conspiracy"
and, in his own unique style, demanded his head:

> Is this man afraid that his terrible face will reveal his
> crimes? That, fixed on him, our eyes will read his soul and
> will uncover the thoughts which it is in his nature to con-
> ceal? Is this man afraid that hesitations and contradictions in
> his speech will unmask his guilt? A man who cannot look his
> fellow citizen in the eye is guilty! I demand that Fouché be
> called to judgment here![20]

The hooded eyes of the cobra were upon another victim, and the
venom was ready. But Joseph Fouché was like the mongoose who
preys on the cobra, quick enough to leap aside when it strikes, and always ready to attack from an unexpected direction. He was the last

person whom anyone would call a knight in shining armor. But Maximilien Robespierre, master of the guillotine, had gone down into the world of men like Joseph Fouché. Justice does not always come from above, with sword held high. It may come from below, like a tentacle reaching up from quicksand.

So, as the rally of the martyrs went forward upon the high ground of the spirit, Joseph Fouché began his campaign underground against the lord of the Terror.

On June 29 Father Vaurs, a non-juring priest discovered in Paris, was martyred by the guillotine along with eighteen others including Nottaire, an old cook for the archdiocese of Paris who had fed fugitive priests in his rooms, and a twenty-year-old girl, Catherine Doublot of Besançon, who was discovered to have among her possessions about a dozen representations of the Sacred Heart of Jesus. Because the Sacred Heart had been so widely used by the Vendeans, Fouquier-Tinville considered any and every Sacred Heart sign to be proof in itself of involvement in anti-revolutionary activities. Early in July Father Férey, who had taken the oath to the "constitutional" church and even participated in the "festival of the Supreme Being," publicly announced his repentance, knowing that it meant death. "May my death be an expiation!" he cried. "I shall end in affirming my inviolable attachment to the Catholic, apostolic, and Roman religion."[21]

On July 7 no less than 59 victims were sent to the guillotine, among them an eighty-year-old retired priest of aristocratic descent, Jean-Baptiste Auguste de Salignac Fénelon. While in Luxembourg prison he had made it his mission to persuade those in the prison who had lost or abandoned the Faith to come back to it, and had succeeded with many. He welcomed martyrdom; "What joy," he said, "to die for having done my duty!" On his way to the guillotine children whom he had helped followed him, crying. "Do not cry, my children," he said. "It is God's will. Pray for me."[22] He urged the others in his death cart to join him in offering their lives for God, giving absolution to those who responded. No reason for his execution appears in the records of the Revolutionary government; he was simply one of 159 prisoners at the Luxembourg condemned as a group for plotting an imaginary prison riot, whose death warrant en masse was casually signed one day by Saint-Just. Eleven other priests were included in this group, all of whom were executed during this week.

On July 9 a layman, Simon-Jude Masse, was executed simply for having attended a Mass said by a non-juring priest. On July 13 some National Guardsmen, on orders of the Surveillance Committee of the local Section of the Paris Commune, burst into the house of Madame

Bergeron on La Barillerie Street, where they found a Mass by a non-juring priest actually in progress. The priest, Madame Bergeron, and several of her household were arrested and taken to La Force prison, where they were awaiting execution under the law of 22 Prairial when the Terror came to an end July 27.

In the Great Persecution of Diocletian in ancient Rome, several of the most celebrated martyrs were young girls about twelve years of age. The Terror produced their equal in a girl of that age named Jeanne-Julie Champy, who was saved from death only by the abrupt ending of the Terror. She worked with her aunt in a house where a non-juring priest, Father Cirriez, who held title to it under the name of Duché, frequently said Mass. Discovered and questioned July 15 by commissioners of the local Section of the Paris Commune, Jeanne-Julie defied them with limpid honesty and shining courage:

> "How do you know the man named Cirriez?"
> "I know him through my work.... I am not obliged to say what I do and what I do not do, in going to his house as I go to others."
> "What did you mean by saying that innocents have died by the Revolution?"
> "I have always thought so; many innocents have been unjustly condemned; in the past, more precautions were taken before condemning a man to death. ... That is my view."
> "Have you been at Mass many times at the house of the man named Cirriez? Who else came there?"
> "I cannot give an account of that, since I came there to work.... In any case, I have no account to render to you."
> "What day do you choose for rest, the old Sunday or the *décadi?*"
> "I hold to the religion my father and my mother taught me; I hold to the feast days and Sundays, and I will not change."
> "Do you like the present government?"
> "Not well.... Not by any means!"
> "Why don't you like the present government?"
> "Because it is not just."[23]

Contemplative religious communities had been among the first targets of the fury of the French Revolution against the Catholic Church. Less than a year from May 1789 when the Revolution began with the meeting of the Estates-General, these communities had been required by law to disband. But many of them continued in being, in hiding. Among these were the community of the Carmelite nuns of Compiègne, in northeastern France not far from Paris—the fifty-third convent in France of the Carmelite sisters who followed the reform of

St. Teresa of Avila, founded in 1641, noted throughout its history for fidelity and fervor. Their convent was raided in August 1790, all the property of the sisters was seized by the government, and they were forced to discard their habits and leave their house. They divided into four groups which found lodging in four different houses all near the same church in Compiègne, and for several years they were to a large extent able to continue their religious life in secret. But the intensified surveillance and searches of the "Great Terror" revealed their secret, and in June 1794 most of them were arrested and imprisoned.

They had expected this; indeed, they had prayed for it. At some time during the summer of 1792, very likely just after the events of August 10 of that year that marked the descent into the true deeps of the Revolution, their prioress, Madeleine Lidoine, whose name in religion was Teresa in honor of the founder of their order, by all accounts a charming, perceptive, and highly intelligent woman, had foreseen much of what was to come. She had said to her sisters: "Having meditated much on this subject, I have thought of making an act of consecration by which the Community would offer itself as a sacrifice to appease the anger of God, so that the divine peace of His Dear Son would be brought into the world, returned to the Church and the state."[24] The sisters discussed her proposal and all agreed to it but the two oldest, who were hesitant. But when the news of the September massacres came, mingling glorious martyrdom with apostasy, these two sisters made their choice, joining their commitment to that of the rest of the community. All made their offering; it was to be accepted.

After their lodgings were invaded again in June, their devotional objects shattered and their tabernacle trampled underfoot by a Revolutionary who told them that their place of worship should be transformed into a dog kennel, the Carmelite sisters were taken to the Conciergerie prison, where so many of the leading victims of the guillotine had been held during their last days on earth. There they composed a canticle for their martyrdom, to be sung to the familiar tune of the Marseillaise. The original still exists, written in pencil and given to one of their fellow prisoners, a lay woman who survived.

> Give over our hearts to joy,
> The day of glory has arrived,
> Far from us all weakness,
> Seeing the standard come;
> We prepare for the victory,
> We all march to the true conquest,
> Under the flag of the dying God
> We run, we all seek the glory;
> Rekindle our ardor,
> Our bodies are the Lord's,

We climb, we climb the scaffold
And give ourselves back to the Victor.

O happiness ever desired
For Catholics of France,
To follow the wondrous road
Already marked out so often
By the martyrs toward their suffering,
After Jesus, with the King,
We show our faith to Christians,
We adore a God of justice;
As the fervent priest,
The constant faithful,
Seal, seal with all their blood
Faith in the dying God....

Holy Virgin, our model,
August queen of martyrs,
Deign to strengthen our zeal
And purify our desires,
Protect France even yet,
Help us mount to Heaven,
Make us feel even in these places,
The effects of your power.
Sustain your children,
Submissive, obedient,
Dying, dying with Jesus
And in our King believing.[25]

On July 17 the sixteen sisters were brought before Fouquier-
Tinville. All cases were now being disposed of within twenty-four
hours as Robespierre had wished; theirs was no exception. They were
charged with having received arms for the émigrés; their prioress, Sister Teresa, answered by holding up a crucifix. "Here are the only arms
that we have ever had in our house." They were charged with possess-
ing an altar-cloth with designs honoring the old monarchy (perhaps
the fleur-de-lis) and were asked to deny any attachment to the royal
family. Sister Teresa responded: "If that is a crime, we are all guilty of
it; you can never tear out of our hearts the attachment for Louis XVI
and his family. Your laws cannot prohibit feeling; they cannot extend
their empire to the affections of the soul; God alone has the right to
judge them." They were charged with corresponding with priests
forced to leave the country because they would not take the constitutional oath; they freely admitted this. Finally they were charged with
the catchall indictment by which any serious Catholic in France could
be guillotined during the Terror: "fanaticism." Sister Henriette, who
had been Gabrielle de Croissy, challenged Fouquier-Tinville to his
face: "Citizen, it is your duty to respond to the request of one con-

demned; I call upon you to answer us and to tell us just what you mean by the word 'fanatic.'" "I mean," snapped the Public Prosecutor of the Terror, "your attachment to your childish beliefs and your silly religious practices." "Let us rejoice, my dear Mother and Sisters, in the joy of the Lord," said Sister Henriette, "that we shall die for our holy religion, our faith, our confidence in the Holy Roman Catholic Church.[26]

That same day they went to the guillotine. The journey in the carts took more than an hour. All the way the Carmelite sisters sang: the "Miserere," "Salva Regina," and "Te Deum." Beholding them, a total silence fell on the raucous, brutal crowd, most of them cheapened and hardened by day after day of the spectacle of public slaughter. At the foot of the towering killing machine, their eyes raised to Heaven, the sisters sang "Veni Creator Spiritus." One by one, they renewed their religious vows. They pardoned their executioners. One observer cried out: "Look at them and see if they do not have the air of angels! By my faith, if these women did not all go straight to Paradise, then no one is there!"[27]

Sister Teresa, their prioress, requested and obtained permission to go last under the knife. The youngest, Sister Constance, went first. She climbed the steps of the guillotine "with the air of a queen going to receive her crown," singing *Laudate Dominum omnes gentes,* "all peoples praise the Lord." She placed her head in the position for death without allowing the executioner to touch her. Each sister followed her example, those remaining singing likewise with each, until only the prioress was left, holding in her hand a small figure of the Blessed Virgin Mary. The killing of each martyr required about two minutes. It was about eight o'clock in the evening, still bright at midsummer. During the whole time the profound silence of the crowd about the guillotine endured unbroken.

Two years before when the horror began, the Carmelite community at Compiègne had offered itself as a holocaust, that peace might be restored to France and the Church. The return of full peace was still twenty-one years in the future. But the Reign of Terror had only ten days left to run. Years of war, oppression and persecution were yet to come, but the mass official killing in the public squares of Paris was about to end. The Cross had vanquished the guillotine.

NOTES

[1]Stanley Loomis, *Paris in the Terror* (Philadelphia, 1964), p. 331.

[2]*Ibid.,* pp. 328-329.

[3]*Ibid.,* p. 328.

[4]R. R. Palmer, *Twelve Who Ruled; the Year of the Terror in the French Revolution* (Princeton, 1941, 1969), p. 316.

[5]*Ibid.,* p. 305; J. M. Thompson, *The French Revolution* (New York, 1945), p. 538; Loomis, *Paris in the Terror,* p. 328; Louis Madelin, *The French Revolution* (New York, 1925), p. 406.

[6]Jacques Hérissay, *La Vie religieuse à Paris sous la Terreur (1792-1794)* (Paris, 1952), p. 242. Translation by the writer.

[7]Madelin, *French Revolution,* p. 404.

[8]Loomis, *Paris in the Terror,* p. 327.

[9]Christopher Hibbert, *The Days of the French Revolution* (New York, 1980), p. 245.

[10]Eugene N. Curtis, *Saint-Just, Colleague of Robespierre* (New York, 1935, 1973), p. 228.

[11]*Ibid.,* p. 229.

[12]Hérissay, *La Vie religieuse à Paris sous la Terreur,* p. 251. Translation by the writer.

[13]*Ibid.,* p. 252.

[14]Palmer, *Twelve Who Ruled,* p. 365.

[15]E. L. Higgins, ed., *The French Revolution as Told by Contemporaries* (Boston, 1938), pp. 350-351.

[16]Madelin, *French Revolution,* pp. 409-410.

[17]Loomis, *Paris in the Terror,* p. 356.

[18]*Ibid.,* p. 359.

[19]*Ibid.,* p. 357.

[20]*Ibid.,* p. 375.

[21]Pierre de la Gorce, *Histoire religieuse de la Révolution* (Paris, 1912-23), III, 528. Translation by the writer.

[22]*Ibid.,* III, 529.

[23]Hérissay, *La Vie religieuse à Paris sous la Terreur,* pp. 278-279. Translation by the writer.

[24]Bruno de Jesus-Marie, *Le sang du Carmel; ou la véritable passion des seize Carmélites de Compiègne* (Paris, 1954), p. 28. Translation by the writer.

[25]*Ibid.,* pp. 418-419. Translation by the writer.

[26]*Ibid.,* pp. 468-470. Translation by the writer.

[27]*Ibid.,* p. 476.

X.

The End of the Terror
(July 18-28, 1794)

That summer was the hottest in Paris in living memory. Day after blazing day the guillotine took its victims: now fifty, now sixty, sometimes as many as eighty. After the passage of the law of 22 Prairial, which authorized denial of all defense to the accused, less and less attention was paid to the most elementary requirements of truth and accuracy in the proceedings of the Revolutionary Tribunal, such as proper identification of the victims. The wife of grand old Marshal de Mouchy, past eighty years old and senile, was brought before the Tribunal with her husband. During the hearing it was discovered that a clerk had made a mistake and that she had never been legally arrested. Fouquier-Tinville was undisturbed. He proceeded with the hearing; Madame de Mouchy was convicted and guillotined with her husband regardless. The famous poet André Chenier was confused with his brother, and guillotined by mistake two days before the end of the Terror. Two women named Biron were being held in the Conciergerie. One day the order went out to bring "the Biron woman" to that day's hearing (the only trial the victims now had). When his clerks asked Fouquier-Tinville which Biron woman he wanted, he told them they might as well take both. A woman of the aristocracy, Madame de Maille, was condemned to death; the prison guards thought a woman with the similar-sounding name of Mayet was she, and put Madame Mayet into a death cart to be taken to the guillotine. Someone got word of the mistake to Fouquier-Tinville. "Since she's here, we might as well take her," was his reply.[1]

The Convention was paralyzed by fear; it was as though its members were all hypnotized. The familiar mannerism of Robe-

spierre, coming into their meeting hall in the Tuileries with his ob-
scuring glasses covering his eyes and then raising them periodically to
his brow to fix his cold green stare on some particular deputy, chilled
their blood; for whomever he looked at in this way might be the next
victim. One of the delegates, in a moment of abstraction, suddenly
started as he found Robespierre's gaze fastened on him, and blurted
out to those standing nearby: "He'll be supposing I was thinking about
something!"[2]

On June 12, two days after passage of the law of 22 Prairial,
Robespierre had issued his maximum denunciation of Joseph Fouché
to the Paris Jacobin Club. Fouché had immediately been expelled
from the Club and marked for the guillotine. But he had not attended
that meeting, and had disappeared at once, like a weasel into a bur-
row.

Now a hidden, hunted fugitive like so many of the Revolution's
victims before him, Joseph Fouché—himself a Revolutionary and a
Terrorist—was brought by his desperate situation to the summit of his
powers. Unlike the earlier Girondin fugitives, he had no illusions to
lose, no sense of humiliation to endure, no false pride to shed. It took
him only a moment to strip down to fighting trim. None was better
than he at manipulating men. And evil as he was, Joseph Fouché had
one great virtue, and one human quality that is rightly admired. He
was a loving husband and father; he would not abandon his wife and
children to the fate of Lucile and Horace Desmoulins. And with his
life on the block, he displayed a cold nerveless unwavering courage
that did not shrink from combat with the lord of the Terror and the
"Angel of Death."

If a Christian had written the script for the ending of the Revolutionary Terror, he would undoubtedly have had it brought about by
a great Christian hero, a Cathelineau or a Larochejaquelein or a Hernan Cortes—never by a Joseph Fouché. But God "writes straight with
crooked lines." The Christian will believe with confidence that in the
realm of ultimate causation the ending of the Terror owed much to
the prayers of the martyrs, perhaps especially to the prayers of the
Carmelite nuns of Compiègne; but the immediate effective agent was
one of the Terror's own men. Those who had ruled the Terror died by
it; and it was just.

For the next six weeks after Robespierre denounced him,
Fouché was constantly on the move. He never slept in the same place
for two nights in succession. He rarely slept much at night in any case.
Night was his chosen time for action, when few were likely to recognize him in the ill-lit streets, and his targets—the Convention dele-

gates—were generally at their lodgings. He knew most of them, and they knew him. He rarely made appointments. Like a ghost he would come knocking unannounced at their doors, in mid-evening or late evening, when the lingering sultry heat made it difficult to sleep. For all of them he had a message; for all of them it was the same.

"Robespierre is preparing another proscription. You are on the list."[3]

Robespierre was indeed preparing another proscription—another list of victims. He always was. He ruled by periodically killing some of those who might rise against him and thereby terrorizing the rest into silence and paralysis of the will. But if all or most were already on his list, then they had nothing left to lose; like cornered rats, at last they would stand and fight. And this was what Fouché intended that they should do.

Robespierre was no fool. He was probably as able a man as Fouché. In less than a month he discovered what Fouché was doing, though still unable to catch up with him. He warned the Paris Jacobin Club on July 9:

> Someone is trying to persuade each member that he has been proscribed by the Committee of Public Safety. He wants to terrorize the Convention. I urge all members to be wary of the insidious remarks of certain people who, fearing for their lives, want others to share their fear.[4]

But Robespierre's fatal flaw was that of all the great tyrants: pride. Knowing what Fouché was doing, he disdained it. He was so confident in the firmness and in the techniques of his rule that he simply assumed Fouché's tactics would not work. He would prepare a great speech denouncing the plots against him, and would promise no one immunity from the guillotine. After all, those he was willing to spare today he might wish to kill tomorrow.

Robespierre's confidence was by no means totally misplaced. As we shall see, his overthrow on the 9th and 10th of Thermidor (July 27 and 28) was, like Wellington's victory over Napoleon at Waterloo, "a very near-run thing."

After Robespierre signalled his knowledge of Fouché's methods and objective in his July 9 speech to the Paris Jacobin Club, Fouché—far from being frightened into desisting—increased the tempo and boldness of his activities. One day Robespierre's spies reported him actually conferring with four Convention deputies in the very corridors outside their meeting hall. He knew of the dissensions and fears within the Committee of Public Safety itself, and worked to promote them. His old associate at Lyons, Collot d'Herbois, was one of his most valuable contacts on the Committee, along with Billaud-Varenne. There were no more blood-stained Terrorists than these maestros of mass slaughter at Lyons in December 1793 and of the massacres of the prisoners in Paris in September 1792, respectively—former Hébertists whom the Committee of Public Safety had co-opted in September 1793 to split that movement and save Robespierre's leadership. But now Collot and Billaud feared for their own heads, and with reason; Robespierre was most likely to move against his opponents within the ruling Committee first, and they had been openly at odds with him since he proclaimed the cult of the Supreme Being, which they saw as a major step toward consolidating his personal dictatorship. On June 29 there had been a violent quarrel in the Committee between Collot and Billaud on the one hand, and Robespierre and Saint-Just on the other; after that Robespierre absented himself from all meetings of the Committee (which were held almost daily) until July 22—meanwhile continuing to direct the Terror through the Police Bureau, which he had established under his personal control immediately after the execution of Danton. So Fouché did not have to work hard to convince Collot and Billaud of their danger, only to put heart in them to resist. That was not easy, for both men were little more than blustering cowards. At the last moment he learned that they were considering a reconciliation with Robespierre by which they would support him in executing more "Hébertists and Dantonists" next, rather than them.

"And when you have let Robespierre have our heads," Fouché reminded them coldly, "who will remain to protect yours? Our corpses will only nourish Robespierre's arrogance and ambition, and when we are gone he will strike you down with the weapon you have lent him."[5]

Apparently beginning almost immediately after the joint meetings of the Committee of Public Safety and the Committee of General Security on July 22 and 23, which he attended and where he seemed to make a reconciliation with the other Committee members, Robespierre began work on a major address to the Convention. It was delivered shortly before noon on July 26, the 8th of Thermidor (the "hot month") in the Revolutionary calendar. He consulted no one in the preparation of this speech, not even his closest and most trusted associates, Saint-Just and Couthon, also members of the Committee of Public Safety. He was up all night putting the finishing touches on it. He came to the Convention wearing the sky-blue coat and the jonquil-colored breeches that he had worn while presiding at the festival of the Supreme Being. His face was drawn from strain and lack of sleep, but his manner displayed no weakness; on the contrary, it was full of indefinable menace. Before he began to speak, he raised his glasses to his forehead and for long, palpitating minutes scanned the hall and the frightened men in it with his pale green glittering eyes.

He spoke for two hours. The speech ranged from the edge of megalomania to sinister threats.

> They say I am a tyrant. Rather I am a slave. I am a slave of Liberty, a living martyr to the republic. I am the victim as well as the enemy of crime. I confess to you that I am sometimes afraid that my name will be blackened in the eyes of posterity by the impure tongues of perverted men. ... I have promised to leave a redoubtable testimony to the oppressors of the People. I shall leave them the terrible truth—and Death![6]
>
> Without the revolutionary government the Republic cannot be made stronger. If it is destroyed now, freedom will be no more tomorrow. At the point at which we are now, if we stop prematurely, we die. We have not been too severe. They talk about our rigorousness, and the fatherland reproaches us for our weakness. ... There exists in your midst a swarm of rascals who are fighting against public virtue. Remember that your enemies want to sacrifice you to this fistful of rogues.[7]
>
> Let us admit the existence of a plot against public liberty; that it owes its strength to a criminal coalition which carries on its intrigues in the very bosom of the Convention; that members of the Committee are sharing in this plot; that the coalition thus formed is seeking the ruin of patriots and country too. What is the remedy for this disease? To punish the traitors, renew the composition of the Committee of General Security, purify that Committee, and subordinate it to the Committee of Public Safety; purify the Committee of Public Safety itself; constitute a united government under the supreme authority of the Convention; thus crush all factions by the weight of the national authority, and raise the power of justice and liberty on their ruins.[8]

But who was numbered and to be named among the "swarm of rascals" and the "fistful of rogues"? Who was to be charged with being part of the "criminal coalition which carries on its intrigues in the very bosom of the Convention"? What members of the Committee of General Security would go to the guillotine to "purify" that body? What members of the ruling Committee of Public Safety would be likewise disposed of? This was surely the new proscription, that everyone had been fearing; these were the charges that would be brought against all whose names were on the "list" of which Fouché had so often spoken, assuring each man to whom he spoke that that man's name was on it.

By giving a list at that moment—any list—Robespierre would probably have saved his life and maintained the Terror; for the essence of the Terror's success, of the ability of one man without a strong armed force behind him to kill so many, lay in the biting phrase long afterward applied by Winston Churchill to the appeasers of Nazi German totalitarianism: "Everyone thinks that if he is the one to feed the crocodile, the crocodile *will eat him last.*" But Robespierre gave no list. He mentioned only one name: that of the financier Cambon.

He could not have made a greater mistake, playing directly into Fouché's hands. To have given a list that would have sounded complete for the moment would have served his purposes best. He might have been able to get away temporarily with giving no list at all. But by mentioning one name only, sentencing that man in effect to death, when everybody in the Convention was sure that he had marked more than one man for death, he gave that one man every reason to fight, and most of the others every reason to follow him.

Still the ingrained habit of submission, that most squalid shield of tyranny, almost saved him. The galleries, packed as usual with Jacobins, applauded. Constrained by habit and fear, the members of the Convention joined in the applause. A motion that the speech be printed was carried by voice vote. Couthon then moved that the printed copies be distributed to the governments of the local departments.

In the back of the hall, among the seats of the "Mountain," rose Bourdon de l'Oise. Known as an ardent revolutionary, he had been among the leaders of the action on August 10, 1792, when the Terror began. But he had been a good friend of Danton; he knew Robespierre hated him; Fouché had assured him that his name was on "the list." Perhaps it seemed to him that he heard the booming voice of his dead leader in his last moments before the Revolutionary Tribunal: "Vile Robespierre! The scaffold claims you too! *You will follow me!*"[9]

"I am opposed to the printing of this speech!" Bourdon cried. "There are many grave accusations in it that ought to be clarified."

It broke the spell, and gave courage to Cambon standing in the shadow of death. He leaped to his feet and charged the rostrum where Robespierre still stood.

"Before I am dishonored," he screamed, "I will speak to France! ... Everyone here should know the truth. One man paralyzes the will of the National Convention. *That man is Robespierre!*"

The great hall seemed to explode with shouting. Billaud-Varenne rushed to the rostrum: "The mask must be torn away!" Panis followed him: "Robespierre has drawn up a list and my name is said to be on it!" Like an amplified echo the cries came back: "The list! The list! Name those whom you have accused! Name them! Name them!" And finally someone named a name of his own: "Fouché? What about Fouché?"[10]

It was the fruit of all those nights Joseph Fouché had spent roaming the streets of Paris, knocking on the doors of the deputies and telling each one that he was on the death list.

Robespierre was caught totally by surprise, but was not as alarmed as he should have been. He was confident that he still held firmly to the reins of power. The next day Saint-Just would speak in his support. "Fine weather for tomorrow!" Robespierre said jauntily, as he made his way to the Jacobin Club for their regular meeting that evening.

When Collot d'Herbois and Billaud-Varenne arrived at the Jacobin Club, it was immediately made very clear to them that, whoever else might or might not be on Robespierre's list, they were. They were actually assaulted with shouts of "To the guillotine!" Billaud took to his heels just in time; Collot was caught, knocked down, and his clothes were torn before he managed to join his fellow Terrorist in ignominious flight.

It now occurred to Robespierre that he might need a somewhat more organized and larger armed force for the morrow than a gang of wild-eyed Jacobins pulling people's clothes off. Totally unmilitary as he was, he may actually have found some reassurance in the presence of the commander of the National Guard of Paris and his promise of support with troops and cannon.

François Hanriot, that most unique of generals, was ready, after the lapse of more than a year, to go into action again.

Meanwhile, in the famous green room of the Committee of Public Safety, Saint-Just had been at work since eight o'clock in the evening on the speech he was to deliver to the Convention the following day, which almost everyone assumed would be a detailed indictment of the men Robespierre intended to kill next. (In fact this speech, though it harshly attacked Collot and Billaud, did not mention anyone else by name; the rest of it was much the same kind of vague generalized menace that had characterized Robespierre's speech.) At about eleven o'clock his two targets came bursting into the room, considerably the worse for wear. We may imagine Billaud panting from his long run, Collot perhaps with a black eye and torn shreds of cloth hanging from his back.

Saint-Just raised his handsome head, which some said he carried as though it were a holy object.

"What's new at the Jacobin Club?" he asked.

"You dare ask us what's new! You!" Collot screamed. "You're the one who would know that! You, who with Robespierre and Couthon, are planning to kill us! You are here to spy on us and to denounce us to your colleagues. You have been drawing up an accusation against us!"

"You are not entirely wrong," Saint-Just replied malevolently.

Collot seized him by the throat.

"Show us the report! You are not going to leave here until you've shown us your report!"[11]

Carnot, always calm, separated the two men, and Saint-Just promised to show them the report before he delivered it.

All night Saint-Just worked on his speech. All night Collot, Billaud, Carnot and Barère of the Committee of Public Safety talked, argued, and perhaps plotted together. It is hard to imagine that they all spent the night together in the green room, though some accounts suggest it; more likely Saint-Just and his targets were in adjoining rooms. And all night Fouché was hard at work putting the finishing touches on his coalition, laying plans for action in the Convention session beginning the next morning, knowing that the following day or two would in all probability see either him or Robespierre dead.

Meanwhile, on the day just done, July 26, 1794, just short of two years from the violent overthrow of the King and the constitution of France on August 10, 1792, fifty-five persons had been guillotined, nineteen of them women, and two of them priests. One was Father Brongniard, the courageous priest who had said Masses all day at the parish of St. Nicolas-de-Chardonnet on the last Sunday before all the churches in Paris were closed.[12]

Dawn came dark red, with thickening clouds and damp blanketing heat. The day advanced with mutters of thunder. By seven o'clock the Convention galleries were already filling up—for once, not only with Jacobins. There were also remnant Hébertists who had come to defend their old leaders Collot d'Herbois and Billaud-Varenne, and old Cordeliers who had come to support the surviving friends of Danton.

The Convention was scheduled to meet as usual at eleven o'clock. Within minutes of the hour a note from Saint-Just was delivered to the Committee of Public Safety in the green room. "You have blighted my heart," the note declared sanctimoniously. "I have decided

therefore to trample my cowardly promises underfoot and open my
heart directly to the Convention."[13] By this Saint-Just meant that he
was not going to let members of the Committee see his speech ahead
of time, despite his promise of the previous night after Collot had attacked him.

An immense crowd had already gathered in the Tuileries, here
at the end as at the beginning of its central events, the main stage in
the grand drama of the French Revolution. The Convention continued to meet in what had been the theater of the palace. The deputies
were still divided into the Right (actually now on the left, and very
thinly populated), the Center (the "Plain" or "Marsh"), and the Left,
or the Mountain. The hideous features of Jean-Paul Marat, whom
Charlotte Corday had sent to the Judgment, leered down upon them
from a large portrait behind and to the right of the president's chair,
which stood above the narrow speaker's rostrum and the wide secretary's table facing it. The presiding officer this day (whether by acci-
dent or by design) was none other than Collot d'Herbois.

Robespierre, Saint-Just, and Couthon arrived in the hall shortly
before noon, followed a few minutes later by Collot and those who
had spent the night with him at the Committee of Public Safety. The
Jacobins greeted their leaders with thunderous applause. The crippled
Couthon, who had lost the use of his legs to a mysterious disease two
years before, moved slowly on his crutches to his seat. Robespierre was
again wearing his Supreme Being outfit—the sky-blue coat and the
jonquil-colored breeches. He took his seat with the Center, directly in
front of the rostrum. Saint-Just wore a brown chamois coat, pearl-gray
breeches, and the immaculate, elaborately ruffled white vest with
stock and scarf that had become his uniform and symbol in major public appearances. He went immediately to the rostrum to give the
speech on which he had worked all night. It was almost exactly noon.
Outside the thunder growled ominously. The contending parties of the
Revolution took their position. Now was the "moment of truth."

Saint-Just began to speak.

"I belong to no faction; I have fought them all. . . . The course of
events has indicated that this rostrum may be the Tarpeian Rock for
the man who . . ."[14]

Then Jean Tallien leaped from his seat, shouting, "Point of order! I demand to be heard!" A lawyer's clerk, born in Paris, son of a
servant of the Marquis de Berry, he had become a Revolutionary
journalist and was a leader in the attack on the Tuileries of August 10,
1792. He had been sent from Paris to Bordeaux to bring the Terror
there to punish those in that city who had supported the Girondins,

who took their name from its region. He had been as deadly and implacable as Robespierre himself until he met in a Bordeaux prison a
beautiful Spanish woman, Teresa Cabarrus, whom he spared; she inclined him toward moderation, and consequently the more violent Jacobins had long been clamoring for his head. Teresa was now in the
Carmes prison of Paris, one of the sites of the September massacres, in
daily danger of the guillotine; but her Spanish blood was up, she was
neither cowed nor resigned, and two days before she had sent Tallien
a dagger with the strongly worded suggestion that he use it. From the
beginning Fouché had selected Tallien as one of the prime movers in
his conspiracy. He had been given the critical assignment of signalling
the attack.

Startled, Saint-Just tried to continue. Collot d'Herbois, presiding,
began furiously ringing his bell. As he rang, Tallien bounded to the
rostrum and pushed Saint-Just aside. "I demand that the curtain be
torn away!" he cried. From the floor rose an answering cry from a
hundred throats, all those whom Fouché had prepared and positioned:
"It must be!"[15]

Billaud-Varenne rushed forward to the rostrum. He reported
some of what had happened to him at the Jacobin Club the night before. "These people are planning to murder the Convention!" he
charged. Then he tested the power of the protest by pointing to an ob-
scure Convention deputy whom he said was one of those who had attacked him at the Jacobin Club. Instantly the deputy was seized and
thrown out of the hall.

Collot d'Herbois stood at the president's chair, sweat pouring
down his face in the humid heat, ringing his bell constantly. All Robespierre's enemies felt it was vital that he and his supporters be given
no chance to speak. Any who tried to reach the rostrum were pushed
aside as Saint-Just had been. Saint-Just himself stood motionless beside
it, refusing either to leave or to fight. Those of the Mountain whom
Fouché, Collot and Billaud had reached were wildly waving their hats.

Tallien came to the rostrum again, shouting at the top of his
lungs.

> I asked a moment ago that the veil be torn aside. It is
> now ripped asunder! The conspirators are soon to be un-
> masked and annihilated. Liberty will triumph!...
> I too was at last night's meeting at the Jacobin Club.
> As I watched, I shuddered for my country. I saw the army of
> a new Cromwell being formed! I have armed myself with a
> dagger which shall pierce this man's breast if the Convention
> does not have the courage to decree his arrest![16]

With a sweep of his arm Tallien pulled Teresa Cabarrus' dagger from his belt and waved it in the air. From all over the hall came cries of "Down with the tyrant!"

The blood rushed to Robespierre's usually pale cheeks—the sign of his rare anger. He jumped to his feet and ran to the rostrum. But Robespierre, thin and small, was no match physically for his opponents, nor could he outshout them with his weak, scratchy voice. Collot rang his bell more lustily than ever, drowning out anything Robespierre might be saying. (The activity of Collot d'Herbois during this critical moment in history was confined almost entirely to ringing that bell with all his might. One wonders if the cynical Fouché, well aware of the virtual void in mind and character that lay behind the ex-actor's handsome face, had given him this assignment after deciding this was the only thing Collot could really be trusted to do.) Tallien came back to the rostrum again; now he moved the arrest of Hanriot and of Dumas, president of the Revolutionary Tribunal. The Convention roared its approval of the motion. The color now drained from his face and great beads of sweat standing out on it, Robespierre made another run at the rostrum. Collot, who had of course stopped ringing his bell while Tallien put his motion, resumed his ringing more vigorously than ever.

From somewhere amid the milling mob on the floor, an almost unknown deputy named Louchet suddenly uttered the decisive words: "I demand the arrest of Robespierre!" He was answered by more shouts of "Down with the tyrant!" Robespierre was still close to the rostrum. His voice rising to a grating scream in an extremity of effort, he finally made himself heard for a moment over the bell. "For the last time, will you let me be heard, President of Assassins!" Tallien, also still near the rostrum, responded at once: "The monster has insulted the Convention!" and called for an immediate vote on Louchet's motion. Collot stopped ringing his bell long enough to signify his assent to Tallien's request.

No one has described, or is likely to describe, what happened next better than Stanley Loomis:

> With a beseeching gesture of his hands, Robespierre now rushed from the rostrum toward the benches of the Left, towards the Mountain, where he had always sat. "Get away from here!" someone cried. "The ghosts of Danton and Camille Desmoulins reject you!"
> He tried again to speak, but his voice was drowned in the pandemonium. "The blood of Danton is choking you!" cried another deputy.
> Rebuffed by the Mountain, he turned in dismay to the Center. "Men of purity," he implored. "Men of Virtue! I ap-

peal to you. Give me the leave to speak which these assassins
have refused me!" But the Plain, which had heretofore sat
"on the watch," by now had had a chance to count the hands
on the Left and on the Right and saw that Robespierre's fate
was already decided. They, too, indignantly repulsed him.
Like a trapped animal he scrambled up the empty seats on
the Right and fell panting onto a bench. The remnants of
this party who had escaped the guillotine withdrew from him
in horror.

"Monster!" one of them screamed. "You are sitting
where Condorcet and Vergniaud once sat!"

Driven from one end of the room to the other, repudiated by all, the frantic creature rose to his feet for the last
time and turned with a despairing glance towards the galleries, where he supposed that the People, the idealized mob
of his vain fantasy, sat. But the People, heedless of what
Robespierre may have imagined them to be, had now disin-
tegrated into their contemptible human components. The
Dantonists and the Hébertists who were among them
screamed down imprecations from the galleries. Those of
them who might have been loyal to Robespierre had the
winds blown in his favor, no doubt the greater portion, now
hurriedly abandoned their doomed leader.

"Arrest him!" they cried. . . .

"Brigands! Hypocrites! Scoundrels!" screamed Robespierre at the Mountain.

"Arrest him!" came the pitiless answer.[17]

It is said that the deputy who cried "Danton's blood chokes you!"
at the trapped Robespierre was Garnier of the Aube, the River of
Dawn, Danton's home territory. And it is said that when Robespierre
heard his words, he stopped stock still for a moment in his wild flight,
as though transfixed by an arrow, and said: "Ah! So he is the one you
wish to avenge."[18]

Amid continuing uproar, the Convention voted the arrest of
Robespierre, Saint-Just, and Couthon. They were brought to the bar
before the president's chair, where the secretary read the decree of arrest to them. The deputies cheered and stamped their feet. The Terror
was over! The shadow was lifted from Paris. It was five-thirty in the
afternoon, and time to celebrate. Collot put down his bell and announced a two-hour recess for dinner.

Stanley Loomis hardly overstates the case when he says that this
action "in the midst of one of the most significant *coups d'etat* of history" "defies all rational explanation."[19] One may imagine Fouché's
searing oath when the news was brought to him. Even in his meticulously careful planning, it had not occurred to him to include instruc-
tions to his conspirators not to stop in the middle of the coup for dinner.

At six o'clock, presumably as they were just sitting down to dinner, the deputies of the Convention heard a sound that many of them
remembered well from August 10, 1792 and from the beginning of the
September massacres. The tocsin was ringing.

Mayor Fleuriot of Paris was confident that he was not on any of
Robespierre's death lists and had no love for the Convention, with
which the Paris Commune had never been on the best of terms. He
was committed to Robespierre, and not at all sure how long his own
head would stay on his shoulders if Robespierre's enemies triumphed.
He directed that no prison in Paris hold Robespierre, Saint-Just and
Couthon in confinement. He called out the *sans-culottes*. He ordered
the tocsin rung. Twenty thousand fighting men assembled before City
Hall. He sent urgently for Hanriot.

It took some time to find him. Having been at the stormy meeting of the Jacobin Club the night before (where he promised Robespierre plenty of men and cannon for the morrow), Hanriot knew that
great events were impending and that he would probably be playing a
central part in them. Whether to celebrate or to fortify himself or
both, he had begun drinking at breakfast, and continued with few re-
missions until three o'clock in the afternoon, when someone brought
him news that the Convention (on Tallien's motion) had just ordered
his arrest. He leaped on a horse and went galloping down the streets
of Paris waving his sword and shouting: "Kill all policemen! Kill! Kill!"
But the only immediate killing he knew about was the daily work of
the guillotine; Fouquier-Tinville was proceeding that day totally without regard to the disturbing rumors afoot about trouble in the Convention. Sanson the executioner suggested postponing the executions
for that day; Fouquier-Tinville refused, and sent off forty-two men
and women in the death carts. Hanriot arrived, with sword swinging
wildly, just as the carts were leaving the Conciergerie, at about five
o'clock, and decided at once that he would guard them on their way to
make sure that all the victims were properly killed. By seven o'clock
they were all dead.

Neither Mayor Fleuriot nor anyone else had thought to look for
Hanriot at the guillotine; but now he came riding back, full of alco-
holic bravado, having lost his hat and with the reddening sun beating
down on his bare head, to deal with the Convention that had dared to
decree his arrest. "Three hundred of those criminals sitting in the
Convention must have their throats cut!" he bawled.[20] Arriving at the
Tuileries totally unescorted, he began haranguing a confused crowd
that had gathered there, whereupon the policemen on duty, who took
their orders from the Convention, arrested him, bound him hand and

foot, and frog-marched him into the offices of the Committee of Public Safety.

It was seven-thirty. The dinner recess of the Convention had ended, and it was reconvening. Scarcely had the deputies learned of Hanriot's arrest when a party of two hundred men from City Hall arrived to rescue him, and promptly did so. The deputies were at Hanriot's mercy; they had only a few arms and no troops. But even when sober, François Hanriot was not mentally equipped to deal with unexpected and unusual situations, of which this 9th day of Thermidor had been very full; and the effects of all he had drunk that day had now progressed from bravado to depression. He took the two hundred men back with him to City Hall to ask Fleuriot what to do. His drunken state was now obvious and left the Commune without a recognized military leader that anyone was willing to follow.

The Convention passed a decree declaring the Paris Commune to be in a state of rebellion and ordering Fleuriot's arrest. Fleuriot received the decree and tore it up. Paul Barras of the Convention, who had formerly been an army officer, began assembling a force of men from the Paris sections who would support that body against the Commune. Meanwhile Robespierre, after having been respectfully refused admission to the Luxembourg prison on the basis of the earlier order from the Commune that he was not to be confined, had been taken at his own request to the mayor's residence near the Palace of Justice, about midway between City Hall and the Tuileries, where he was out of communication with everybody. Never a man of action, profoundly shocked and staggered by what had happened to him that afternoon, Robespierre remained there for several hours, unwilling or emotionally unable to come out. Finally at eleven o'clock Fleuriot prevailed on him by a series of messages to come to City Hall. But by that time Barras had brought together a substantial force, while Hanriot's men were beginning to slip away into the night.

Almost exactly at midnight, the thunderstorm that had been muttering and threatening all day finally broke in a torrent of rain. Hanriot's men had not seen their leader for two hours; most of them knew his condition. They were confused and undisciplined. Rumors were spreading that many of their friends and neighbors were supporting the Convention and Barras. Most of them knew nothing of Robespierre's arrival at City Hall. Despite Fleuriot's urging, he had not yet agreed to sign an appeal to the people of Paris to come to his aid; he protested that he was not sure in the name of what authority he was to sign it. The slippage of an hour before became an ebb tide.

By one o'clock in the morning the Revolutionary army of the Commune had entirely dispersed.

At two o'clock in the morning Barras' troops arrived in the square before the City Hall and entered the building without resistance. There was a moment of wild confusion as they burst into the third-story room where the leaders of the Terror were gathered. A shot broke Robespierre's jaw. His brother Augustin tried to escape by crawling along a window-ledge; he fell off, breaking almost every bone in his body. Philippe Lebas, one of the very few Convention deputies who had supported Robespierre to the end, pulled a pistol. Saint-Just asked Lebas to kill him with it; Lebas replied, "Fool! I have more important things to do!"[21] and blew out his own brains. Couthon crawled out of his wheelchair and under a table, from which someone dragged him to the head of a staircase; he fell down it, severely injuring himself. Dumas, president of the Revolutionary Tribunal, also tried to hide under a table. Coffinhal, vice-president of the Revolutionary Tribunal, seeing that all was lost, vented his rage on the now dead-drunk Hanriot; he seized him by the shoulders, dragged him to a window, and threw him out into a manure pile.

An hour later Robespierre, covered with blood, was brought into that very green room of the Committee of Public Safety from which he had ruled as lord of the Terror. His head with its shattered jaw was laid on a wooden army ration box. He lay there more than six hours. The room was unguarded in the confusion; many of the ordinary people of Paris who had heard that Robespierre was there came to see him. Some mocked and jeered; others simply gazed in astonishment at how the mighty can fall. Two remarks were particularly remembered—one by one of the curious observers, the other by Robespierre himself.

The observer looked at Robespierre in silence for a long time, and then declared in a quiet, solemn voice: "Yes, Robespierre, there is a God."

But for all that Maximilien Robespierre had been and done, he was now a helpless and doomed man in agony, and another observer was moved to pity, and brought water to bathe his gaping wound. "Thank you, monsieur," Robespierre said, forgetting—or ignoring—that by Revolutionary decrees which he had totally supported, all men were to be called only "citizen," never "monsieur" as in the bad old days of the monarchy.[22]

At ten o'clock in the morning Robespierre and those arrested with him, including Saint-Just, Couthon, Fleuriot, and Hanriot, were taken to the Conciergerie, where Marie Antoinette had endured the agonizing last weeks of her life by order of the regime these men had done so much to impose and maintain. Early in the afternoon they were convicted under Robespierre's own law of 22 Prairial, without opportunity to make any defense. Fouquier-Tinville, with mottled features, pronounced their death sentence; no one needed to tell him that the Public Prosecutor of the Terror could not now have long to live himself, that soon the shadows of the dead that he had felt following him would catch him up. At four o'clock in the afternoon they began the long ride in the death carts, to which they had condemned so many others. At seven o'clock they reached the guillotine. Of the twenty-two who died by it that day, July 28, 1794, Maximilien Robespierre was the twenty-first. As he tied him to the plank under the knife, the executioner jerked the dressing from his wound, and Robespierre "gave a groan like that of a dying tiger, which was heard in the far corners of the square."[23]

The great shining blade crashed home. The lord of the guillotine had died by the guillotine.

But the Lord of the Cross gives life through the Cross, and final victory is His.

NOTES

[1]Stanley Loomis, *Paris in the Terror* (Philadelphia, 1964), p. 334.
[2]Louis Madelin, *The French Revolution* (New York, 1925), p. 403.
[3]Loomis, *Paris in the Terror*, p. 376.
[4]Jean Matrat, *Robespierre, or the Tyranny of the Majority* (New York, 1971), p. 270.
[5]Loomis, *Paris in the Terror*, p. 378.
[6]*Ibid.*, p. 385.
[7]Matrat, *Robespierre*, p. 272.
[8]Madelin, *French Revolution*, p. 418.
[9]*Ibid.*, p. 398.
[10]Loomis, *Paris in the Terror*, p. 387.
[11]*Ibid.*, p. 389.
[12]Madelin, *French Revolution*, p. 416; Jacques Hérissay, *La Vie religieuse à Paris sous la Terreur (1792-1794)* (Paris, 1952), p. 288. See Chapter Seven.
[13]Loomis, *Paris in the Terror*, p. 390.
[14]Matrat, *Robespierre*, p. 275; Loomis, *Paris in the Terror*, p. 391.
[15]Loomis, *Paris in the Terror*, p. 391.
[16]*Ibid.*, p. 392.
[17]*Ibid.*, pp. 393-394.
[18]Matrat, *Robespierre*, p. 277.

[19]Loomis, *Paris in the Terror*, p. 394.
[20]*Ibid.*, p. 396.
[21]*Ibid.*, p. 399.
[22]*Ibid.*, pp. 400-401.
[23]Matrat, *Robespierre*, p. 288.

Afterword

The end of the Reign of Terror did not bring an end to the French Revolution. The forces it had unleashed, though to some extent harnessed and stripped of their most obviously evil and Satanic elements, continued to batter Europe and threaten the whole world for no less than twenty-one years after Maximilien Robespierre died under the guillotine. Even then, when by an immense, heroic effort Christendom had apparently defeated decisively the Revolution and its heirs, its spirit soon reappeared. It is with us still, now in our time when a third of the world lives under the tyranny of its direct descendant, the Communist Revolution, and all the rest of the world is touched and twisted by its legacy in thought and action—often misunderstood, but no less and perhaps more potent for that.

Yet after July 28, 1794 the worst was over—at least until the Communists took power in Russia more than a century later. The immediate heirs of the French Revolution, chiefly Napoleon Bonaparte, for all the oppression they inflicted and all the destruction they wrought, were clearly within the pale of humanity. Not even their most dedicated foe or worst enemy could reasonably have said of their rule, as sober historians we have quoted have said of the Reign of Terror, that "one is here confronted with forces more powerful than those controlled by men" or that "a spirit was abroad which contemporary conservatives truly described as satanic."[1] As de Guerry had called upon the Vendeans at Montaigu and Saint-Fulgent to do, the devils had been driven back into Hell—not perhaps so much by the Vendeans themselves, though surely they played their part, as by the great rally of the martyrs.

The very day after Robespierre's execution the Convention ordered that one-quarter of the members of the Committee of Public Safety should retire each month, with no retiring member eligible for re-election for at least one intervening month, thereby preventing this Committee from continuing to be a seat of tyranny. On July 31 six new members to the Committee were elected to replace the three who had been executed and three more who became the first to be retired in the new rotation. All the new members had strongly supported the overthrow of Robespierre (as indeed, nearly everyone in the public eye in Paris, or hoping to get there, was now claiming truthfully or untruthfully to have done). On August 1 the Convention repealed the law of 22 Prairial, arrested Fouquier-Tinville, and threw him into the Conciergerie. Almost killed by the prisoners there when they saw who he was, he was rescued from them barely in time, and put into a small unlit cell alone. "There, at the mercy of his own thoughts, in the dark, like a wild beast shut in his den, he waited and thought."[2] He who had brought so many from arrest to execution in twenty-four hours was given weeks and months to prepare and present his defense. Only after two lengthy trials was he finally convicted and brought to the guillotine, under which he died on May 7, 1795.

On August 24, 1794 the Convention abolished the local revolutionary committees, which had been among the chief agents of the Terror. On September 1 Billaud-Varenne, Collot d'Herbois and Barère were removed from the Committee of Public Safety; on March 2, 1795 they were arrested, and soon afterward Billaud and Collot were deported to Cayenne in French Guiana on the steaming equatorial jungle coast of South America, later famous as the locale of Devil's Island and known as the "dry guillotine." Collot soon died there; Billaud spent twenty years there and ended his days in Haiti, unrepentant. The slippery Barère escaped and lived until 1841, in abject poverty during his later years, the last survivor of the Committee of Public Safety. On November 12, 1794 the Paris Jacobin Club was closed by order of the Convention, an action generally seen as a final repudiation of the Terror and its authors.

All this left France without any government that could even reasonably pretend to be legitimate; but too much both of human and of material capital had been invested in the Revolution for most of its leaders to abandon it completely. On August 22, 1795 a new regime was proclaimed, with a two-house legislature (Convention members were guaranteed occupancy of two-thirds of the seats in each house) and a five-man executive Directory. An attack against it by the Paris mob was driven off by Napoleon Bonaparte, now a general who wrote his name in the French rather than the Italian fashion, with a "whiff of grapeshot." Over the next four years General Bonaparte established himself as the premier military commander in Europe; he conquered

Italy and brought Pope Pius VI a prisoner to France. In November 1799, despite a major reverse in Egypt due to the great victory of England's Admiral Horatio Nelson over the French fleet at Aboukir Bay, General Bonaparte became head of state in France as first consul. Four and a half years later this Corsican peasant's son was proclaimed Emperor of France, already the most powerful single man on earth at the age of only thirty-five, and set out to conquer Europe and the world and to rule the Catholic Church as well. It was his plan to fuse the heritage of the Revolution with a new aristocracy of talent to create the mightiest empire the world had ever seen.

He almost succeeded. Only a unique alliance of the Catholic people of Europe (forged and annealed when Pope Pius VII, like his predecessor, was seized by Napoleon and carried off a prisoner to France), the Eastern Orthodox Tsar of Russia, and the stalwart Protestants of England and Prussia brought him down at last, after a titanic struggle through ten years. That struggle was finally decided at the Battle of Waterloo, June 18, 1815, with the Duke of Wellington peering through the late afternoon haze, every man of his staff dead around him, the charge of the Scots Greys broken in slaughter and his last reserve under Colonel Maitland lining up behind a protecting slope as Napoleon prepared to launch his Old Guard in a final charge. But Napoleon lacked ten thousand men who could and probably would have given him the victory at Waterloo ("the nearest-run thing you ever saw," as Wellington said all the rest of his life) because Louis de la Rochejaquelein, brother of Henri de la Rochejaquelein and second husband of Marie-Louise Victoire, had led another rising in the Vendée which drew those troops away from the decisive combat at Waterloo. Louis de la Rochejaquelein fell in battle against Napoleon's men at the Pont des Marthes June 4, 1815, and Marie-Louise Victoire was widowed for the second time; both her husbands had died fighting the Revolution and its heir.

From 1789 to 1793, it seemed that heroism was dead in France and in Europe. But Christian heroism had revived; first in the Vendée, then among the martyrs of the Terror, then on through the great war against Napoleon, which was also in a real sense a war of religion and a crusade—and a war that Christendom won.

But the greater, deeper war of the spirit goes on, and is being fought still. The Revolution still rises, armed and deadly, against the Faith: the power of man and Satan against the authority of God and the workings of grace. Sometimes we can see the battle lines clearly drawn, as at Paris on the day of the tocsin or at Nantes on the day of Cathelineau's attack, or when Kornilov and Denikin faced the armies of Lenin and Trotsky on the Kuban in 1918, or when Colonel Moscardo stood against Largo Caballero with the prayers of six thousand martyrs rising about him like incense in the blazing summer of 1936. Sometimes we can only barely glimpse and guess them, as in the struggles for the souls of Georges-Jacques Danton and Jean-Baptiste Gobel and Whittaker Chambers and Igor Gouzenko, or in that arcane arena where the prayers of the Carmelite nuns of Compiègne met the malevolence of Robespierre and Saint-Just. There is no better symbol for that war than the guillotine against the Cross.

NOTES

[1]Stanley Loomis, *Paris in the Terror* (Philadelphia, 1964), p. 328; R. R. Palmer, *Twelve Who Ruled; the Year of the Terror in the French Revolution* (Princeton, 1941, 1969), p. 316.

[2]Alphonse Dunoyer, *The Public Prosecutor of the Terror: Antoine Quentin Fouquier-Tinville* (New York, 1913), p. 129.

Bibliography

Battersby, William J. *Brother Solomon, Martyr of the French Revolution* (London, 1960)

Billaud, A. *La Guerre de Vendée* (Fontenay, 1972)

Bowers, Claude G. *Pierre Vergniaud, Voice of the French Revolution* (New York, 1950)

Bruno de Jésus-Marie, Rev. *Le Sang du Carmel, ou la véritable passion des seize Carmélites de Compiègne* (Paris, 1954)

Bryant, Arthur. *The Years of Endurance, 1793-1802* (London, 1942)

Cambridge Modern History (1st edition), Volume VIII: "The French Revolution," ed. A.W. Ward, G.W. Prothero and Stanley Leathes (New York, 1908)

Chandler, David G. *The Campaigns of Napoleon* (New York, 1966)

Christophe, Robert. *Danton* (London, n.d.)

Cronin, Vincent. *Louis and Antoinette* (New York, 1975)

Curtis, Eugene N. *Saint-Just, Colleague of Robespierre* (New York, 1973)

Dawson, Christopher. *The Gods of Revolution* (New York, 1972)

Dunoyer, Alphonse. *The Public Prosecutor of the Terror, Antoine Quentin Fouquier-Tinville* (New York, 1913)

Dupre, Huntley. *Lazare Carnot, Republican Patriot* (Oxford, Ohio, 1940; Philadelphia, 1975)

Ellery, Eloise. *Brissot de Warville, a Study in the History of the French Revolution* (Boston, 1915)

Furneaux, Rupert. *The Bourbon Tragedy* (London, 1968)

Hardman, John, ed. *French Revolution Documents [in French], Volume II: 1792-5* (Oxford, 1973)

Hérissay, Jacques. *La Vie religieuse à Paris sous la Terreur* (Paris, 1952)

Hibbert, Christopher. *The Days of the French Revolution* (New York, 1980)

Higgins, E.L., ed. *The French Revolution as Told by Contemporaries* (Boston, 1938)

Jordan, David P. *The King's Trial; Louis XVI versus the French Revolution* (Berkeley CA, 1979)

Kennedy, Michael L.   *The Jacobin Club of Marseilles, 1790-1794* (Ithaca NY, 1973)
La Gorce, P. de.   *Histoire religieuse de la Révolution,* Volumes II and III (Paris, 1909-23)
La Rochejaquelein, Marchioness de.   *Memoirs* (tr. Sir Walter Scott) (Edinburgh, 1816)
Loomis, Stanley.   *The Fatal Friendship* (Garden City NY, 1972)
————————.   *Paris in the Terror* (Philadelphia, 1964)
Louis Philippe d'Orléans.   *Memoirs 1773-1793,* tr. John Hardman (New York, 1977)
Madelin, Louis.   *The French Revolution* (New York, 1925)
Matrat, G.   *Robespierre, or the Tyranny of the Majority* (New York, 1971)
May, Gita.   *Madame Roland and the Age of Revolution* (New York, 1970)
Morris, Gouverneur.   *Diary of the French Revolution* (ed. Beatrix Davenport), Volume II (Boston, 1939)
Palmer, R.R.   *Twelve Who Ruled; the Year of the Terror in the French Revolution* (Princeton, 1941)
Patrick, Alison.   *The Men of the First French Republic; Political Alignments in the National Convention of 1792* (Baltimore MD, 1972)
Pratt, Fletcher.   *Empire and the Sea* (New York, 1946)
Ross, M.   *Banners of the King; the War of the Vendée 1793-4* (New York, 1975)
Saint Pierre, Michel de.   *Monsieur de Charette, Chevalier du Roi* (Paris, 1977)
Scott, Otto J.   *Robespierre, the Voice of Virtue* (New York, 1974)
Scott, William.   *Terror and Repression in Revolutionary Marseilles* (New York, 1975)
Taine, Hippolyte.   *The French Revolution,* Volumes II and III (New York, 1881-85)
Thompson, J. M.   *The French Revolution* (New York, 1945)
Tilly, Charles.   *The Vendée* (Cambridge Ma, 1964)